IN SHORT

IN SHORT

A GUIDE TO SHORT FILM-MAKING
IN THE DIGITAL AGE

Eileen Elsey and Andrew Kelly

First published in 2002 by the
BRITISH FILM INSTITUTE
21 Stephen Street, London W1T 1LN

The British Film Institute promotes greater understanding of,
and access to, film and moving image culture in the UK.

Cover images: (left to right) *Kill the Day* (Lynne Ramsay, 1996); *Is is the Design on the Wrapper?* (Tessa Sheridan, 1997); *Cherish* (Winta Yohannes, 2000); *The Queen's Monastery* (Emma Calder, 1998); *To Have and to Hold* (John Hardwick, 2000)
Set by couch
Printed in the UK by Bell and Bain, Glasgow

British Library Cataloguing-in-Publication Data
A catalogue record for this book is available from the British Library

ISBN 0–85170–893–5 (pbk)
ISBN 0–85170–892–7 (hbk)

Contents

Acknowledgments   *vii*
Foreword – Glimpse Culture: Celebrating Short Film – Gareth Evans   *viii*

1. INTRODUCTION: SHORTS IN THE FIELD OF FILM   1
   The invisibility of short film   1
   A definition of shorts   2
   The scope and function of the book   3
   The role of shorts in contemporary practice   4

2. A SHORT HISTORY OF SHORTS   5
   Short film and film history   5
   Education   8
   Animation   11
   Advertising   13
   Music video   16
   Avant-garde   18
   Conclusion   19

3. CONVERSATIONS WITH FILM-MAKERS   21
   Introduction   21
   Nick Park   23
   Emma Calder   32
   Tessa Sheridan   41
   Lynne Ramsay   52
   Damien O'Donnell   60
   Anthony Minghella   71
   John Smith   77
   Jonathan Glazer   86
   John Hardwick   93
   Winta Yohannes   102
   Keith Wright   110

4. CONTEMPORARY FILM-MAKERS AND SHORTS PRODUCTION   120
   The creative process   120
   Commissioning and funding   122
   Exhibition and distribution   125
   Digital film-making   127
   Conclusion   128

5. HOW SHORTS (CAN) GET MADE AND SHOWN   129
   Getting the film made   130
   Getting the film shown   132
   Television   134
   The short film and the digital revolution   134
   What should be done?   139
   Conclusion   139

6. SHORT FILM-MAKING RESOURCE GUIDE   141
   On-line films   141
   On-line film directories   145
   Funding sources for short films in the UK and the Irish Republic   146
   Cinema exhibition   152
   Selection of festivals showing short films   152
   Other Internet sources of information   156
   Print publications   156

Bibliography   158
Filmographies of Contributing Film-makers   159
Index   165

Acknowledgments

We thank the following for their help and support: the Arts and Humanities Research Board (AHRB), the University of the West of England, all the film-makers interviewed here and the companies interviewed for research; Mel Kelly for preparing the resource guide, the anonymous reader for the BFI who provided many valuable comments, Andrew Lockett, Erich Sargeant and Sarah Wilde at the BFI, Les Blythe, George Brandt, Helen Brunsdon, Andrea Calderwood, Sophia Contento, Maggie Ellis, Robin Gutch, Martin Hammond, Joost Hunningher, Helen Langridge, Carlotta Mastrojanni, Cassius Matthius, Clive Meyer, Meabh O'Donovan, Janine Partington, Colin Pons, Maita Robinson, Dick Ross, Janet Thumim and Liz Wells. We would also like to thank the board and staff of the Encounters festivals who have been helpful in providing advice and comments, especially Jeremy Howe.

Foreword – Glimpse Culture: Celebrating Short Film

O God, I could be bounded in a nutshell and count myself a king of infinite space.
Hamlet, William Shakespeare

Imagine a room. It is decorated in a style familiar to Paris in the 1920s. In it sits a woman, attired in the fashion of the times. A tango plays. In the same room a man sharpens a razor. He is casual, relaxed but nevertheless attentive to the task in hand. Above, a full moon is cut briefly by clouds. The man then turns to the woman, opens wide her eye (she does not resist) and slices the eyeball with the blade. Sight spills out and runs to darkness.

Luis Buñuel and Salvador Dali's 1929 surrealist debut *Un Chien Andalou* contains perhaps the most challenging image in, or rather, to cinema, the most radical action that the medium has delivered. In that gesture, film violates itself by neutering the chance of its own reception. Light is cancelled, the world is unmade. The audience is 'assaulted' in the most pointed way possible.

Now imagine a woman asleep. She lies on her side. A man is looking at her. Then she wakes. She opens her eyes. She looks at him, and briefly us, the viewer. It is an act of definitive mundanity. However, the film we are watching is Chris Marker's 1962 *photo-roman La Jetée*, whose science-fiction narrative explores memory and desire through a sequence of still images, montaged fluidly together to suggest motion where none is present. Except, that is, for the unique and epiphanic moment described above. We can relax again.

One might propose that these two images mark the outer (and opposite) limits of an arc along which all the possibilities of cinema rest. By defining the spectrum of vision, and its erasure, they hold between them all else that can be observed, by the camera, a director and by the audience to their stored shadowplay.

It is also worth noting that they are both short films.

Un Chien Andalou clocks in at sixteen minutes, Chris Marker's epic (really) at twenty-nine. Is length an issue? Does size matter? Do those two moments, lasting only a couple of seconds apiece, owe their potency and significance in any way to the fact that they occur within what are brief works? On one level, not in the slightest. They are simply instants in films, that work effectively (or not) dependent on the ability of the constructed narrative to generate interest in, even empathy with, the events depicted. To separate shorts out for praise or critique is unhelpful to them and the medium itself. Cinema has after all a most democratic of definitions – 'a medium of the moving image' is, I would hazard, just about all that can be pitched without being asked for serious qualification. And anyway, as the historical introduction that follows makes clear, the story of cinema is very much the story of short films. Shorts are cinema, they were in its birth, and so to make exceptional claims beyond that ancestry and based solely on running time is perhaps ludicrous.

And yet … when you consider the Lumière Brothers' train arriving, Méliès' man in the moon, the first appearance of Mickey Mouse, the chilling footage of the Warsaw Ghetto (or Alain Resnais' *Night and Fog*, 1955), Kenneth Anger's *Scorpio Rising* (1963), Jack Smith's *Flaming Creatures* (1963), Franju's *Le Sang des Bêtes* (1948), Humphrey Jennings' *Night Mail* (1936), Maya Deren's *Meshes of the Afternoon* (1943), Stan Brakhage's *Dog Star Man* (1964), *The Simpsons* even …

Enough. Enough, in fact, has been made in the short form of such importance that there is clearly a case to be put for not only why short films matter as a thing distinct, but also how.

My first remembered encounter with cinema was with a short film. It was, however, none of the above. I saw it in the cavernous single-screen Embassy Cinema, in the Hertfordshire dormitory town of Harpenden. The picturehouse sat on the main road, just out of the town centre, huge and apart, slightly disconcerting in its solidity. It really did seem like a fundamental part of the environment. To a youngster barely able to see over the seat in front, it was a cool hall of great promise, secrets and surprise; from the faded – I realise it now – grandeur of its façade through the tiled lobby to the high, vaulted auditorium. It seemed almost to be enough in itself, for me simply to be in there while the day continued outside, within the chosen community of an anticipatory audience. I can remember then being awestruck by the way that this imposing building seemed to dissolve as the room dimmed and the wall we were all fixed upon became a dance of forms, of people and places conjured from a pathway of light. Which perhaps makes this specific memory all the more unlikely. It isn't of a matinee cartoon or a Disney featurette, of a made-to-order Western or Children's Film Foundation outing. Rather, it is of a black bull being winched aboard an open fishing boat off the Scottish coast. This creature, the titular *Duna Bull* (1971) (as I remember it), was making the rounds of the islands for reasons of insemination, and the short documentary – part of a mixed supporting package for the main feature (long since forgotten) – followed the animal on its seminal work, commenting briefly along the way on any settlements visited.

Only twice since then (watching Tarkovsky whilst reclining on the cushioned floor of the Hare Krishna cinema in Sydney, and being transported by the opening of *Paris Texas* [1984] in London's late, lamented Lumière cinema) has the act of watching itself proved such a revelation. I shall never forget the image of this jet-black bull hanging in space between quayside and vessel. It seems, in a quietly pivotal way, to contain the essence of cinema and its *raisons d'être*. It revealed something previously unseen (to me at least), it located its subject in the believable and materially-anchored world without removing its mystery and it generated a brief intimacy while simultaneously suggesting great scale, great arcs of potential expansion. It was in itself both a result and the first step on a path, a journey into sight and insight. And, as a neat dovetail with the chronology of cinema itself, it seeded my encounter with film through a form that is, as noted, the medium's founding work.

However, this particular memory also appears, when set in the context of a volume celebrating the short film, to point towards several other guiding frameworks. Viewed now from the perspective of diverse professional involvement in the film industry, it signals the moment (the early 1970s) when most people's experience of short film outside of advertising, and most significantly in the context of opening a feature-length presentation – whether documentary, fiction or animation – was beginning to be threatened by changing policies in theatrical programming and scheduling. Such removal of diversity in exhibition strategy – whether considered in terms of length, genre, content, language or origin – is of course a direct challenge to all of cinema, and one we are living through in an even more explicit way at the moment. But it struck a body blow to widespread viewing of short film, one which only now, in the last few years, it is recovering from. And, with this volume as partial case for the defence, the shift can be seen as much more than mere recuperation. An entire short form industry, with all component elements discrete and intact, is now networking globally to generate product in all genres and media and at all levels of financing. From supporting acts once again, through broadcast compilations to Internet streaming, let alone concentrated in festivals proliferating worldwide, less is most definitely more as larger and larger audiences are watching *less*.

Many infrastructural shifts have of course contributed to this filmic fecundity: the development of the music promo (with MTV the mansion on the hill), the prohibitive cost of feature production and the attendant need for reasonably risk-free, 'calling card' evidence of talent before the cheques are signed. Which is not to claim that shorts are only technical exercises notable only for the promise they suggest will be realised later and at length. Consider Scorsese, Lynne Ramsay, David Lynch, Polanski and Jane Campion (to name only a handful) for evidence of complete achievements within the short form by directors famed more for features. It's this calibre of lineage that works of course as a compelling spur for aspirants.

Add such reasoning to the subsequent break with the celluloid absolute in light of the digital age's unarguable street-level financial and creative advantage – its cameras, post-production and distribution opportunities – and you have a climate, increasingly sponsored by varying structures of exhibition, where concise image-making can flourish. In such a hothouse atmosphere, short films can reveal particular qualities of the *zeitgeist*. With technology now on their side, they also display that hardware's key component – speed – in aesthetic terms and regardless of pace. They embody acceleration and contribute to it. As, almost literally, there is less time available because, paradoxically, society's velocity has increased, so 'short' artworks become messengers and message of that change. Just as with similar developments in publishing, short films are 'attention-sensitive' to the contemporary moment. Their response times are faster. They allow themselves an audience partly by being less intrusive than artefacts longer or bulkier.

Traits emerge then. The best short films are crystalline creations of precise, prismatic intensity. The worst are desperately compressed in their banality and lack. Simplistically arranged, they offer enough tedium to empty cemeteries. Surprising maybe, given the duration, but in this arena all elements are amplified, not reduced; noticed, not overlooked. The principle of magnification reveals flaws and gems. Trace and testimony, all films serve as a witness statement, all cinemas become the incident room of the investigation. The shorter the evidence the more imagination plays detective, the more any problems frustrate solution. The greater the yearning for the (literally) cursory epiphanies short film can offer.

Short films are long films that finish earlier. Short fuses to a large result.

In Britain, the short film has a particular and gleaming tradition. A luminous lineage if you will, exemplified by a handful of key practitioners who have expanded the language of cinema generally, let alone simply the reach of the short form. As with other territories, and before reaching the top dogs, a national pitch becomes reasonably evident early on, albeit with numerous exceptions rupturing the 'rules', once serious viewing is pursued. There's a tonal or atmospheric level, almost a thematic yardstick, against which titles might be considered. England (Britain even, although the Celtic edges bring a certain conceptual wildness and 'otherness') has always felt most at ease with a social naturalism, a heightened realism of the everyday. The world is there – all the messy business of hierarchies, parties, industry, labour and letdowns aplenty – but filtered through the personal, the impacted lives and domestic spaces rather than in grand, unanchored gestures of empowerment and betrayal. The story might be lean, an incident under the lens, a brief walk into narrative with perhaps a digression or two, but real success lies in the implications between scenes, in the pressing social frame coded or carried through a chamber tale.

Inevitably, and even in the dramas, there is a documentary aspect to this position, a sense that certain realities, positive as well as negative, are too close to be ignored or imagined away; and indeed many fine short works of non-fiction have been made and have often re-energised the short form (think of the Free Cinema movement of the 1950s, blending observation with a vibrant polemical urgency). But the concern here is with the dramatic short, with the creative lifting of daily business into empathetic and imagined realms of fine attention. In this regard, are there any better exemplars of such an attitude than the 'childhood' trilogies of Bill Douglas and Terrence Davies? For any short to stand sustained gaze (and indeed receive primary interest) its style must be both its own and absolutely confident – without affectation and undue or excessive 'borrowing'. Both Davies and Douglas belong recognisably to native traditions of telling and seeing, but imbue their tri-partite narratives of hard lives and losses with the singular intensities that mark them from the first frames. There are significant similarities (as well as differences) in these autobiographically motivated works: both were shot over almost a decade – primarily the 1970s – and focus on childhood progression as a way into the personal and collective stories of communities under certain kinds of siege. For Douglas, the setting is the Scottish mining village of Newcraighall in the 1940s. The memories are hard and unflinching, but the scenes in *My Childhood* (1972), *My Ain Folk* (1973) and *My Way Home* (1978), delivered in stark monochrome, keep sentimentality at bay and provide an enduring document of lives too often overlooked. The films have been hugely influential, not least on the work of Lynne Ramsay.

For Davies, the milieu is urban, working-class Liverpool, but the sense of difficulties to be overcome remains equally prominent. Add in the spiritual confusions engendered when Catholicism meets an emergent gay identity and the journey of protagonist Robert Tucker through *Children, Madonna and Child* and *Death and Transfiguration* becomes a stirring account of dignity quietly triumphant, observed in a way that is exacting, occasionally surreal and finally transcendent. However, the brightness of a lasting faith is here as likely to come from the set lights or the terraced dawn as it is from the altar's spreading arc.

These works are masterpieces of observation and memory charged by considered, accepted suffering. Their authenticity, their authority as 'documents' (the transformed real) comes from their grounding in the passage of actual lives. Screen them alongside the encyclopaedic, Borgesian structures and artifices of Peter Greenaway and it would be hard to imagine the directors hail from the same celluloid nation. However, the polymath archivist Greenaway's idiosyncratic shorts are in their own way as British as Douglas or Davies (like them, and around the same time, he went on of course to feature film direction, but established his filmic signature in the shorts). His fascination with forms of the foreign in object and thought, his rigorous classifications, a dry and mordant wit and not least a strong strain of landscape romanticism, evident in works like *A Walk Through H* (1978), *Vertical Features Remake* (1978) and *Water Wrackets* (1978), support a vision of the world quite as compelling as the more explicitly realist approaches mentioned above.

These three directors have produced seminal works in the short form, all in their own way experimental, and yet still accessible. There is no question, however, that they benefited enormously from the imaginative public funding of their times, a subsidy that recognised their underpinning attributes of innovation and curiosity: democratic, voice-enhancing, bringing the overlooked central. Risk, (self-)expression, 'freedom'. It's a crude breakdown perhaps, but workable.

Those qualities are of course still in the air, but the formal support structures have altered considerably. The private and the proactive are now traits required in the top drawer, not last on the list of approaches. Where once the young sat in cafés working earnestly on heartfelt verse for their debut slim volumes, now the latter's lounge is the location of an impromptu screening, a video projection of scattergun titles, missives from the first minutes of the future. Their shorts live fast on the cusp between self- and formal finance, marginalisation and sponsorship, private statement and public assembly, outlaw status and in-house operation. But wherever you squat on the scale, of one thing you can be sure. The factors that allow you to breathe also permit a million others to do the same. Volume is now the greatest threat to satisfactory exposure.

It is crucial therefore that distinctive strategies (in the work's aesthetic and thematic intentions, and its dissemination) are adopted to guarantee reception. Such strategies, beyond being more or less amusing/effective marketing campaigns, also engender a certain, admittedly unflagged, *political* position in the work being pushed. There's the interventionist role: surprise them when their guard's down and hit the retina hard. Or there's community building, teasing slowly at attention within the script and in a 'united we stand' grouping with others. The family of mavericks and individualists that make up the experimental or avant-garde wing of film have of course long known that the functioning reality lies somewhere in-between, both in business organisation (think of the pioneering London Film-maker's Co-op) and in shaping themes. Money here has generally not been a defining option. The late Orkney magus and mobiliser Margaret Tait made almost all her work effectively unfunded, so far from the centre it was no longer a source of concern. It and she did not share the same map. Figures like her – and there were numerous, solitary in shed studios across the territories – effectively kept the secret pulse of short film beating whenever it faltered more officially. As the novelist Bryher wrote in the avant-garde film journal *Close Up* as far back as 1931: 'If the cinema is to survive it will be only through a few groups refusing to visit commercial kinos ... They will have to make scraps of film that every commercial producer would refuse and project them on kitchen walls ...'

They knew lack of finance and hours meant their work would almost always be short and so they turned it to advantage, didn't resist the framework but used it. Anyway, too much of a good thing and it all goes under. Because there is less distance to travel between form and content, image and intention, opening and closure, an attention to frame and exposition, regardless of whether a plot is in place or not, becomes crucial. But a guiding line is only part of the 'story' in shorts. The product of patience *and* pressure, made often on borrowed or liberated time, with the urgency of hours pulled clear of the grind, they are adept at the sensual, at surfaces and atmospheric impact, at remarkable concentrations and degrees of shift in tone. They can wander but any drift must be *organised*. Meditative and reflective, lyrical certainly, but focus is the key. It's about the concentration of idea, the layering, metaphor on metaphor. Only what is necessary, but never merely functional. Idea determines length. Form and content collaborate beneficially in a system where omission becomes a pivotal principle, the ability to edit (out) an index of talent. Ignoring content or mood, short films are first and foremost 'poems' when considered against the general 'prose' of features (this quality, and the tradition from which it chiefly springs, is celebrated in film-maker Peter Todd's various BFI touring programmes of 'Film Poems').

Idiosyncratic approaches can often be formulated simply from a relevant updating of avant-garde approaches. Where meagre finances prompted certain production and distribution schedules, now similar constraints result in a sequence like Jem Cohen's *Chain*. It's the acclaimed New York diary film-maker's most ambitious – and also realistic – project: thirty short films on aspects of globalisation, to be made as funding allows, and presented in various configurations, in diverse media, reflecting the various readings of the issue and the linkage/convergence of elements within it.

Cohen presented this proposal to producers at the 2002 Rotterdam International Film Festival, an event not dedicated to shorts but certainly to innovation. A fine harnessing of imagination to a certain industrial pragmatism, it stands out especially for its clarity of intent. In the annual smorgasbord of shorts gatherings globally, this is an essential quality. Whether at agenda-setting Euro-fests like Tampere, Clermont-Ferrand and Oberhausen or any number of round-ups across the planet, the density of viewing that attracts both industry and punters also threatens to jade, if not erase, distinction altogether. Too many 'self in a city' pics, too much relationship melancholy. Too many kids in crisis, too many one-twist ponies. Too much 'atmosphere' alone. They stack, accumulate, blur.

Since it is often harder to watch shorts en masse than it is features – it's not just the filmic volume but the increment of switches between titles that challenges – a handful of titles very quickly emerge in any given period that do the rounds of the fairs riding a wave of general relief. When too many worlds are on offer, too many jolts between dimensions, what the mind retains are titles that refuse to be scored exclusively to the (sometimes) concealed music of trusted national approaches. Works that blossom out of detail and the sensibility of their origins in place and creator while simultaneously reaching further make, of course, the difference. Think here of – just to name a clutch of Brits who come readily to mind – Phil Mulloy, Paul Bush, the Brothers Quay (honorary islanders if not naturalised) and Leytonstone's John Smith, regular prizewinners who give their all to shorts and travel with their traits intact. Artists who can shape the mood of a festival and provide its enduring peak.

But such festivals – those extraordinary clusters of images, transports of light, of virtual worlds scattered across a real geography – pale in scale when considered next to the product of the www. This volume will examine the Internet display of wares (produced elsewhere) as the evolutionary 'next phase', but the Web itself has spawned demented and entirely unpredictable shards thrown up, as it were, by the machinery itself and umbilically dependent on it. At Sheffield's 2002 Lovebytes Media Art Festival, Ben Slater and Jon Harrison presented 'Search Engine Cinema', a subversive, often no-budget trawl through the subcultural fringes of the system, taking in Hungarian remakes of *Star Wars* (1977), dynamited whale carcasses, tofu shooting ranges, 'truth in advertising' and, perhaps most presciently when it comes to realising Net potential, location recordings of the 11 September attacks uploaded less than twenty minutes after the first plane hit (the URL itself no longer exists).

However, if these admirably idiosyncratic projects shared anything theoretically, it was the way they provoked an expanded interrogation of what is meant by 'animation'. Since animation, like the avant-garde, is a grouping that, for all the obvious reasons of time and labour, majority-inhabits the short form, these test-tubes of the viral digital become weighted with a significance beyond themselves. They echo an observation made by producer Keith Griffiths in a recent essay (see *animateonline.org*) that, through its systematic manipulations, often on a frame-by-frame level, contemporary movie-making in the digital could be considered animation, almost regardless of declared aims in that direction. Similarly, the 'hallucinations of reality' Griffiths admires in innovative visual practice, harking back to cinema's founding traits of magic and illusion as exemplified by Méliès, also found their place, beyond a mere eccentricity of content, in the 'Search Engine' package, when the desired delivery came up against the limits of technology transfer to a suitable projection format. The result: even live action or news footage became, in the jerkiness of passage, pixellated, vulnerable to signal loss, texturally altered and shifted into a quasi-heightened realm when lifted out of its environmental (Web-based) context.

This full circle return to the primary dictionary definition of the digital, to an origin in the hand and a manual (albeit keyboard) operation as much as that of the eye, seems not only to underscore the artifice of film and its craft component but also, in the case of short works, helps explain why they will continue to matter. Just as the Net pieces proved fragile and often insubstantial, yet somehow terribly poignant, so shorts, in their proximity to the sketch, the notebook entry, the short story, reveal a similar vulnerability *and* hope. However much they claim to contain a world, they inevitably can only aspire, only suggest. They're like the shrapnel paragraphs of newspaper round-ups, which seek to convey the dimensions of an entire news item in a couple of lines, in a threshold incident, in an aftermath, with all the build (and the perhaps long life to follow) implied in a turn of phrase, a look, a response to certain weathers.

Yet these are the fragments, layered and fired, that lodge in the heart and mark us. Grace notes. The haiku opening from detail towards sublime revelation, or even the subliminal, if one of the media in question – advertising – is taken to its logical endpoint. A whole narrative of unconscious desire in a split second. But isn't this what occurs in the viewing anyway? In November 1993, writer-director Chris Petit penned 'Flickers' for the BFI's journal of record *Sight and Sound*, in which he listed simply his key moments of cinema, from 'Anna Karina cycling in *Bande à Part*' to 'Robert Vaughan catching flies in *The Magnificent Seven*'. In the final analysis, these perhaps are shorts as key as any, the remembered experiences of film (and life), of sequences lifted by love out of a work; a history of pictures, the way we make cinema our own, and the world. And they show, as this book argues throughout, that the briefest of time frames can catch, carry and change everything.

It's something that writers have known, whether Shakespeare or Jorge Luis Borges. In his short story 'The Aleph', the latter describes the titular object, several centimetres across and located in a cellar in Buenos Aires, as 'one of the points in space containing all points ... the place where all the places in the world are found, seen from every angle ...' And he goes on, 'if all the places on earth are in the Aleph, the Aleph must also contain all the illuminations, all the lights, all the sources of light'.

Could this not be a description of the potential of just a single frame, a site where, as visionary poet William Blake once observed, you might 'see a world in a grain of sand, and a heaven in a wild flower, hold infinity in the palm of your hand and eternity in an hour'.

Or even less.

Gareth Evans is a freelance writer and film programmer. He contributes regularly to *Time Out* (London), *The Independent* and *Sight and Sound*, and edits the film magazine *Vertigo*. He works as a programme advisor to the London Film Festival and Brief Encounters International Short Film Festival, and has served on juries at Tampere and Oberhausen short film festivals.

1

Introduction: Shorts in the Field of Film

The invisibility of short film

Between 1999 and spring 2001 British and North American newspapers began to take an interest in the short film. The news covered first, the establishment of many digital short film websites and, second, the release of nineteen films, many of them shorts, of the complete works of Samuel Beckett. For a brief time, short films had a profile that had not been present since the early days of film-making. For many readers, indeed, it may have come as a surprise to learn that shorts still existed: even regular cinemagoers rarely see short films outside of festivals and television, still less see reviews of them. Despite this interest, the Beckett on Film project failed to secure more than a few screenings, and most saw the films on television, not at the cinema. Beckett's literary fame, and the publicity surrounding their release, were not enough to guarantee distribution. And after an early flurry of activity – when the best shorts were in huge demand – the Internet has still to deliver quick and easy viewing of films, and will not do so until broadband is widely adopted. The dot.com collapse has also led to retrenchment and less coverage.

Short films are nothing new, though, they have been present since film-making began. Shorts were the only films in the early days of cinema. National governments made them a tool of official propaganda in the First World War. During the development of sound, they became an experiment for the new order. Some of the great short films appeared in the 1920s and 30s – especially in cartoon animation and the comedy of Keaton, Chaplin, Laurel and Hardy and Langdon – and many of the best propaganda shorts in the Second World War have become cinema classics. It was only in the 1960s and 70s that the decline began, when short films went from being a staple part of the cinema experience to being present only in specialist cinemas and festivals.

More than one hundred years on from the birth of film, shorts remain a key part of cinema, however. There has been a small renaissance in recent years and some of the most innovative, exciting and thought-provoking short films that we have seen are being made today.

Short films are easy to ignore because they are hard to see. We lose a lot because of this: creativity and innovation, inspirational storytelling, and, simply, some great films. We believe it is time to look at short films so that we can celebrate the achievements of short film-makers and help new film-makers learn from current practitioners, to encourage the production of more and better short films in the future. We also believe it is time that the economic and creative importance of shorts within the British film industry is recognised.

Our book is the first for many years on the short film in Britain. Apart from a growing body of work on avant-garde film, books about the cinema are generally about features and their stars. The most popular short films – cinema and television commercials and music videos – receive little critical attention and their role in providing experience and income for film-makers is largely unacknowledged.

Following a short history of short films – which looks at education, animation, advertising, music video and the avant-garde – film-makers talk about their work. We are fortunate to have gathered together such an excellent group of film-makers, all of whom provide inspiration and vision as well as important information on the basics of short film production. Short films provide an ideal opportunity for a close investigation of the individual creative process, from initial idea to finished film, and that is what the interviews in Chapter 3 set out to do. Chapter 4 pulls together the main points raised, and the final two chapters look at the practical aspects of getting short films made, and includes a resource guide with details of websites, magazines and funding opportunities.

The authors are both involved in short film exhibition, production and teaching. Andrew Kelly founded Brief Encounters, the Bristol Short Film Festival, and we have both been on the board of the festival since the start. Eileen Elsey is also a screenwriter and principal lecturer in Time Based Media at the University of the West of England. Together, we bring such concerns as scripting and storytelling as well as management, marketing and funding to the discussion.

A definition of shorts

What is a short film? Sometimes, the term is used to describe any film under feature length. Most film festivals rule that a short must have a maximum duration of thirty minutes, and this is the definition we use here. A definition based purely on duration is arbitrary, and many superlative shorts are often very short. The impact of Anthony Minghella's *Play* (sixteen minutes, 2000), or Tessa Sheridan's *Is it the Design on the Wrapper?* (seven minutes, 1997) or Jonathan Glazer's *Surfer* commercial (one minute, 1999) is related to their dominance of the form and the dense layers of meaning built up in such a short time. The possibility of Web distribution – which we look at in detail in Chapter 5 – has raised interest in the very short piece of five minutes or less. But longer films may also use the space well. For example, Damien O'Donnell's *Thirty-five Aside* (twenty-seven minutes, 1995) is a beautifully sustained film which is both touching and funny. John Smith's *Black Tower* (twenty-four minutes, 1987) has a slower, more reflective pace. What all these shorts do share is the opportunity they offer film-makers to practise their art outside the pressures of feature film and television production. Unfortunately, what they also have in common – apart from the advertising commercial – is limited distribution, which means that most readers will not have had an opportunity to see them.

The scope and function of the book

Here we concentrate on narrative drama films of thirty minutes or less produced in Britain. We have omitted documentary, work for children and – in the main – abstract avant-garde work. We have included music videos and advertising commercials. These omissions and inclusions have come about in an attempt to draw a line round a subject area on which so little has been written, and represent an attempt to locate a community or network of film-makers. Because Britain does not have a sustainable feature film industry, most drama film-makers – both live action and animation – have worked on music videos and commercials. Although avant-garde production tends to be separate, their work is viewed by other film-makers at film courses and festivals and is often a source of innovative ideas or approaches. It may seem madly optimistic to aim to cover this breadth in one book after the long silence on short film, but it is important that the interconnectivity between drama and animation shorts, commercials and music videos is acknowledged.

Shorts are an important part of the film-making culture of Britain, but are largely ignored in both critical and distribution terms. It is time to re-evaluate their position and to raise their profile. We want to see more discussion about short films in their own right and not as a calling-card for a feature production (although this has a role). We want to see more high-quality short films made. To encourage this we need information and examples of good practice. Above all, we need to know, directly from those involved, how to make successful short films.

If you like short films, teach about them, make them now or want to make them in the future, this book provides the essential details. It is not a guide to short film production, though there is much guidance here, and the websites listed in Chapter 6 will provide information on commissioning and funding opportunities. As these details can become out of date quickly the book's centre is elsewhere – we look for advice and inspiration from today's film-makers. Through our interviews with contemporary short film directors in Britain and Ireland we discuss the creative and commissioning process of film-making, and the relationship between funding, distribution and creativity.

We cover a wide range of work including artists' film and video, live action, animation, commercials and music videos. There are huge differences in budgets, distribution, exhibition and working practices in the films we discuss. But all use sound and image to communicate a story to an audience in a short space of time, and do so creatively. Often, the people we interviewed work across different areas, with commercials and music videos helping to fund their independent productions. The combination of diversity of product and interconnectedness of practice is an important aspect of short film production.

The role of shorts in contemporary practice

Advertising commercials and music videos play an important role in sustaining a film-making culture in Britain, and most film-makers have been involved in their production. Commercials are more lucrative, but are usually more creatively con-strained; there is more opportunity for film-makers to see their own ideas on the screen in music videos. But commercials have the highest production values and budgets (in relation to their duration) that film-makers will ever have the oppor-tunity to work with. Thus they give the opportunity to try out expensive equipment or processes and to reward cast and crew who have worked on low-budget produc-tions. They provide opportunities to build production teams and develop skills. They also reach a much wider and more populist audience than shorts which are often restricted to film festivals and late-night television.

Production experience is essential for film-makers to hone their skills, but there is a difference between developing the craft of film-making and finding an author-ial voice (although the two are closely related). Films that have evolved from the creative processes of a writer/director or production team are also an essential part of development. Short films, with their limited production time and lower budgets, provide an essential space for experiment and innovation where directors can try different structures, different ways of working with actors, different subject matter, without feeling that failure will bring an end to their careers. The right to fail is an important aspect of all experimentation.

Short films can be emotional, funny, experimental, poetic, open-ended: a play space for both film-maker and audience. Experimentation and a powerful personal vision must be at its centre, and the best shorts have a resonance that lingers with the audience long after viewing. Recognising the high quality of films made in this area may help us protect them from being turned into inferior copies of Hollywood-style narratives or mini-soaps.

2

A Short History of Shorts

Short film and film history

In one hundred years short films have gone from being the only form of cinema to being marginal, and from a commercial venture to, presently, being made only through the generosity of public subsidy or business sponsorship. The first films were shorts. They were all about one minute long – fragments of documentary, music hall acts or dramas which relied on the audience's amazement with the new medium for their impact. As people became used to the wonders of the moving image, the complexity and length of films were increased, and a programme would be made up of a variety of films.

The Lumière Brothers gave the first public film show in Paris in 1895. It came to London in February 1896. In the following month, the first public showing of British work took place, organised by R. W. Paul. Interest in the moving image was high in Europe and the USA, and ideas for equipment, technique and content spread between countries. (Méliès, who became a specialist in fantasies using trick photography, bought his first camera from Paul when the Lumières refused to supply one.) Many film-makers were involved in the production or exhibition of older technologies – stills photography, magic lantern shows, theatre and vaudeville – which informed the film-makers' and audiences' approach to the new medium.

Moving image composition often used photographic conventions, while drawing on theatrical devices for framing and staging action. One of the films from that first show, *Sortie d'usine* (*Workers Leaving the Factory*, Lumière Brothers 1895, 48 seconds),[1] begins and ends with the opening and closing of the factory gates, like theatre curtains to the action. The camera remains static, but the workers move towards and to one side of the camera, thus using depth of field in the manner of still photography.

Between 1896 and 1906, thousands of short films – drama and documentary – were produced by film companies scattered across Britain. The Hepworth Manufacturing Company at Walton-on-Thames, for instance, produced 100 films a year. More complex dramas, using spectacle or emotion to appeal to the audience, appeared. 'Trick' films using double exposure particularly appealed to audiences; for instance, G. A. Smith's *The Corsican Brothers* (1897), *The Fairy Godmother* (1898) and *Faust and Mephistopheles* (1898). The popular film *Rescued by Rover* (Hepworth 1905, 6 minutes 34 seconds) uses camera movements, low-angle camera, two studio sets and four different locations, and editing included elisions and parallel action. It shows filmic narrative structure in the process of development, including the use of continuity editing, and it works to emotionally involve the audience through the use of a baby victim and a dog hero. The story is of a baby from a respectable middle-class home being abducted by a gypsy while the nursemaid is canoodling with a soldier. When the family learn what has happened they are hysterical. Rover the dog tracks the gypsy to a slum area, and returns home to lead the father to the rescue. The gypsy has got drunk and fallen asleep, so she doesn't put up much of a struggle, and the baby is brought home in triumph.

Some of the elements of this plot, particularly the portrayal of the respectable middle class contrasting with the criminal working class, may point to the problems which British drama faced as narratives became more extended. British society was divided by class and was paternalistic in nature. Although technically advanced, middle-class film-makers were often making entertainment for working-class audiences and a moralising attitude could often result. Working-class heroes were usually restricted to comedy.

Increasing competition, particularly from the USA, led to both the number of British films being shown and the amount of money invested in the industry falling. Erratic funding – particularly of short film – and low investment has been a feature of the industry ever since. The 1914–18 and 1939–45 wars saw a decline in the European film industries. Cecil Hepworth's studio continued until 1923, when it went bankrupt. From 1927 onwards legislation was brought in to try to protect local product against imports and to encourage investment.

Since 1939 state subsidy in various forms has ensured that short films continue to be made. Government commissions – particularly of documentary, animation and feature films – became increasingly important during wartime. The National Film Finance Corporation was set up in 1949; new directors and makers of short films were among those helped. Their priority was feature film production, however, and in the years 1973–81 they contributed to the funding of only six shorts. The Eady Levy began in 1950, a percentage of which went to the BFI Production Board. The Board has been a strong advocate of shorts and has helped to promote more culturally diverse productions. Both the National Film Finance Corporation (NFFC) and the Eady Levy were dismantled in 1985, and British Screen set up in 1986. Funding was also channelled through the Arts Council and regional arts boards. Television companies and, after 1995, the National Lottery, which has supported seventy short films, became increasingly important in short film funding. Business sponsorship of films has fluctuated with profit levels and the amount of government-sponsored work. The launch of the new Film Council in 2001 has already led to increased budgets being devoted to short films.

Documentary and animation tended to develop further than live-action drama in British shorts. Drama was often seen as more suitable for features, although comedy shorts and serial films – particularly for children – continued to be popular. The dramas of the 1920s and 30s are often unsophisticated comedies and spoofs, for instance Ivor Montagu's *Bluebottles* (1928, 29 minutes).

Part of the reason for the superficial nature of much British output may have been censorship. The Russian Revolution and growth of the Communist Party, the General Strike and economic depression created a government nervous about anything which might cause unrest, particularly in a medium popular with the working class, and films portraying 'relations between capital and labour' were banned. Although film clubs were set up to provide an alternative to commercial cinema, films shown still had to be passed by the censor. In this context, the influence of, for instance, Eisenstein's montage editing and approach to film, was limited. Where it did occur – he gave two lectures at the Film Society, London, in 1929 – it has often influenced form not content. In Desmond Dickenson's *C.O.D. – A Mellow Drama* (1929, 11 minutes), for example, low lighting, angled camerawork and montage editing are used to tell a spoof pass-the-parcel melodrama with no character development. This contrasts with *Everyday*, directed by Hans Richter (1929, 17 minutes), where form and content mesh to create real impact.

Gradually, in the face of official censorship and bland commercial cinema at a time of economic hardship for so much of the population, short film began to be used by radical groups. Often made on low budgets, film-makers would use animation, documentary, archive footage and live action to make a political statement. In the 1930s, the Workers' Film and Photo League and Kino were set up and, although poorly funded, produced such films as *Bread* (1934, Kino London Production Group) and *Peace and Plenty* (1939, Ivor Montagu and Kino). Helen Biggar and Norman McLaren's strongly anti-war *Hell UnLtd* (1936, Glasgow School of Art) is a powerful mix of animation and live action which aims to incite civil disobedience. Some of the most radical film-makers joined John Grierson's group at the General Post Office (GPO) Film Unit, and so became dependent on government funding. Other groups were disbanded during the Second World War.

The 1950s saw the beginning of a revival of independent film-making with films such as Lindsay Anderson's *Oh Dreamland!* (1954), Karel Reisz's *We are the Lambeth Boys* (1958), Richard Lester's *Running Jumping Standing Still Film* (1959) and the development of the Free Cinema movement. Although many of the productions were documentary in nature, the approach also fed in to the 'working-class realism' features of the 1960s, such as *Saturday Night and Sunday Morning* (1960). The London Film-makers' Co-operative was founded in 1966 to provide an alternative to mainstream cinema, but its members tended to be more interested in abstract experimental work. In general, there has been a distrust of narrative film in Britain. A divide opened up between mainly conventional television drama and experimental work. Commercials and animation became the areas where new narrative techniques and dramatic forms were explored.

Although there is little data available to make a definitive judgment, the contribution made by film schools, regional arts boards, media development agencies and, in some cases, local authorities cannot be ignored. All of these have helped to make and fund short films – often through elaborate collaborative ventures.

The 1970s and 80s saw the expansion of media education and the evolution of feminist, gay and black film-makers with their own agendas, whose work often bridged narrative and abstract forms. Occasionally, particularly with the advent of Channel 4, film-makers like Sally Potter and Isaac Julien reached a wider audience.

Today we still see that divide in drama shorts between glossy, high-quality productions and a more disrupted form and less perfect aesthetic as in the animation of Joanna Quinn. There is a deep ambivalence around production values, film form and political meaning which is not solely about the size of the budget: Lynne Ramsay, for example, comments on the division between glossy drama and fast-moving documentary production at the National Film and Television School in her interview. There are moments – for instance, around Hugh Hudson's election film for the Labour Party, or the physical attractions of Lara Croft – where this boils over into public debate. Tension around the political meaning of perfection is unlikely to go away, particularly with the increasing fusion of computer-generated images and live action.

Education

A vast amount of short film and video production takes place within the educational system, where shorter durations are found to be ideal for the limited time and low budgets available. The growth in the use of video in the 1970s and 80s and the resulting lowering of production costs and simplification of process have led to widespread use at all levels of education. Often linked to theoretical studies in media or communication, the majority of these productions reach no audience beyond students and staff. Nor are they designed to be seen by a wider audience, as it is usually the process of planning and production, rather than the end result, which is regarded as educationally important. Awareness of the process which lies behind the persuasive television and cinema screen, and the ways in which meaning can be manipulated through sound and moving image, are now seen by many teachers as being important basic knowledge in today's society.

Film and video production within higher education has a longer history. Apart from the London Film School (opened in 1957), opportunities to produce film appeared within existing educational institutions and at first were connected to existing subject areas. British art schools, which traditionally have the aim of enabling individual creativity, allowed students to explore film as another medium. It was at Glasgow School of Art, for instance, that Norman McLaren and Helen Biggar produced *Hell UnLtd* (1936). The Royal College of Art and the Slade offered post-graduate courses in film. At polytechnics, where craft or technical process tended to be foregrounded, film courses often grew out of the photography subject area. An example of this is Regent Street Polytechnic (where the Lumière Brothers gave their first British film show), which has a long record of film education broken only by the Second World War and despite a couple of name changes – to the Polytechnic of Central London in 1970, and then to Westminster University in 1992. Originally, film was offered as part of the photography course and gradually evolved a separate identity.

Traditionally, polytechnics and art schools have enabled practice whilst universities specialised in a theoretical approach, and opportunities for film production at universities were rare. An early exception to this was Bristol University, where film and television production grew up within the Drama department from 1956. A common thread throughout education, however, was the importance of the relationship between theory and practice rather than a skills-based approach.

The film industry depended on a tradition of apprenticeships for training, while most television training was provided by the BBC. There was also vocational courses offered by trade organisations and commercial companies (for example, the Royal Television Society, the British Kinematograph Sound and Television Society, Kodak). The industry favoured practical skills-based courses, and were generally suspicious of film-makers coming from college or university with their more analytical approach. The relationship between the media industries and education has frequently been marked by distrust and lack of understanding on both sides, and the debate on the merits of 'training' vs 'education' has been long and heated.[2] Strong unions meant that it was extremely difficult to work in the media without union membership, but it was difficult to acquire membership. The ability of some colleges to offer a union card to their students could add immensely to the popularity of the course and the success of its graduates, but by the late 1980s only seven educational institutions in Britain had received Association of Cinematograph, Television and Allied Technicians (ACTT) recognition.[3]

The National Film School (NFS) opened in 1971, and both the government and industry were involved in its evolution and funding. The initial free-wheeling approach of learning through practice developed into a more structured curriculum with industry involvement in the 1980s. It became the National Film and Television School in 1982, aimed at providing in-depth film and television training at post-graduate level, and the change of name reflected the growing involvement of the television industry. The National Short Course Training Programme, for retraining freelance professionals, was financed by the Eady Levy. Government and industry financial support has waxed and waned over time. As early as 1977 the Film Production Association criticised the NFS as an unfair burden on the Eady Levy, and the axing of the levy in 1984 was a blow to the School's finances. Industry sponsorship has become increasingly important. The 1990s saw an increased focus to the curriculum, with student enrolment into specialist departments and tighter production controls.

The British Film Institute (founded in 1933) has actively encouraged film culture in Britain, particularly through education. It has promoted and disseminated the main debates around film (from structuralism in the 1960s to digital technologies in 2001) through seminars and conferences, as well as its publications – *Screen* and *Sight and Sound*. It funded the first university appointments in the new discipline of Film Studies in the early 1970s. Today, it provides resources, training and advice for teachers at all levels of education, as well as maintaining the national moving image library and archive.

The 1970s and 80s saw a rapid growth in courses across the country, particularly within polytechnics. This was part of the wider growth in higher education as well as meeting a particular demand for media education.[4] On many film and video courses in the 1970s, there was a shift to an anti-establishment stance, which was fuelled by technological changes (lighter cameras, low-light film, the advent of video), the influence of the French New Wave, as well as the political unrest of the times. There was a move away from studio production, a questioning of traditional approaches, and a striving towards political meaning in their work by film students. Jim Cook and Jim Hillier, writing in 1976, remark: 'Politicisation has meant a great interest in ideology and the aesthetics of realism as well as in militant and revolutionary cinema – hence the interest in realism and documentary and in the industrial nature of film production and exhibition.'[5] There is a marked difference between earlier film graduates – such as Ridley Scott, Alan Parker and David Puttnam – and film-makers who studied during or after this time of upheaval – for instance, Peter Greenaway, Sally Potter, Derek Jarman and Isaac Julien – and their attitude to mainstream cinema. Many film-makers today – both within and outside the avant-garde – continue to work to deconstruct filmic conventions and encourage audiences to take an active, critical stance to what they see.

The destruction of the unions' power base in the 1980s has led to increased opportunities for graduates, but also has led to the casualisation of the workforce with negative effects on career progression and job security.

Because of its history in different subject areas and different types of institutions, media courses in higher education today provide a rich diversity of approach. Art colleges have often been subsumed into polytechnics, and polytechnics have become universities, but the evidence of their histories is often evident in the work being done now. Animation courses, for instance, are often based in places with an art school background. A concern with the relationship between theory and practice is common within education, however, as is the realisation that people with the potential to develop as film-makers must be able to analyse and learn from their own and others' work.

With the growing pace of technological change and shifts in the use of media, industry is also becoming aware that the people able to cope with such a fluid way of working need to be able to think beyond specific skills. The relationship between industry and education continues to improve as an increasing number of people throughout the industry have graduated from media courses. They are often happy to continue their involvement with education through visiting professorships, part-time lecturing and other formal and informal links.

Animation

Animated images were used before film was invented. Sequential drawings were used in research on persistence of vision and its uses, and optical toys, for example, the zoetrope, were created. In Paris, Emile Reynaud patented a projected version, and gave public performances of his optical theatre. Arthur Melbourne Cooper made the first animated film, *Matches, An Appeal*, for a public appeal during the Boer War in 1899. He later made shorts by animating children's toys, including *Noah's Ark* (1906) and *Dreams of Toyland* (1908).

Lightning sketches or chalk talks were popular entertainment where the animator was also a performer – giving a monologue and modifying the drawings on screen – and some of the earliest animators came from this vaudeville background. James Stuart Blackton (born in Britain, emigrated to the USA) made *The Haunted Hotel* in 1907, a film that mixed live and animated action. This provided the inspiration for Emile Cohl in France, the first specialist animator, who made hundreds of animated shorts in France and in the USA from 1908 until 1938. Arnoldo Ginna, in Italy, was experimenting with colour over time by painting directly onto film in 1910, and Ladislas Starewich made the first three-dimensional animated film – *Lucanus Cervus* – in Moscow, also in 1910. In the USA at this time, Winsor McCay, an artist who produced newspaper comic strips as well as performing chalk talks, animated his cartoon character *Little Nemo* (1910) and started a popular and lucrative animation genre. His work became increasingly complex. One of the most popular – *Gertie the Dinosaur* (1914) – was an interactive performance with McCay as the dinosaur tamer before it was turned into an animated film.

The labour-intensive nature of animation meant short formats were more viable, and feature-length animations rare, until the rise of the Disney Studio. Cartoons were popular in both Europe and America, and often had their character and narrative sources in children's comics or stories. They were ideal for comedy shorts to be shown as part of cinema programmes or at specialist cartoon cinemas.

By the 1930s the majority of animators in Britain worked in cinema advertising, but cartoons were also produced. Cecil Hepworth's studio produced *Kiddigraphs*, a series which included *Little Red Riding Hood* and *The Three Little Pigs* (both 1922). However, these did little to challenge Disney, which grew from employing six people in 1928, to 187 in 1934 and 1,600 in 1940.[6] Along with other film-makers, animators of all styles emigrated to the USA before and during the Second World War when much of the production infrastructure in Europe was destroyed and, for many, the political situation became oppressive or dangerous.

Through the 1930s and 40s, British Government departments became increasingly important as commissioners of work. The GPO Film Unit helped both Len Lye and Norman McLaren to develop as animators. Lye's *Tusalava* (1929) and *A Colour Box* (1936) – still influential today – are products of this unit. McLaren made films for the GPO Film Unit, including *Love on the Wing* (1938), before going to Canada in 1941 to head up the animation sector of the Canadian Film Board. His rich and inventive work continues to be an inspiration to animators.

The long-lived animation studio Halas & Batchelor was set up in London as an independent arm of the advertising agency J. Walter Thompson in 1940. Their first two films were cinema commercials – *Train Trouble* (for Kelloggs Cornflakes) and *Carnival in the Clothes Cupboard* (for Lux toilet soap). They made a large number of series and shorts and a feature-length film for the government, and built up an excellent reputation for this and their independent work.[7] For the Festival of Britain, Halas & Batchelor made two colour 3D films, and from 1955 onwards they were producing television commercials. In the 1960s they made the first animated series for television, and became the first in the world to work with computer animation. Halas & Batchelor employees continue to influence British animation today.[8]

Bob Godfrey (MBE and Academy Award winner) has also collaborated with and trained a number of British animators. He started in animation at Larkins – a studio founded in London in 1940 – before setting up Biographic with Keith Lerner in 1954 and his own independent studio later. Now in his eighties, he continues to work as an animator and teacher. His popular children's series *Roobarb* and *Henry's Cat* contrast with the adult humour of *Polygamous Polonius* (1959), *Karma Sutra Rides Again* (1971) and *Great* (1975) – a thirty-minute musical about Isambard Kingdom Brunel.

Since the 1960s there has been a period of growth and diversity for British animation in advertising and feature films, including animated feature films such as the hugely popular *Yellow Submarine* (1967). By 1987 there were over thirty studios in London, and others in Bristol, Cardiff, Glasgow, Manchester[9] and Leeds.

Aardman Animation, set up in 1972 by Peter Lord and Dave Sproxton while they were still at school on the strength of their first BBC commission, is now one of the biggest studios in Britain, employing around 300 people on shorts, features, advertisements and music videos. Famous for their clay animation, they have also diversified into work in a variety of animation methods.

British animation studios are economically underpinned by advertising, children's programmes and overseas distribution. They now face increasing competition from cheaper films from overseas. Computer animation has brought down production costs (although updating equipment and software is often a major financial consideration) creating a less labour-intensive way of working. Television companies, particularly the BBC, Channel 4 and S4C, have become involved in financing animation, and film festivals play an important role in sales, as well as providing exhibition opportunities for less commercial productions. The use of the Internet to show short animation also reinforces the international nature of animation practice.

Today there are a number of independent animators or small studios, like Emma Calder and Ged Haney's Pearly Oyster, and a large number of freelance workers. As the possibilities of creating films on computers increase and the line between animation, computer graphics and special effects becomes blurred, the numbers involved are difficult to quantify with any accuracy. That there is a shortage of skilled, talented animators and scriptwriters for animation is agreed, however.

Right from animation's inception we see certain qualities that remain – a diversity of styles and methods, use in both commercial and artistic sectors as well as public information or propaganda films, and an international creative community. Also, the line between live action and animation has often been blurred. The original hand-cranked cameras were very adaptable to the stop-frame techniques and trick effects that were particularly popular in silent comedies, which enabled the mix of fantasy and reality that still draws audiences to the cinema today.

Advertising

The potential for cinema to sell to its captive audience was recognised early: Cointreau commissioned the first cinema commercial in 1898. Advertising, like other forms of cinema, evolved from existing entertainment – especially music hall acts, popular songs and cartoons – and adapted the testimonial format from print advertising. British advertisers often felt that they should inform as well as entertain, and short pieces showing the raw material, the production process, or dramatising the company's history were produced. Advertisements ranged from simple announcements to camera or a photomontage with voiceover or jingles, to elaborate animations, live-action mini-dramas or ersatz documentaries. The use of public information shorts grew as well, particularly during wartime.

Cinema audiences were worth reaching. In 1936, total admissions to the 4,300 cinemas in Great Britain were 963 million and box-office receipts totalled £41 million. It was also a growing market – a year later, the number of cinemas had increased by nearly 700. But the cost of reaching the audience was high compared to other forms of advertising. A complex production might cost £1,000 or more to film with cinema bookings, printing and distribution taking the cost up to £6,000.[10]

The advent of independent television in 1955 offered more advertising opportunities, although creatively it was slow to develop. For at least the first ten years, television was seen as augmenting print advertising, and many commercials simply turned print advertisements into a moving image. This was a confusing time. Television companies' projections of audience size proved to be over-estimated and both broadcasting hours and rates had to be cut. Creative producers tried a variety of styles – 'thinly adapted radio and cinema advertisements, transplanted US commercials, mini television programmes, presenter sales pitches, documentaries, simple animation, unsophisticated jingles and occasional forays into experiment' according to David Bernstein.[11]

British creators of commercials watched American examples but often found them too brash, too direct. They were working in a different environment – a polite, restrained and class-conscious society – and had to find a different way of selling to the public. In the USA, television and advertising had arrived together; in Britain, public service television had existed since 1936, and social commentators were ambivalent about television advertising. There was widespread concern that commercial television would lead to lower standards in public entertainment, and that British culture would become infused with American idioms. Partly to allay these fears British advertisements had a different style, which the *New York Post* described as 'a paragon of phlegmatic British understatement and restraint'.[12]

Advertisers also had to deal with the nuances of class divisions in their representations of society. Actors were trained to rid themselves of any trace of regional accent and adopt the upper-middle-class Received Pronunciation (RP) English. This was fine for the mainly middle-class theatre audience, but often alienated the major market that the working class represented for cinema and television. One of the reasons for the popularity of American films was that they were perceived to be classless by the British public. ITV (Independent TeleVision) programming had an American influence that contrasted sharply with the BBC's output.[13] There was also uncertainty about how to deal with the short format of commercials (initially between one and three minutes), particularly for live-action drama. The theatre or feature film provided the models for performed drama, and tended to be slow-moving three- or five-act structures.

Animation was useful in solving these problems. Animators had worked with shorter formats and knew how to communicate economically through the moving image, and animated figures – particularly animals – were more neutral in class terms. In the first years of commercial television, nearly one third of all advertisements were animations. Some of the most popular characters – the Murraymint guardsmen, the Esso Blue dealer, Sammy and Susie Sunblest – were created at this time. The first Oxo cube advertisement featured Sooty, a glove-puppet teddy bear. Typhoo Tea got round the problems by shooting live-action dramas starring chimpanzees, which became the longest running television advertising campaign. It was finally dropped in 2001.

Unlike American television, British regulators were concerned that advertisements should be clearly indicated to the viewer, and advertisements were gathered together into commercial breaks. They were not allowed to exceed 10 per cent of transmission time. Outside this quota, however, were advertising magazines, again a TV version of a print format where advertisements were thinly disguised as editorial material. The most popular one was *Jim's Inn*, set in a pub with Jimmy Hanley as the landlord. Advertising magazines were not allowed after 1963. Corporate television advertising was important as one aspect of creating a favourable public image. For instance, Shell was promoted through print advertisements, guide books, maps and three-minute television shorts presented by John Betjeman. Beautiful countryside and architecture were featured; petrol stations were not.

Transmission of commercial television gradually improved through the 1960s and by 1970 covered 90 per cent of homes. As the planning and production of advertising campaigns became more complex, specialist advertising agencies developed. The idea of a creative team for each brand was imported from the USA. Made up of an art director and a copywriter, on a commercial they initiate and script the idea and handle the liaison with the film director.

Most commercials were cut to fifteen, thirty or sixty seconds, with an occasional two-minute epic. Advertising agencies became more confident in their use of this format. Gradually, television became the dominant medium in advertising, and with the advent of colour in 1969 budgets and production values soared. Commercials became glossier and faster than the programmes around them and, with little happening in the national film industry, became a major creative outlet for writers, art directors, film directors and producers. Terry Gilliam, David Puttnam, Alan Parker and Ridley Scott all worked in advertising at this time.

Through the 1970s and 80s the British advertising industry was internationally regarded as highly creative and successful, and able to solve marketing problems. When two instant mashed potato mixes – Wondermash and Smash – were launched at the same time, it was Smash, the brand with the funny and popular Martian puppet characters, that won the battle. The Cadbury's Milk Tray advertisements, showing a mysterious man risking danger in order to deliver secretly a box of chocolates to a woman, rivalled the James Bond movies for fast-moving stunts and spectacle. Many commercials of this time contained mini-stories with witty dialogue and characters who often developed over a number of advertisements. The Oxo family evolved into a mini-soap without the tragedies, and has run for thirty-four years.

What were regarded as the best commercials often sold obliquely, using humour, mystery, conundrums and spectacle to involve the audience, as creative teams learnt how the repetition of commercials enabled, even demanded, a more complex style which called on the audience to unravel the message. The opening of a new commercial television channel in 1982 – Channel 4 – did little to challenge the cohesiveness of the television audience, and the popularity of characters, jingles and catchphrases from TV commercials.

Recently, successful advertising has become more problematic. People are perpetually surrounded by advertising in a variety of media and so stop noticing them.[14] Television advertising's greatest challenge has come from the splintering of audiences resulting from the impact of new technologies and an escalating number of channels available in the home. Internet and video games take up screen and leisure time. Cinema audiences have been increasing for the past decade. Such diversification of activity and breadth of media choice make it difficult for television advertising to have the same impact as before. Companies prefer brand stretching (offering new products or versions under an existing brand name) to attempting to make an impact with a new brand. Website publicity, often as an adjunct to print or TV, is increasingly important. And some companies, such as BT Payphones, Levis, the *Daily Telegraph* and BMW, have turned occasionally to short films to sell their goods indirectly to niche markets.

TV commercials have lost their dominance as a marketing tool, and the average company spend on television advertising budgets is going down. However, the advertising industry still manages to keep some of its previous creative status, and occasionally grabs the public's imagination.

Through the 1990s and into the new century there has been a general move away from character and dialogue towards spectacle and mood, using computer-generated effects. Animation remains important, but today it is more difficult to know where live action ends and animation begins. The advertising industry is continually looking for new ideas and ways to communicate, and has always trawled widely for these. New techniques laboriously developed by experimental film-makers or digital artists are pressed into the service of publicity.[15] Advertising often incorporates styles from groups that are marginal, even oppositional, which raises questions for many film-makers about the relationship between form and content.

Music video

The music video is a recent phenomenon, but music and film have worked together since the start of cinema. From the 1850s onwards, lantern slides were designed to accompany popular songs. The development of moving image projection and syn-

chronised sound were also used to bring music hall performers to a wider audience
– the first talking feature film, *The Jazz Singer* (1927) starred the singer Al Jolson.
Jazz shorts featuring black performers were produced for showing at American all-
black theatres. The 1940s, 50s and 60s saw the development of juke boxes with
accompanying films, usually of the performer lip-synching the songs.

The growth of pop music and the youth market led to pop singers having feature
films built around them: Elvis Presley from the 1950s onwards and in Britain, Cliff
Richard and then the Beatles. The feature films *A Hard Day's Night* (1964) and *Help*
(1965) were a breakthrough in bringing together the art school consciousness so
prevalent in British pop performers and commercial feature films. The tendency to
reflect the psychedelic popular culture in the style as well as content of film (jump-
cuts, odd angles, film run backwards) became especially noticeable in the *Penny
Lane* and *Strawberry Fields Forever* promotional films (1967).

Short films made to promote a single pop song and using the song as a soundtrack remained slow to take off in Britain, where there was a lack of broadcast
opportunities for the material. There were few pop music programmes on the three
heavily controlled television channels that existed. These programmes often used
live studio performances because of union agreements to limit the amount of
recorded material used, so record companies saw film-making as a promotional
expense unlikely to reap a profit. This attitude changed in 1975, when Queen
released *Bohemian Rhapsody*, and the single was at the top of the UK pop music
charts for nine weeks. Many record promoters saw the strong visuals in the video as
an integral part of its success, and were prepared to put increasing amounts of
money into pop promo production. Initially they were transferred to video to be
used as a media pack, and sent out to television companies for possible broadcast,
but there was a growing demand for these promos to be available on video for the
public to buy. The pop promo became the music video as the primary purpose
moved from promoting the music recording to becoming a product in its own right.

Throughout the 1980s and 90s, music video benefited from the lifting of restrictions on the use of pre-recorded material on television, and the growth in the
number of channels British audiences could view through cable, satellite and digital technologies – including MTV (Music TeleVision).[16] The Internet has provided
another way of seeing music videos. Relatively cheap, good-quality digital video
cameras, CDs, DVDs and the Internet together provide the possibility of turning
the recording and dissemination of music and music videos into a cottage industry.

Music video has become an alternative area to cinema, television and commercials for directors, animators and computer graphics artists to work in. Less well paid
but also less constrained than advertising work, it provides income as well as the
potential of a more individualistic approach for film-makers. An eclectic variety of
styles are on show. This may partly be to do with its history – the connection between

art and pop as mentioned above – and partly to do with its form. Limited to the length of the piece of music, usually about three minutes, this is an ideal time for an abstract work, a short narrative or a mixture of the two.

Pop music enables film-makers to gain access to a young and diverse audience, as well as cutting through the cultural elitism of other film and video output. Abstract images are as acceptable as live-action narrative to this audience; there is none of the negativity that marks the popular reception (or dismissal) of the avant-garde. The music provides a ready-made structure that encourages the poetic or abstract use of pattern – rhythm, repetition, variations of pace – and foregrounds those qualities in the audiences' perception, and at the same time provides a justification for such a structure. Animation of all types, and computer-generated animation and special effects, have continued the experimental element in music videos which excites the interest of film-makers.[17] It is an area that will allow different production values and styles, and all will receive the same airtime and follow one another in MTV's flow of content.[18] This open, flexible space gives much freedom to the film-maker. Five of the eleven directors featured here have been involved in music video production.

Avant-garde

Unlike other short film genres there is a body of writing on this subject area, the most recent and thorough example being A. L. Rees' *A History of Experimental Film and Video*.[19] So we will not attempt to go beyond the general history provided at the beginning of this chapter, but would prefer to draw out the most interesting aspects within an overview of short film – experimentation, a questioning of the role of film, and cross-fertilisation.

Experimentation is central to avant-garde film-making. Rees mentions techniques which are 'ciphers of resistance to normal vision',[20] and there is a questioning about what is suitable subject matter, how to use the medium and how we make sense of film. Part of the questioning of the role of film has resulted in exhibition moving from cinema to clubs to art galleries to challenge viewing assumptions and cinematic conventions. Now websites, CD Roms and DVD have enabled experimentation with the moving image and interactivity, and have opened up the potential for far larger audiences than avant-garde work reached in the past. Lower production and distribution costs and a freedom from traditional gatekeepers have also provided opportunities for work from the margins to be published.

Avant-garde work is seen by film students and influences their work, and often the influence is extraordinarily long-lived. *Un Chien Andalou* (1929) still retains its impact seventy years after its first showing. Lynne Ramsay cites Maya Deren's *Meshes in the Afternoon* (1943) as an influence on her work. John Smith's *The Girl Chewing Gum* (1976) – which seeks to deconstruct the relationship between image and voiceover, director and film – is still a popular film school text. Clearly the avant-garde is one of many influences, including commercials, music videos, feature films, and material on the Web. But its self-aware innovatory approach makes it an important one.

Conclusion

Though short films no longer occupy the highly visible place they once held – after all, few can be seen in a cinema nowadays, when cinema was once made up only of short films – they remain important. Certain films, like *Un Chien Andalou* or *Hell UnLtd*, continue to live on long after they were made as powerful examples of the potential of cinema. Shorts production also offers film-makers experience, career opportunities and most of all a chance to experiment and create new work. The rise of advertising and of music videos has allowed new creative outlets for film-makers. What is clear is that throughout the history of cinema, short film-makers have used live action, animation, documentary, fiction and fact to create new and innovative work. They continue to do so today as our interviews – which make up the next chapter – testify.

Notes

1. Many of the films mentioned in this section are available to view on the BFI video collections *Early Cinema: Primitives and Pioneers* Volumes 1 and 2, *Britain in the Twenties*, *Britain in the Thirties* and *Free Cinema*.

2. See *The Journal of Media Practice*, vol. 1 no. 2, Intellect Ltd, 2000, for examples of the continuing debates on the relationships between theory and practice, industry and education, and education and training.

3. By 1988 the ACTT had recognised the Drama Department of the University of Bristol, Bournemouth and Poole College of Art and Design, the London College of Printing, the London International Film School, the National Film and Television School, the Polytechnic of Central London and West Surrey College of Art and Design.

4. In Britain, the provision of media education is student-demand led, and this has driven the expansion of courses. Film and video courses attract very high numbers of applicants. In contrast, many film schools in Eastern Europe were developed in response to the demands of the industry. For instance, before the advent of free enterprise the Polish Film and Television School only selected a very limited number of students which related to the needs of the industry. Graduates would never be out of work, but on the other hand most applicants were rejected.

5. Jim Cook and Jim Hillier, 'The Growth of Film & Television Studies 1960–1975' (London: Film & Television Studies in Secondary Education Conference Paper, 1976), p. 15.

6. Giannalberto Bendazzi, *Cartoons: One Hundred Years of Cinema Animation* (London: John Libbey, 1994), p. 66.

7. Their wartime commissions included *Dustbin Parade* (on recycling waste), *Digging for Victory*, *Handling Ships* and *Submarine Control*. Their independent work included *Magic Canvas* (1948), *Animal Farm* (1951), *The Tales of Hoffnung* (1964) and *Ruddigore* (1967). For more detail see Roger Manvell, *Art & Animation* (London: Halas & Batchelor, 1980).

8. For instance, Alison De Vere, Geoff Dunbar, Jerry Hibbert and Graham Ralph, among many others.

9. The Manchester-based Cosgrove Hall, one of the largest animation studios in Europe, specialises in children's drama.

10. Sydney Box, *Film Publicity: A Handbook on the Production and Distribution of Propaganda Films* (London: Lovat Dickson, 1937), p. 31.

11. David Bernstein, 'The Television Commercial' in Brian Henry (ed.), *British Television Advertising, The First 30 Years* (London: Century Benham, 1986), p. 260.

12. Ibid.

13. For instance, the popular music programme *Oh Boy!* featured American rock'n'roll artists, a variety show hosted by the American singer Connie Francis was laced with a very un-British effusiveness, and the series *Robin of Sherwood* was largely written by Hollywood scriptwriters blacklisted under McCarthy – although the lines were delivered by the actors in perfect RP English.

14. Winston Fletcher, *A Glittering Haze: Strategic Advertising in the 1990s* (NTC Publications, 1992), p. 23.

15. One example of this is Zbig Rybazynski's *Tango* (1980), which compacts the use of one room over years into a short sequence where different characters live without seeing each other. The production process, using film, was painstaking and innovative. The idea was used in the Ariston *On and On* commercial, using computer-generated imagery.

16. The MTV channel became available in Britain in 1987, and the majority of its programming is music videos. The European arm of MTV has commissioned a number of channel idents from animators and graphic artists (including Emma Calder). It also runs music video competitions for new directors. To be banned from MTV or have a watershed limitation placed on a music video may severely affect the audience reached (see the interview with Jonathan Glazer). However, coverage in the music press of the event may bring both music and artist to public notice.

17. See the work of Zbig Rybazynski and Chris Cunningham, for instance.

18. 'The Art of Pop Video' programme at Brief Encounters 2000 featured music videos with budgets from £30 to £100,000, and one of the favourites was a camcorder reality-style piece – Fatboy Slim's *Praise You*, directed by Spike Jonze.

19. A. L. Rees, *A History of Experimental Film and Video* (London: BFI, 1999).

20. Ibid., p. 6.

3

Conversations with Film-makers

Introduction

This chapter contains interviews with eleven different film-makers – ten British and one Irish. Each interview concentrates on the creative process behind one or two short films, from initial idea to final cut and distribution. In choosing the directors to interview we looked for an exceptional ability to use the short form creatively. Directors who made films that looked like features squashed into ten minutes were excluded. We wanted also to highlight the diversity of people working in different genres and at different stages in their careers. Those interviewed range from Winta Yohannes, a film school graduate, to Anthony Minghella, now working on his fourth feature and whose second film, *The English Patient* (1996), received nine Academy Awards.

Two animators appear here – Nick Park and Emma Calder. Nick's popular clay animation characters, Wallace and Gromit, appear in three shorts as well as his forthcoming feature. We selected *Creature Comforts* (1989), which brings to life interviews with zoo animals, as it offered a concentrated creative process conducive to analysis. Although many people have seen the commercials based on *Creature Comforts*, fewer have seen the Academy Award-winning original film. Nick discusses the fine line between structure and improvisation, talks about the way he makes characters come alive and the joys of working with plasticine.

Emma Calder's beautiful watercolour animation, *The Queen's Monastery* (1998), will be less well known. It is an impressive technical achievement as well as an exploration of emotions. Our discussion centres on the way in which style and content evolved together. *Is it the Design on the Wrapper?* (1997) by Tessa Sheridan, packs every second of its seven minutes of parallel narratives in an entertaining and moving way. *Alien Corn* (1992) – her second short – is slow paced, elliptical, and explores the potential of sound and image. Tessa analyses the creative process, the way she brings the subconscious to the surface, and the importance of an integrated approach to all elements of film-making. Lynne Ramsay (director of two feature films, *Ratcatcher* [1999] and *Morvern Callar* [due for release in 2002]) talks about two of her shorts, *Gasman* (1997) and *Kill the Day* (1996), her experimentation with the short form and the importance of taking risks. Her brutal aesthetic contrasts with her exploratory, even meditative, camerawork. All three film-makers discuss the way in which personal experience and emotion feed into their work.

The Beckett on Film shorts are considered in two interviews. Michael Colgan, artistic director of the Gate Theatre in Dublin, asked nineteen directors to make a film version of a Samuel Beckett play. Damien O'Donnell (director of the feature *East is East* [1999]) and Anthony Minghella discuss the way they approached such revered and complex texts. Damien, who made *What Where?* (2000), discusses the need to provide a symbolic setting for the play, and the intriguing pub conversations about Samuel Beckett that the project led to. Anthony discusses the reasoning behind his controversial treatment of *Play* (2000), the modernity of Beckett's work and its relation to filmic forms.

The growing potential, or problem, of the Internet for short films is covered in a number of interviews. Damien O'Donnell talks about his work on the website linked to Mike Figgis' feature film *Hotel* (2002). We discuss also digital technology and its impact on both film-makers and distributors, which may offer hope for the future of short film. The prolific John Smith – director of thirty-three films, including the film school favourite *The Girl Chewing Gum* (1976) – adds his view of the pleasures and pains of digital technology, and the opportunities it holds for gallery exhibition. Although he usually works in a different funding area from the other film-makers interviewed here, in artists' film and video, his exploratory way of working and use of material can be compared to Emma Calder, Tessa Sheridan and Keith Wright. He describes his collaboration with the composer Jocelyn Pook that led to *Blight* (1996), a film that provides an insight into the true costs of road building. Another of John's films discussed here, *The Black Tower* (1987), plays with our perceptions of landscape without the use of any special effects.

Jonathan Glazer's commercial for Guinness, *Surfer*, has had a bigger audience than all the other films featured here. A dream-like mix of surfers, horses and a hypnotic voiceover, it was voted best commercial of all time by the Channel 4 audience. Jonathan discusses the complex special effects in *Surfer*, the development of his music video *Rabbit in Your Headlights* (1999), and the experience of working in these different areas. John Hardwick talks about music video from a less well known director's point of view and how his favourite – *The Sweetness Lies Within* (1998) – evolved from disaster. As a contrast, he describes the process behind the strange, cold award-winning film *To Have and to Hold* (2000).

Winta Yohannes is that rarity: a black woman film-maker who stands at the beginning of her film-making career. In her graduation piece, *Cherish* (2000), she dares to slow the pace and give the actors time to act. The film will resonate with many young people who stand at the borderline of youth and adulthood, modern life and tradition. Keith Wright made *Where's Bingo Betty?* (1998) for £50, and its positive reception helped him to go on to make *Stan's Slice of Life* (1999) and *Long in the Tooth* (2000). He describes the way in which discarded film stock became the catalyst for the style and story of *Where's Bingo Betty?*

Five of the eleven directors interviewed have made feature films, but all say they will continue to make shorts. This goes against the notion that shorts are a stepping stone to features, and that feature-makers never return to short film. The opportunity to make a film fast, with a small crew and more control over the process, is an experience which is needed to counterbalance the investment of years of time and weight of responsibility of large budgets which feature films impose on the film-maker.

By focusing on directors here we are not suggesting that they are the sole creators of their films. Most of these film-makers work in collaboration with people they know and trust. They are dependent on their producers for many aspects of the process, and many work very closely with their cinematographers, editors and others. For example, Lucia Zucchetti, Lynne Ramsay's editor, says that she enjoys working with Lynne because she 'wants to collaborate and is open to suggestions and improvements'.[1] Anthony Minghella commented about the benefits of having to argue his point with the people he works with. The nature of the short form – which requires fewer people to be involved – does enable the director to have a strong creative input, however. Apart from the Beckett on Film examples, all the interviewees are discussing work where they have been both writer and director. The clarity of the authorial voice is often one of the pleasures of shorts, as if the film-maker is standing just behind the screen as we watch. A filmography for each director is included at the end of the book.

Nick Park

Nick Park is a model animator whose creations have gained immense popularity. He joined Aardman Animations in 1985, where he completed the film he had started at the National Film and Television School – *A Grand Day Out* (1989), the first of the Wallace and Gromit films. He is at present working on a Wallace and Gromit feature film. Here we are talking about one of the *Lip Synch* series, *Creature Comforts* (1989), which won an Academy Award for best short animated film.

What drew you to Aardman?

I was a student at the National Film and Television School and they invited me two summers on the run to work with them. I was doing work on *Morph* and that kind of thing, and I remember at first being so thrilled that they'd asked me out of all the people in the country. It dawned on me by the next time that I was the only person in the country that did the work they needed.

Do you know why you're attracted to model animation?

I think it's partly seeing the work of Aardman. I used to see *Morph* on television. I was already doing plasticine animation as a hobby at home as a kid, when I was twelve. I used to copy it a bit, or be inspired by it. I used to do things that were very similar, especially the early things I did for *Vision On*. I just loved the way you could use plasticine. It was so real and yet you could use it in a cartoon way as well because of its flexibility. It's got that organicness to it. I'd do a little sketch, for instance someone in the living room hoovering up. This person just suddenly started sucking up the carpet and then she sucked up her cat, then her sofa and then her husband until she'd sucked up the whole world all around her. I just loved the way you could just start off and not quite know what you were going to do. You'd just work through the sketch and do it. You don't quite know what the story's going to be.

Where did the idea for Creature Comforts *come from?*

It started in 1989. There were only about six of us on staff at Aardman then, and we'd been talking about getting a series off the ground of five or six short films. Then along came the opportunity to talk to Channel 4 about it. At the time they were the only people really doing this sort of thing, and we knew that they were open to be approached. We sat round a table trying to think what would we do? We had many ideas. The only thing that we could think of that would unify this series was if it used found voices on tape, the way that Aardman had done in the past when it was just Peter Lord and Dave Sproxton. This would be like *Conversation Pieces* for Channel 4 and before that *Animated Conversations* for the BBC. We decided to call this series *Lip Synch*, and *Creature Comforts* was one of them. And so I thought I'd use found voices but with animals.

Why animals, when up to then Aardman had used human models?

I suppose that was my way of saying 'I'm not doing the same thing. I want something to make my own mark here.' I think I've always loved drawing animal characters. I like humans as much but it just seemed right.

At the very beginning the plan was to go into a place with a hidden microphone so that people weren't aware that they're being recorded. I went into Bristol Zoo with a tape recorder hidden in my bag and a microphone pinned on the strap. I stood near to people who were talking about the animals in the cages, saying things like, 'Look at that little fat hairy one' or 'Oh, they don't look well do they?' – that kind of thing. And then I was going to put those voices in the mouths of the animals looking at the people, so it was about who was observing who – reversing the roles. But it was so hard to get any good conversation. I recorded a couple of days' worth of it, but people just don't say much, except when the giraffes are pooing, and then you get a lot of comments from the kids – 'Look at that! Look at the size of that!' and all that kind of thing. And that's the most entertaining part to the kids. And then you'd have problems with background noise – a waterfall or a heater fan going, and so you couldn't record there. So in the end I thought, 'I've got to go up to people and stick the mike in their faces.' That's when it got interesting actually, because then it became more like a documentary, or a comment on documentaries, I think. Then you got the self-consciousness of the characters, which was an added dimension that I hadn't thought of. Whenever you see a person interviewed I always find it interesting, how they are in front of the camera and in front of the microphone.

How did the interaction between animals come about – for instance, the polar bear with two cubs, and one starts getting embarrassed about what the other one is saying?

I found I could invent that sort of thing. I added bits, like the polar bear putting his hand up and waiting for his turn to speak. I tried to keep a lot from the original recording as well, like the woman I made into a gorilla, the woman from Northern Ireland who talked about it raining a lot. While she was talking I don't know what happened but something hit the microphone, and so I used that as her hitting the microphone. I didn't mind if it was an imperfect recording as long as I could hear it. I then had to think what is like a zoo, because a lot of the animals are from foreign climes. I met this Brazilian guy who hated the weather and the food and everything in the student halls of residence, so I went there and asked him all these questions. Then I also asked him what it was like for the animals at the zoo and edited the answers all together, so it sounded like all of a piece.

You start with a shot of the tape recorder and then you put the microphone in shot. What made you decide to do that?

It was about it being like a documentary – it suddenly became a comment on that kind of thing. And it gave the feeling that these were live, real recordings, improvised, and they were ordinary people being interviewed and not actors and not scripted.

We recorded so much. Some of it I recorded and for efficiency and speed I had a journalist from the BBC go out and get some stuff for me as well. She went to retirement homes, because we thought they might give similar answers to animals in a zoo might give, because they talk about being looked after and that kind of thing.

If I'd set out to make an animal rights film, I'd have probably structured it and scripted it more, and it would have been less interesting. People said whatever they really felt about the confines of their space – some looked on it positively, others negatively, and that's what people are like. That's what gave the film, for me, an extra feeling of truth, because people are complex and don't give the answers you want them to give.

How did you present the ideas to Channel 4?

Some of the other films in the series were more scripted – it was possible to

Creature Comforts (1989) (© Aardman Animations Ltd)

present in storyboard form because they were stories. I remember when we
presented them probably the least likely to be any good was *Creature Comforts*,
because it was simply a series of shots, quite unrelated shots really, and I didn't
have any recordings at the time either, so it was all very speculative. I had to
guess the kind of recordings I might get. I did some rough recordings with
some friends to give the idea, but they weren't very impressive at all. And I
sketched out what the animals might be and presented them. It was a very thin
presentation really, and I don't think it impressed the commissioning editor at
the time very much. But it was seen as one tacked onto the series so it got
through. It was a difficult thing to present because the recordings didn't exist
properly, so it was one of those things where you could only show what you
mean once you've got it recorded, which means halfway into production, so it
was a bit of a tricky one.

But we'd got the track record of Aardman – of what Pete and Dave [Peter
Lord and Dave Sproxton, the founders of Aardman] had done before – and it
was in the early days of Channel 4 when it was quite easy to get commissions
through. So I had that sense of freedom to work on this without feeling like I
had to prove anything.

Were the original characters that you put into the proposal in the film?
I remember drawing a handful of characters initially, but some weren't in. The
jaguar on the log, I remember originally was a leopard sat on the floor. I think I

drew penguins at one point. For some voices, I'd have an animal in mind as I was recording them, but then that might change when I got home, or I'd then start to juggle them around thinking 'I've got enough meat eaters' or whatever. I had to put them all up on the wall and vary them again because there was too much of one sort of animal. The ape was the last recording I did. She wasn't necessarily going to be an ape when I was recording her, but then when I got back to the studio I felt that in order to have a good range of zoo animals you needed to have an ape in there. Everything kept changing all the time as I kept standing back and looking at it.

I remember shortly after making the film and the adverts that followed, people were always saying 'Oh the voices fit so well with the animals' but I think you can fit any voice with any animal. For example, the Brazilian jaguar seemed to demand to be a wild cat or a meat eater because he kept talking about eating meat, but then I thought it could be equally funny for a penguin to be saying those lines. It can work either way, like it's quite funny to make a child with a little voice be a big animal.

One thing that amazes me about your work is the way you use the depth of field. There is so often something going on in the background, which is very unusual for animation because of the complexity of the process. Where did that come from?

It was following in the footsteps of what Pete and Dave had done. For example in one of the *Conversation Pieces – On Probation*, about kids in borstal – there's a committee meeting and one of them is putting his glasses on but they fold up as he puts them on and pokes him in the eye. I wouldn't know about that because I don't wear glasses, but Pete does. These little things, to me, are what clay animation or plasticine animation is so good at, because it's a medium where when you start a shot you very much start at the beginning and work through it, like a performance. It's not as if you can keep re-doing it until you get it right, or add cells or drawings here and there, or even like computer animation where you do your basic action or your keys or whatever and then run down. It's not a continuous process like that. You start the finished thing at the beginning, if you see what I mean. Each frame is the finished frame. And because you're handling the puppet every frame, because of the improvised nature of it, you're constantly changing your mind as to what to do. One of the great challenges is to keep on track, to stick to the point of the shot. It's great because it's very tempting to put things in all the time because you can do it, you know make a character start drumming their fingers, just because it's got fingers and they're static you feel like doing something with them. So, whereas to do that in something like drawn animation you've got to put quite a lot of work into each frame to make that happen, with this type of animation the puppet's there, all you have to do is move it.

Do you think you get more involved with the characters because they are there?
They've got a sort of reality to them.

Yes, there's something about this technique. I think it's because the character really exists and it has gravity and all these natural laws affecting it that they have a certain weight on screen. And of course their eyes are real. I always think that eyes are probably the most important part of the character, and this is again where clay animation comes in. You've got to go in there and it's not just a matter of moving the character every frame, you've actually got to feel it. So something of you, your personality, in very subtle ways starts coming through into the character. You're not only moving it, you're nudging it, and you're sort of teasing the character out of it because of that contact. That's where I think computer animation to be good has to have people who are very aware of that human contact working on it, otherwise it will seem robotic.

But it is like they become a character on their own, isn't it? They somehow develop.

Yes, that's true. It certainly happened in the Wallace and Gromit films. There's been very much an evolution. You feel nervous when you're animating a character walking across the screen, you feel like someone stepping out onto the stage. It's very hard to start off a shot sometimes, you've got to psych yourself up. If you start off on the wrong foot so to speak, almost literally, the whole shot will go badly. You've got to be in control completely, but there's that element of improvisation all the time too. Once you get confident you can improvise.

On Creature Comforts *you got the commission, and then did you do a complete story-board?*

No, I wasn't really able to do a storyboard until I got all the recordings done. So yes, we got the commission through and then we knew that the project was green-lighted. I had the drawings that I originally did, but then I put those aside and I went out and just recorded tonnes of stuff, maybe seven hours' worth of material, and spent about three months recording and editing. As I started to home in on the recordings I liked, I started sketching animals that would fit them, and I didn't do any filming until I'd completely edited the soundtrack. It was completely edited almost frame accurately, and so I'd got a five-minute film just in dialogue. It took a lot of editing of the soundtrack, cutting out sentences and chopping and changing a lot, so all the editing was really done at that point.

And while you were doing that you were evolving the characters in sketches etc?

Yes, and in my head I was imagining.

Were you thinking of events and actions as well?

Yes, things started to come to mind there, but not yet fully. The actions almost happened on the set. If you want a gag where one bird pulls the beak off the other bird, you've got to prepare for that, but it doesn't take long. I'd obviously got to know that there had to be two birds in the background, so some planning went into that part of the action and what would happen, because you have to have all the bits made. And then I worked with an old friend, a sculptor called Debbie Smith, and she took my sketches and made the characters up in plasticine. I had a lot of chance to comment on them and change them.

Is it all sketches or do you do any writing, any notes?

Not much writing really. Once the soundtrack was edited each shot would be broken down into a dope sheet, where it's all broken down frame by frame, into syllables so they can do accurate lip synch, and on those dope sheets I'd start marking down the action. The dialogue always acts as a good framework to base the actions on, and inspires us as well. For example with the jaguar, whenever I'd play the track, obvious things would come to mind. I started to love the way he kept repeating the word 'space', so to make that repetition even funnier I planned an action to go with it. I didn't plan any other action except him chatting because I found the dialogue interesting in itself. Really the picture was there to support the dialogue in that film.

When do you decide to put something going on in the background?

It's so easy to think things up all the time. This is what happens with commercials. Quite often people say 'Oh we love all the background details, we want loads', and we end up with so much background detail that they're completely distracting and the viewer doesn't know where to look. In commercials, the shots are too short for that kind of stuff. It was partly that we had these long shots really, as well as watching those things on TV like *It'll Be Alright On The Night*. When someone's being interviewed in the street, sooner or later someone's bound to pull their trousers down in the background or fall over or something. Because it was a documentary we thought it would be great to do that kind of thing. And it's really funny how unplanned it was. I had no idea whether it would work or not. It was fun – with a touch of fear. A good fear, that keeps it entertaining and stops the film from getting bland.

And where do all those ideas come from? Are they all coming from you or are other people suggesting things?

I think that's all me on that, all the content of it was my own. There were people doing the lighting, the modelling, set building and all that kind of thing. Once I got the soundtrack edited then I did a proper storyboard and some of the animals got changed, and that was it really. I didn't do any of this thing that we do now where we pretty much film the storyboard and put a soundtrack with it and music and everything. Because some of the shots were forty-five seconds long you just had one board for that forty-five second shot and the rest was 'Well, I'll do something at the time.' Like with the polar bears, I didn't know what was going to happen. Maybe on the day I was shooting I'd have ideas, and then when it came to the actual shoot, because some of the shots took five days to do I had many chances to change my mind, and I often did. In fact sometimes I'd start an action and then decide not to do it or think 'No, it's too early' and change the action to something else. You often get into that situation where as an animator you start thinking, 'I'd better make them blink again, they haven't blinked for two days,' but that two days was only three seconds ago on film, so it's easy to pack it with too much.

When I look at *Creature Comforts* now I think I was so confident back then just to trust in the sound and looking at an image. I'd love to get back to that sort of thing. You didn't feel it had to constantly hit you with new images.

How long did it take to make?

The shoot was two months in preparation, three months in shooting. Then an editor, Will Ayles, came in to edit it and he cut out a few frames here and there in between shots, but nothing within the shots was edited, and he put the sound on as well. There was no music.

And what was the response at Channel 4?

They loved it.

It sounds like a good way of working – you had quite a basic plan and you improvised within that.

I think that's an accurate way of saying it. It was planned because I had to know how many characters were in there and where they might stand, what they might do, like the bird pulling the beak off. Then when you have an idea like that you have to know where to put it. If it gets a laugh you don't want the laugh to go over a vital bit of dialogue. So I had to decide where the key points in the dialogue were that were funny in themselves, where you were looking at the foreground character. I also started to realise at some point that the audience doesn't necessarily look at the person talking, they accept them as just being there and as soon as they see them their eye starts to wander.

Especially if there's movement.

Yes, a lot of the film was trying to understand where the audience might be looking at any point and not stepping on things, like not putting action on jokes in the dialogue, or giving time for someone to recover from a certain joke before another one happened.

Can you remember what you hoped to achieve with that film? What you wanted to get out of it creatively, in career terms or whatever? Was it money?

Not at all. Back then we didn't even think that film-making could be profitable. It was just a chance to make your own film and to have it shown on television.

Did you have a creative aim?

It was really for the sake of it, wanting to try it out. Having an idea that seemed really funny. I didn't know I'd get such good dialogue when I got the idea.

Did you feel there was a more serious intent appearing underneath as you worked?

The content developed very organically with the piece. It's almost like I'd discovered what it was about quite late on. I think that often happens with writing – you don't know what it is you're writing. Quite often you'll find you've written your own story in some way or other. I think that's how it always works with me. You start off with a basic funny idea and just let it develop and it starts to take on more layers. After it was made I found that even though it was taken as very funny, people also took it quite seriously. It moved people a lot, feeling for those animals.

I'd spent the last seven years doing *A Grand Day Out*, which was my college film that I took to Aardman. I was in the last stages of filming that when I took time out to make *Creature Comforts*, and then came back to *A Grand Day Out* months later. What's funny is that *Creature Comforts* came in and stole the limelight from the film that I'd spent seven years thinking, 'This is going to be great when it's finished.'

I thought after all that time making characters with their eyes close together and great big wide mouths, 'I'm going to do something with a different style so I don't get typecast.' And Debbie, who normally makes very realistic sculptures of animals, looked at my designs and made these big, round, quite robust characters. I said, 'Make sure the eyes are more naturalistic, in the right place and everything.' But as soon as I got hold of them I couldn't help it, my hands just naturally went and pushed their eyes together and pulled out the mouths, and suddenly they had these big coat-hanger mouths again. It's just a natural instinct.

But it's a very clean aesthetic that you have. There's lots happening on screen, the characterisation is very rich, but within that you have these clean lines.

Yes, there's a bit of that in Wallace and Gromit but in *Creature Comforts* it's more so. I think there's a bit of influence of *The Far Side*, keeping big simple shapes. I wasn't sure, using quite naturalistic voices, documentary style with a slightly more cartoon world, how that would all work really. I wasn't sure at all. And there's lots of texture in the landscapes. The place where the birds are is just like being in an actual chicken run, with real mud.

Creature Comforts went to television. What other distribution did it have?

It went all around the festivals. That was great for me because I suddenly had two films out which I think caused quite a big splash at the time that we hadn't planned. It always amazes me that a five-minute film that took five months to make went all round the world and picked up an Oscar and all these awards. I got so much satisfaction from that short film. I often think of that when I'm making a feature film with the amount of effort and the payback that you get.

You said that you felt you were freer in those days, why do you think that is? You would think you would be more free to improvise the more you did, because you learn what will work.

Yes, and the more success you had the more you proved how well you could do it. You'd think so, but it doesn't work like that I find. It's because more people get on board, and everybody becomes an expert at what you do. I think it's just a case of structuring it so that it doesn't go like that, that's what I'm learning. So far I've done bigger and bigger things, so there's more money involved and so more people want a say in how that money's spent.

And how do you see your future from here?

I've got ambitions in feature films, I'm writing a Wallace and Gromit feature with Bob Baker and Steve Box. It's funny talking about *Creature Comforts*, though, because I'd love to do something else like that again where you work with a very small team and work much more hands on. I long for those days of just doing it myself again and just really enjoying the plasticine.

Emma Calder

Emma Calder has been an animator since 1981. Her work has been shown at art galleries (including the ICA and the Tate) as well as film festivals, cinema and television. She has also made commercials, music videos and channel idents. In 1989 she and Ged Haney set up Pearly Oyster Productions, an independent animation studio. Also mentioned in the interview are her partner Julian Cripps, their daughter Coco, her assistant, Fiona Woodcock, and Claire Kitson (then at Channel 4). We are discussing her watercolour animation *The Queen's Monastery* (1998).

Tell me about The Queen's Monastery.

The film is centred on a woman whose lover has returned from war a changed man. She can't fully understand what he's gone through, so life becomes unbearable. She starts to fantasise about the man in his former life when he was an acrobat, and she remembers the day when she first met him. Her lover starts to think she's having an affair with somebody else; he tries to kill the acrobat. But the whole thing is seen through the woman's mind, and she's really in control of all the actions. It's a projection of herself and the conflict between the acrobat and the soldier is a manifestation of her guilt. In the film you're not sure whether or not she is having an affair with somebody else. The central idea is that she can't cope with the fact that she no longer loves the man that she's with and she loves the way he used to be. The cathartic staircase fight is an illustration of that sort of anxiety, almost bordering on madness.

The Queen's Monastery (1998)

Some people might look at the film and think it's overly sentimental, almost like a fairytale or a bit sugary. But the very romantic style of the film – the watercolours and the music – is deliberate. At the end of the film, the woman has got over the worst of that situation and perhaps she is going to try to adjust and learn to love the man. And the man has to come to terms with the fact that maybe he's just imagining something about the woman that's incorrect, or maybe he has to come to terms with the fact that she doesn't love him in the same way that she used to.

Why did you choose to use watercolours?

When I started on ideas for a new film, I was working with Ged Haney on his film and I was very instrumental in getting the technique working. We were using very flat inks and watercolours. This is in the days before computers were really taking hold, and we wanted to use ink but we didn't want it boiling. So I spent my whole time working out these flat washes, mixing all the colours. At the end of each day towards the end of the project, I was getting very frustrated and bored because we'd done all the animation and were just basically running a whole team of people to do this laborious watercolour work. Someone had given me these old sketchpads, they had nice faded paper. I'd get my

paintbrush that was loaded with ink left over from doing Ged's stuff and I just
started splodging and splashing and doing the exact opposite to the style in
Ged's film. In each splash I'd draw in a character or a face, and I got into
doing these sketchbooks for a period of about three or four weeks, and that is
how the technique evolved.

The monastery itself, I'd been doing a lot of stuff with black ink that day
and I got my sleeve in the ink and it left this mark that looked like a Rorschach
ink blot. I thought, 'Yes that looks like a monastery.' The monastery in a way
represents the prison of her mind. People probably don't get it when they see
the monastery, but I like that because it's quite abstract and it also had hidden
connotations.

Did the creative process start with these notebooks, or did you have a plot idea first?
I did all these sketchbooks and around that time S4C had a competition for
animators to fit a story idea to a piece of out-of-copyright classical music. I went
through lots of music and found this Janáček piece that was out of copyright –
but I didn't know that the copyright laws were going to change from fifty to
seventy years. I chose the Janáček music because it was the only one that gave
me any really strong feelings.

I imagined the whole story from listening to the music. I thought of the
monastery and there were lots of funny piccolo noises and I thought that
sounded like a monkey, then I made a leap and thought, 'Acrobat!' I knew I
wanted to make a film about infidelity and about a woman who loved two
men, and so I started working on the idea of this acrobat lover. There was all
this marching in the music and so I thought, 'The soldiers.' And it sounded
very much like a bandstand and trumpets and things like that. I started thinking about, I don't know why, a big town square. There was this running sort of
sound in the music, so I was thinking about the staircase scene. After listening
to the music for about a day, I just wrote the story from beginning to end,
starting in the monastery, each scene in order. I was really excited – it came
together so quickly. I started to design the characters the following day, and
over about five to six days I had all the characters designed and I had the
story.

Then I researched Janáček and had a complete shock. There were all these
links that I'd seen visually while listening, so I was extremely excited about that.

Because the copyright laws were changing and it wasn't going to be out of
copyright, S4C turned it down, but they really liked the proposal. I did think
about changing the music, but I couldn't. That was the point when I decided
I'd keep going with it, even though normally I wouldn't want to do something
to a piece of classical music. But this seemed so magical that I had to pursue it,
and I carried on trying to get the money.

*You say you just sat down and wrote it. Do you think it was sorting out in your mind
as you were working on the sketchbooks?*

I think writing was the second stage. The sketchbooks were to do with the
technique primarily and within that there may have been certain anxieties
about how I was feeling about myself that might have come out. But the key
thing was that as soon as I had the music I knew I wanted to do something
about a woman who loved two men. I was looking for a piece of music that
had that kind of feeling.

Most of the films that I make have evolved like that, it's the way I work. I'm
not a great believer in the western approach to script – for animation anyway.
Many broadcasters are anti a lot of animators because they don't write proper
scripts, and they think that's bad. I think it is bad with some people because
they make crap films, but I think if you're a good and talented film-maker you
can actually work the other way around. At the moment I'm storyboarding my
next film and I haven't written a script, and I've been doing lots of drawings
and messing about a lot with images. I think that it is tapping into the subconscious. Most people don't make good films because they don't have the ability
to see when they come across something that could be a good idea. I think the
process that I go through is probably closer to art than the majority of artists,
because it's to do with discovery. It's also to do with really being honest about
the subject matter, but not being inward either, projecting it outward and being
able to give the audience something back.

What was the next step on The Queen's Monastery?

I wrote a storyline, a couple of pages.

And do you do character profiles or notes?

I always analyse the characters – I might not write it down but I know exactly
what the characters are like.

What did you submit to S4C?

The drawings I'd been doing in those few days, a storyline, a treatment and a
few of the images from the sketchbook that kind of related.

After the S4C refusal I gave it a break, then sent it to Channel 4 – the same
pack. Each time I sent it out I would do a bit more work on it. Claire Kitson
thought the story was unclear, but she liked it and told me to get back to her in
six months and I thought, 'I can't be bothered.' Because Channel 4 had rejected
another project, I was a bit off. She was right though, it probably wasn't clear.

I'd been involved with this group called Cartoon, which came out of an
initiative in Brussels. We'd been trying to get them to subsidise and promote
short films, and they asked people to submit projects. The idea was that they
would get all these European broadcasters together and see if they could choose
some projects to fund. So I sent it off to that. I did a bit more work but because

they specified a limited number of drawings and different things I didn't put
everything in. Colin Rose from the BBC was on the panel, and he picked my
project. He also picked another British project and Claire Kitson picked two
other British projects, but no European broadcasters picked any because they're
not interested in short films.

Colin Rose had a small sum of money left in his budget, and he really liked
my drawings and the story. He came to the studio and went through everything. I showed him other drawings of the woman, he said, 'Why haven't you
got a big picture of the woman.' I said there wasn't enough room in the pack.
He asked, 'What does the monastery mean?' I said that it represents the prison
in the woman's mind. He said 'You've got to express that, you're not conveying
that in the treatment.' I spent a lot of days on the computer going over and
over the treatment until I perfected it. I included all the things he said were
missing and I sent it back to Colin with all the additional visuals. He suggested
trying to get London Production Fund and Lottery funding. I sent the stuff off
to the London Production Fund and they said they would also give me money.
And then I had to do the Lottery application.

By that time I was pregnant. I knew I was going to get BBC and London
Production Fund money but I didn't know if I was going to get Lottery money,
and I had to take a chance that I'd get it. It was a big chance because we
started production. The first contract was signed around the date of Coco's
birth, and I was still finishing my Lottery application. Ged and Julian [Emma's
partner] brought the computer home, I'd had a caesarian and Coco was only
eight days old. I'd had general anaesthetic and I was on all these drugs, and I
was finishing my Lottery application. I would have liked to have postponed the
project for six months, but we had no other work and we didn't have any
money, we were completely flat broke. So I had to say that I'd start on 1 April.

I had three months off, but meanwhile I had to do more research and I
took Fiona on. She'd already started working for me because she wanted to
work on the film, and I knew she'd be perfect for the backgrounds. We trained
her but we couldn't pay her. We got her doing exercises and things, and then
she started to help me on research and I'd send her out with a camera to video
things. We went together to the various museums like the Imperial War
Museum, so I could look at war footage. We went to the BFI to look at old
footage of acrobats. I would be sitting there with Coco breastfeeding whilst the
blokes brought more cans in, and Fiona would help me draw. It was unfortu-
nate that I had to do it at that time, but we couldn't do without the budget. It
was a gruelling experience.

After about six months, I realised that I was never going to get it finished in
time and that I'd under budgeted. Maggie Ellis at the London Production

Fund was great. She was very supportive and she knew I didn't have enough money. The BBC and the London Production Fund put in some extra money, and she helped me raise the additional cash.

Were there any conditions from the funders?

We had to negotiate over a couple of points. A standard BBC contract has control over the final cut, but they were not putting in enough money to justify this. It was a problem very easily solved. Although the Lottery had no creative input they do own 70 per cent of any money the film makes, but only after Pearly Oyster has recovered costs. It's very unlikely to go into profit because of the amount that we put into the budget. The London Production Fund asked for nothing back.

Was there a deadline?

I said when it was going to be finished, but I'd based it on the old Emma, the one that used to work seven days a week, twelve hours a day, and suddenly I wasn't that same person. So I had to change that and put a much more realistic deadline.

Looking back, how do you feel about that process? These applications take a lot of time and thought. Do you think that was useful or a waste of creative energy?

On *The Queen's Monastery* I didn't write the script until after I'd more or less got all the money on board. Colin asked for a script to show the people at the BBC, so I wrote it after I'd done the whole storyboard, but it wasn't a waste of time. I'm finding that process more useful; do the storyboard, then do the script because then you're analysing the visual material in a different way and it certainly helps with cuts.

I think Colin's input was good because I think he picked out all the weak things. I realise now why I hadn't got money for other projects. Colin Rose is one of the most visual of all the commissioners, I have the greatest respect for him. I think the main problem I learnt from him was that many people who are looking at these proposals are visually illiterate, and I suppose I always kind of knew that but I didn't realise exactly the sort of detail you need to provide. I had my latest project, *Beware of Trains*, turned down by Channel 4 and I know it's for exactly the same reasons, so I should have learnt by now. I feel that I should be seen as someone who can make the films from my previous work. I was hoping they might give me some development money because that's what it needed, but of course they don't want to give you any development money now. The proposal had all the same faults in it as *The Queen's Monastery* did initially – it's not saying things specifically enough. Now I'm working through the storyboard so I can give them a more detailed treatment. I might not even show them the storyboard.

When I do the drawing I spend half the day writing as well, writing ideas.

They might not be in the script though. They'll be trying to get inside what the idea's about, analysing what it is I'm doing, trying to justify each idea in terms of how it's going to work in the context of the film.

Do you take anything from the real world in this creative process, or do you have any-thing that you bring into your studio?

The mirror is probably the best thing that I look at to help me with the characters. But most of it comes out of my mind. Obviously I go and do research at a certain point, for example looking at footage of acrobats and doing lots of drawings from that. And then my drawings of the footage would act as a basis for the starting point for maybe that pose for that particular bit of action, but I only did that for certain tricky bits of acrobatics. I'm good at drawing people from memory and I can design different characters one after the other, but I'm useless at backgrounds. A lot of that came from finding photographic references of the buildings in Czechoslovakia, and I also researched the political history of the Czech Republic.

I had my storyboard with the basic sketches of perspective and the sort of composition I'd want. Then Julian, my partner, who's an architect, did a proper drawing because I can't imagine backgrounds very well. He'd do an architectural sketch to help set up the composition. And then Fiona, who had this great use of the pencil, would trace over Julian's drawings in her style, and then it would go back to Julian and he would modify it, because we didn't want the perspective to get too realistic. He would alter things back and then she would do the final drawing. We'd work very carefully, and they were nearly all based on a rough sketch that I'd done.

Ged helped with getting it to work with the soundtrack when I had problems with the story and it wasn't working. I hated having to ask Ged because we fight all the time in terms of who's got the best idea when we work together, and because it was my film I didn't want to ask him. It would always be after having spent hours trying to sort out the problem that I would ask him, and he would come up with a solution normally quite quickly, sometimes not a solution I liked, and then we'd battle it out. But he really did help, it was great, because the way our partnership works is that I tend to have many of the initial ideas for projects, and I can think of a basis to work and I can think of the characters. When it comes to the narrative and the story I'm a bit all over the place and he will say, 'That isn't clear.' I think he likes things too clear, I wouldn't like to go completely with what he says. So on *The Queen's Monastery* he acted as a critic.

How long did it take to get the film made?

It was about four to four and a half years from initial idea to getting the funding, and two years to make.

What did you hope to achieve by doing the project?

I wanted to make a film that people would think was the most beautiful film they had ever seen. I didn't necessarily want people to understand it completely. I wanted people to see themselves in the film to some extent, and to have an emotional experience. From the moment they started to watch it to the end they would be drawn into the film, it would change the way they physically felt for the duration they watched the film. And then I wanted, although it's probably asking too much, instead of the audience just forgetting the film, I like the idea of somebody a couple of days later or that night thinking about the film; thinking, 'What did that mean – was the acrobat the soldier? And who did she really love?' Things like that.

But I wanted the film to be absolutely perfect and to work with the music in such a way that no-one would have known that the music hadn't been composed for the story. And lots of people who have seen it do think the music was done specifically for the film.

It's interesting the way you don't differentiate between your own creative achievement and the communication with the audience.

I couldn't bear it if it just worked for me and nobody else, that's part of the challenge. I suppose because I was trained as a graphic designer. I haven't got that amount of confidence to think that I've made a brilliant film but everybody else hates it. I do want people to like it.

Was there anything you wanted to achieve technically?

I'd never seen a film that had used watercolour in a way that wasn't just boiling all over the place at random. I've seen lots of films done with watercolour and ink but they always tend to have this very rough feel, and what I wanted to do was to make something that was almost like the appearance of one melting watercolour. So from a technical point of view it was a real achievement, and I don't think anyone else has done anything like it.

And how do you feel about the finished film now?

When it was finished I thought, 'Well, if I get run over now and I never did another film, I've done it.' I was more pleased with it than all the films that I'd made up to that point, because I had the money to do it well. It was as perfect as I wanted it to be. Now I'm not so pleased with it and I find it difficult to watch at the moment. I know that I wanted to please the audience when I made that film and I wanted it to be appealing. It was to do with visual poetry, and that was what I wanted to achieve.

Now I do see faults in it. There are little bits of animation that I think could have been better, but most of the animation was of a reasonably high standard. Now it doesn't quite mean what it meant at the time, but one's state of mind changes all the time. You might look at it one day and still think it was brilliant, and then you look at it another day and think, 'I don't like that.' But I think I achieved more with that film than any other piece of work. Colin Rose said he couldn't believe how closely it had stuck to my initial vision but was ten times better than he ever imagined it was going to be. So there wasn't a lot of digression really.

What distribution did the film have?

Oasis got it on with the feature *Love is the Devil* (1998). So that was shown at Notting Hill Gate, Brixton, Finchley and Croydon for two to three weeks. And then they put it on with *My Name is Joe* (1998) and with a South American film as well. It went to Brighton and Scotland – it was shown a lot. And it's done hundreds of festivals and won quite a few prizes; the last one was Zagreb. And Spike and Mike bought it and they've been showing it for two years in fifty cinemas in North America. Now it's finished the festival round it's gone to video. They sell it on the compilation video of the 'Best of World Animation', so that's good.

Do you feel it has reached its audience, the people you wanted it to reach?

The fact that it's been shown as a short in the cinema has meant that it has reached a fairly mixed audience. It hasn't been shown on BBC yet and the BBC hasn't got a slot for any short animation at the moment so that's a real pain. Obviously that's an audience that you hope for as well, although my film looks so much better in the cinema.

Were you concerned about distribution? Did you have it in mind during the planning and production stages?

Yes. When I did *Springfield* (a film I made a long time before *The Queen's Monastery* [in 1986]), I went round all the main distributors in London and tried to get it distributed. There was no interest at that time in shorts at all. Although some people said they would take it I didn't have enough money to pay for 35mm prints, and a lot of cinemas weren't interested in projecting 16mm. It was just shown at one or two places and I was so disappointed. But with *The Queen's Monastery* it was a big remit of the Lottery to get the films into the cinemas. Oasis was also involved in the Lottery and I was lucky that they liked it – because they don't like everybody's film – and it fitted with the feature. It was perfect with *Love is the Devil* for various reasons; there was a spiral staircase in the film and it's all about an artist, so it fitted in with the painterly nature of my watercolours. Then someone saw it at its first screening and told Spike and Mike to get hold of it. I sent it to them and they loved it. I was lucky, because it is quite an appealing film, it got the success from that.

Do you feel The Queen's Monastery *led to anything for you?*

It hasn't led to anything directly, and I don't think that any of my films have led to anything. That's difficult because each time you finish a film you have all these expectations that it will lead to something, and it doesn't seem to. I suppose it strengthens your reputation, but that is very short-lived anyway. People only really know who Emma Calder is for the two years your film is on the circuit at festivals and in the cinemas. After that anyone new coming into the business, unless they get the opportunity to see the film, will not have heard of you or the film. That's a bit of a drag really.

I did think that it might generate some commercial work, because we need the income to keep the studio going. Ironically it hasn't generated any commercial work at all. Although I've done a lot of pitches based on the style of *The Queen's Monastery* for adverts, I haven't won any of them. People really like it in advertising agencies, but once they've seen the style of the film and the subject matter together they can't seem to split them apart. And because some people think the film is dark – I don't think it's particularly dark, but some people do – that makes it unattractive to them, though I think the style would be great.

And what's happened since completion?

We took on an agent and we tried very hard to get commercial work. We also had an offer from this company called Passion Pictures, they wanted to represent me because they liked my film. I turned them down because we'd just set up an agreement with someone else. We spent all that year pitching for jobs and we also did a couple of little pieces, but we had a really bad time. Then Passion asked again if they could represent us, or represent me primarily, they were most interested in *The Queen's Monastery*, and we agreed. At the same time we'd been working on this series, *Bonehead*. We put in for development money for a pilot, and it took ages to come through. To get some income, Ged went to Germany to work on pop videos for a few months. We put them on our showreel and Passion loved them, we immediately got loads of responses. We started work on the *Bonehead* pilot last April, then we got four commercials in the style of Ged's pop video. I'm also developing an IMAX film with Fiona, which we're trying to get the money for. We've got some interest on that.

Tessa Sheridan

Tessa Sheridan worked as an animator, a camera operator and a theatre director before making her first film in 1990. She has made six shorts and is now working on her first feature film, *Blindfold*. The films we discuss here are *Is it the Design on the Wrapper?* (1997) and *Alien Corn* (1992).

Your biography is strikingly colourful – a family of musicians, living on a riverboat. Do you think this background is important to you?

I think the most important influences are usually the early ones. My first language is probably sound because that was around me much more than words; people weren't really speaking but there was a lot of listening going on. I spent a lot of time just looking out over the river – which is very blank and gives very little back. Or you could say it's open and accepting. Water's indefinable – always shifting, tidal, not a solid shape – but it's also something you can trust to be there. It creates a speculative space. I think something about the way I understand the world comes from that very early environment. Other influences are easier to understand in that I trained as a musician and then started taking photographs. I then worked in animation, which is really an education in cutting. You don't create excess material – you only animate the bits you're going to use. You've got to cut in your head, and that's a good education in live-action editing – and in conciseness as well. Then I became a film camera operator, which gave me a sense of live-action, movement, framing and so on. I've always written short stories and poems, and they began to mutate into scripts. So I had an education in the parts of film-making – in sound first, through music; in story, through my own writing; in editing, through animation; in the visual sensibility, through camerawork. It took me a while to realise that all of these together added up to film. I didn't realise that until fairly late because it wasn't the sort of thing I was brought up to do.

How would you describe yourself as a film-maker?

This is difficult to do, and maybe it's not my job. It's certainly not a style thing. Stylistically my films are very varied. *Is it the Design on the Wrapper?* is verbal, colourful, cutty, narrative. *Alien Corn* was sounds and music – no words, black and white, elliptical. I've learned a lot from all my films and I'm happy with their different styles. For me form and content seem to develop side by side, individual to each project.

In terms of the way I work, all my work begins underground and rises to consciousness through stages. First it bursts through as a rhythm or image or word or whatever, then by working and playing it becomes conscious and slowly forms itself into something that exists separately from me – in whatever shape feels natural.

In terms of what drives me: I believe in ideas – that place where emotions and thoughts swirl around together to make something new. It's natural for me to think and feel in film language – as opposed to conversation, say. I've got to do something with the overcrowding in my head! For me there's no point in making something that's just a story. I'm interested in theme more than in anything else: the story underneath the story which supplies the central metaphor. That's what drives it, what gives it guts for me. And that's where all the rest comes from: story, environment, characters, visual style, soundscape. If that theme and central metaphor isn't there, there's no film in it for me. I try to

make films that work on a first viewing, but which hopefully have other meanings or depths that won't become apparent until a second or third viewing. I
like to leave gaps so that the audience has space to create their own meanings.
But most of all I just want to bring ideas and emotions and characters to life.

Why did you decide to make Is it the Design on the Wrapper?

The situation was unusual in that the funding was already in place – but for a
different project. I had applied to the London Film and Video Development
Agency (LFVDA) for a grant to make *Bug Boy Gull Girl* (a Kafkaesque love
story about an insect collector) and had been awarded a grant of £11,300. But
my previous film over-ran – I was six months behind schedule. We realised the
budget for *Bug Boy* was too low to create the effects I needed. Often an idea
can be reworked to fit a limited budget, but in this case that would have been
very difficult – insects don't take direction well and I needed masses of them. I
went back to the LFVDA, took a deep breath and said 'I know you've waited
for this film for a long time, and I want to make it, but I don't want to make a
bad film: what I can do is make this other idea well instead.' I thought, they
can only say no. But, amazingly, they went with it. But that's a very unusual
situation in two ways; one because I was allowed to keep the funding from one
year to the next, and two because I swapped horses, which nobody usually gets
to do. It was the only time I've been in the situation where I've felt the funders
wanted me to make something more than they wanted a particular film to be
made. And that's the kind of faith you don't find very often.

Describe the creative process on Wrapper.

The original impulse for the script came from a book of 50s cartoons by Jules
Feiffer. I'd read it again and again as a child and found it very funny – even
though it was for adults. When I found the book again it still made me laugh,
but in a different way, and that in turn made me curious – both about the
book, and about me as a child. Remembering why you laughed is an odd thing
to research, but I think that's what I was doing. So with *Wrapper* the original
impulse was analytical and investigative. But then the more surreal, playful side
of me kicked into action and the story and characters grew out of that. In retrospect I can see that I was interested in exploring a reversal of the power
balance between adult and child; but it wasn't so conscious or articulate at the
time. It's a cliché but it's true that most writers write to find out what it is
they're writing about.

But *Wrapper* was unusual for me in having some external 'hook' that pulled
me in. Usually I work only from my own subconscious or half-buried material,
and that emerges in different ways: often an early indication that a film idea is
brewing is an image that sticks in my mind and won't go away. But it might be
a line from a poem; or a key word that seems to pop up in whatever I'm read-

ing; or a location with a particular, evocative soundscape. I'll gather these clues in an instinctive way, getting a strong sense of the tone of the film before any solid plotting is done. Without a sense of its tone I can't make any other meaningful choices. The film's form and content then develop together.

For instance, throughout *Wrapper* we cut between past and present, between two parallel narratives. We get the feeling of two simultaneous and different mental spaces, one where the child is telling a story, and the other is a story happening in front of us which the child isn't conscious of but we are. I didn't think consciously about finding an intercutting device, it just arrived along with the idea. The story – the content – is ironic, but so is the structure – the form: because there are two versions of events. The meanings hang between the two versions, and that gave me a sense of its pacing. It would have a jagged, accelerating pace and its tone would be ironic, or even sardonic sometimes – she's quite a sardonic child. So that tone gives you a feel for everything else. It starts to give you the sense of what the casting must be. It gives you a sense of the kind of location – there's an ironic aspect to watching a saleswoman trying to sell you something that guarantees success in an environment which screams failure. If the scene had taken place in front of Harrods it wouldn't mean the same thing. Also, the saleswoman's outside her own environment, she feels displaced, so she's already vulnerable. The crosscutting gave me clues as to what I was getting at, which was a disjunction, a twist on the truth or whatever. Even if you don't say to yourself, 'Oh, this is an ironic story,' it gets that feel to it and that can feed into the casting, the locations, the costume, and back into the dialogue. So you rewrite around that structure which itself is telling you what it's about underneath what it's about. It's about trying to root out the essence of it, the resonance, the theme.

Do you think it partly grew out of the character of the girl as well, because the girl is displaced, the girl is homeless in some way, she's got no place?

The tone didn't develop from her, because she didn't exist before or separately from the film's tone or form: she developed along with everything else. I never make characters that I bung against backgrounds, it never works that way for me. They are part of the *mise en scène*. Character develops throughout the filmmaking process. The camera style and the visual environment and the costume and the cutting and so on don't just illustrate character – in film language they also create it.

How did you cast the role of the young girl?

There was something about Bianca Nicholas that I kept coming back to and I didn't know quite what it was. She was the least adept actress of the five we shortlisted, the one who couldn't remember her lines, seemed least interested in doing the role, couldn't maintain eye contact with the camera – any logical

Is it the Design on the Wrapper? (1997)

sense would have told you 'no'. But after weeks I was still coming back to her
going, 'Yes, but …'. Which meant there must be some other reason. I kept asking myself 'What is it that she has that nobody else has got?' And of course it
was that unusually ironic world view, that very throwaway quality that's so frustrating in casting sessions. That little gesture in the penultimate shot – a
dismissive flip of the hand – is pure Bianca, and pure adult. You can cut
around problems of performance, but you can't put in qualities that aren't
there, and this was the quality I really needed. But it's not like you're going, 'I
need an ironic child, I'd better go and find one.' It's more that by finding
someone you're interested in you find out *what* you're interested in. You don't
know what you're looking for when you start, but when you see it you recognise it, and when you recognise it you try to make it conscious so that you can
build on that.

How do you develop characters?

Names are very important to me. Usually they just arrive unannounced, but
sometimes I'll make little random forays like looking up the etymology of a
word in the dictionary. I also use objects. I collect objects that 'speak' in some
way – pebbles, discarded buttons, anything – and gather them together without
thinking about them. I just let them hang about the flat, play with them, stick
them on the wall, whatever.

   I think I use objects as metaphors for emotional states. Simple objects are
often best; their meanings are open. A pebble for instance can 'mean' a lost
happy memory, something to shatter a pane of glass, a weight you carry
around, an impossible balancing act, etc. If something that holds a multiplicity
of meanings comes to mean one thing for you, it's clear you're making choices.
That's why it's important to find open objects.

Is there an example you can remember from Wrapper *on the use of an object?*

Actually in *Wrapper* the central metaphor is a process rather than an object – the blowing of bubbles. In that film the ability to blow bubbles equals social success, and the rest of the narrative follows from that. It didn't have to be bubblegum of course: they could have been talking about – or doing – skipping or archery or a burglary or whatever. But I liked the histrionic feel of a child getting so het up about something no adult could find important. And to the child it really does matter, because it's success or failure; either you can or you can't blow bubbles, there is no middle ground. But it's not just a childish problem. This is a world in which those who can seem to be specially blessed. Those who can't are enraged but secretly feel there's something wrong with them.

Could you give an example of an object from Alien Corn?

That film was originally called *Snail Trail*, which I probably should have kept to. I like the sound of the word, the rhyme. My own definition of a snail trail is that it's the lasting evidence of slow progress. I think that's quite nice, and maybe I was interested in that idea of imprint, the film being a small fragment of somebody's slow progress and also the lasting evidence of it. Also, I was interested in snails because they live in a shell and they come out slowly and with difficulty. All you have to do is touch one of those beautiful horns and they shrink in again, and it will be a while before they re-emerge.

When you say it rather than see it, it sounds crude, but many deaf people live naturally inside a shell. The question the film posed was, how does a deaf child come out of that state and move on? The child is like this creature which is trying to emerge, trying to go somewhere, and that's a delicate and slow process. That's why the film opens with a shot of a snail and the snails are there throughout, right up to the end. Snails get used in all kinds of other ways in that film as well – they're jangled in a jar to make a sound, and they make a visual parallel with the spiral-shaped earpiece of a hearing aid.

How long did it take to develop Wrapper?

It was very fast. The finance was already in place. I wrote it in a couple of weeks, and then spent a week on the storyboard. Within a month of submitting proposal, storyboard and complete script we were off. But I rewrote that script six times during the course of pre-production, honing the structure, story and dialogue repeatedly. Some of those changes were responses to location, casting or lack of cash, but it was mostly a case of sifting and resifting my material to make sure the film was as lean and sharp as it could be, without losing the essential tone and ideas I'd started with.

Usually short film projects take much longer. My first film took two years to get financed. My second film took a year to develop and – incredibly – nine months to finish. Both my short films were turned down the first time I submitted them, and several others I've written have never been made – like *Bug Boy*. But I've learned such a lot from writing them that the process never seems wasted. And characters or situations you've worked on for one unmade project often turn up magically transformed in another.

Is visual material important when submitting a proposal?

Yes. I think if you're a film-maker you assume everybody else can think visually but usually they can't. That's easy to forget. And something that seems glaringly obvious to the film-maker isn't at all obvious to someone else, especially when they've had twenty scripts to read that afternoon. The storyboard was the visual support material on *Wrapper*. With *Alien Corn*, I just found one image and stuck it on the front of the script, and that helped people lock into the core of the story.

What was your production schedule on Wrapper*?*

We had six weeks pre-production. We begged office space from Sankofa Films to provide a base. I went out wandering round London to find locations. Then I spent a long time casting the child and adult and rallied my friends as extras. Meanwhile the production team were finding crew and begging for freebies – equipment, facilities, transport, props, film stock. The process accelerates and expands very fast and there comes a point where there's no turning back. If you hit a big problem at that stage you simply have to overcome it.

We'd planned only three days for the shoot – very tight indeed, especially with a young child. This expanded to four days (after more begging) – except that it rained torrentially on the last day and nothing I'd planned to do would work. So we still had pick-ups to shoot. For example, in the original rushes the saleswoman's questionnaire on which she marks her crosses was soaked with rain: the shots were unusable. So we begged a camera free for half an hour and Gerry Floyd (my cinematographer) and I reshot them together. So the close-ups of the saleswoman's hands are my own hands – in false fingernails – shot in the camera hire company's car park two weeks later.

Did you rewrite dialogue during production?

Yes, repeatedly. I gave Bianca different versions of each line to say both during rehearsal and on the shoot. That was partly to find out what was comfortable for her and what she could remember; partly to combat shoot tedium – a big problem for small kids. Some alterations got written into the script; others didn't. Incidentally, she was the one who insisted on saying the line 'Is this lady bothering you, girlie?'. Initially I'd planned to cut away from her just before this moment but you can see in her eyes that she just loved the line. I'm always prepared to rephrase a line to suit an actor's accent or rhythm or just their mood – often it comes out more naturally. But more often I'm rewriting because I'm never quite satisfied that I've expressed myself as well as I possibly can. And it's true – when I look at the early drafts now I wince.

And how long did you have for post-production?

We had three weeks for the picture edit – which was pretty generous, but the cost of a Steenbeck (now everyone cuts using Avid) is low, and thinking and rethinking at this stage can improve the film immensely. It gave us time to think clearly, to try out experiments, and to show various cuts to friends to check out their reactions. We locked down the narrative pretty quickly, so the rest of the time was devoted to pacing and to 'what ifs'. We didn't reject any ideas, however mad, until we'd tried them once.

We also had terrible sound problems at this stage – most of the child's words were inaudible. So halfway through the picture edit I took Bianca up to Hampstead Heath and got her to perform every line again several times. We cut the new lines in over her visuals as a rudimentary post-synching device. Luckily the fast pace means we get away with it for the most part. Of course I used this opportunity to rewrite some lines yet again.

I usually work very intensely and creatively with sound: I think its effect on a film is terribly underestimated. In *Alien Corn*, which is about a deaf child, there were no words at all. We created a highly stylised internal soundscape made up of vibrations, muted noise and mismatched sounds (for instance, for the sound of a pan of milk boiling over we used the sea breaking on the shore). But in *Wrapper* there was very little room for subtlety – it's almost wall-to-wall words. There are a few subconscious devices hidden in there – a train passes by as the child's angry monologue builds up; a boxing match on the television is mixed with the sound of the child's parents arguing, etc. – but generally I concentrated on the quality of real sounds. We spent an hour trying to recreate the heavy wet plop of stones hitting the canal mud in the opening shot – and made it eventually by chucking metal objects into a tub of strawberry yoghurt.

On location, we had three train lines running in various directions around that wasteland and the sound was pretty awful, so we had a small post-synching session. We got an afternoon in a studio for footsteps, sound effects and so on. The sound post-production was a nightmare – it's very hard to get facilities free. We had to grab available time whenever it was offered, which might mean a couple of hours before midnight and then waiting days for a new slot to become available. The dubbing mixer walked out in frustration and had to be persuaded back to finish it off. The pencil-scrape sound which accompanies the opening credits is again something I just thought of during the dub. The mixer, halfway through his 'nervous breakdown', said, 'I suppose you want that sound travelling right to left?' And I said, yeah, great! We had no cash to clear music for the end credits so Bianca hummed us the only song she knew, and that was that.

How did the source and level of funding affect the project?

As to source, the LFVDA were very open about what we did – they didn't want to see a rough cut or to have any editorial control. As to level, with a budget that low, you have to be very clear about your priorities. After a lot of discussion we decided to shoot on 35mm because we planned to screen in cinemas. It would have been just as expensive to shoot on 16mm and blow it up. My producer spent ages negotiating for free stock and good deals on processing and printing. We couldn't afford a proper art direction budget, so we gave ourselves a limited palette to work with – turquoise, eau de nil, violet and sand. I think most of our art director's tiny budget went on paint, if I remember. We really worked to stay within those limitations – even the car is turquoise.

We couldn't afford tracks or cranes, so I knew I needed to find a simple shooting style that would work with the frequent cutting backwards and forwards between past and present. Sometimes when you've got restrictions it's fun to restrict yourself even further. I had the idea of using an offset grid pattern – the sort of thing you'd use on acetate for animation – as a blueprint for the camera movement. We restricted camera moves to little jerky horizontals and verticals (no drifting or zooming), in order to give the feeling that we're always in the wrong place, always about to slip over to the 'other' story. The framing shifts constantly but is never manic. Originally I planned to always cut from a horizontal movement to a vertical to a horizontal. In the event I couldn't maintain that, but there's enough left of the idea to give the feeling I was aiming for, I think.

More generally, I think funding does have quite a lot of effect on projects. The worst aspect of it is self-censorship. Funding is scarce and arguably more conservative now. As a result many film-makers try to sell ideas they think other people will like, rather than making what they really want to do into something that other people understand and want.

What did you hope to achieve by making Is it the Design on the Wrapper?

For me the film is its own achievement – I do it to do it. I certainly wasn't trying to make a showreel film: I don't think in terms of career moves. Each project should have its own integrity. I think it's a mistake to make a short 'in order to' make a feature, or to imagine that if you can do one you can do the other – they're very different forms. Feature films need much more narrative work, they're complex structures and develop in a different way. Shorts are a challenge to find the essence of an idea or situation. People tend to think of feature films as visual novels and shorts as equal to a short story. But features are much more like short stories – they usually have one main character, one

self-contained story, and stay within one time frame. And they're read/viewed
in one sitting. Shorts on the other hand can be more elliptical, more open, like
poems – or in the case of *Wrapper*, cartoons. They can make you laugh, think
or just wonder, and they thrive on experiment, intensity and conciseness. And
like a poem, if they've got nothing to say they'll be boring.

Do you like to work alone?

Yes, I develop the idea and script on my own. Once the storyboard and script
are in place, other people get involved – especially my producer, Stella Nwimo.
The production office for *Wrapper* helped me learn to delegate much more
than I had before, and that freed me up creatively. It's important to keep the
lines of communication open, expressing doubts about a location or being hon-
estly confused when you are, so you don't spring surprises on people when an
idea they thought was essential is suddenly dumped. Conversely, if you know
the production team is having terrible problems trying to get hold of a prop,
you can go home and try to come up with an alternative. But it's best to draw
clear chalk marks between your area of responsibility and someone else's. It's
dreadful if you rush around trying to do everything. The creative decisions are
mine, and the organisational ones belong to the production department, and
hopefully we both support each other.

Did you keep control of the project?

Yes, and perversely that's because I trusted my producer enough to delegate to
her. I kept to my set of priorities and defended them throughout. It's vital for
the director to know what's important and what's just a wish-list. When something's essential I can really dig my heels in, but I can be oddly happy with a
really awful turn of events. Some things you can't control – you just concentrate on those you can. The weather on *Wrapper* was terrible. It was non-stop
rain on the last day, and that meant nothing we'd planned to shoot would cut
together with what we'd already shot in sunshine. Then one of our two lights
failed so we couldn't recreate sunshine convincingly over any large area even if
the rain stopped for a minute. So I dumped my storyboard of supposedly
'essential' shots and we shot everything very close up, where we could light just
a small area and cover the actors' heads with umbrellas. When I got back to
the cutting room Tina (my editor) expected me to be suicidal, but oddly I felt
fine. You need to be prepared to improvise when you've really got no choice.
That kind of situation is a terrifying prospect if you think about it in advance.
But when it's happening on the day and everyone's waiting for a decision, you
just have to go with it and trust yourself.

How do you feel about the finished film?

I like it – it's fast, funny, weirdly adult: overall I think it worked, and it's very
near to what I set out to do. One exception is the character of the saleswoman.

When I originally cast her, she was giving a different performance – quieter, lisping, with a lower-middle-class accent. It gave her a vulnerability that made her more sympathetic and 'real'. But on the shoot I had to concentrate so much on directing the child that I didn't realise the woman's performance was suffering – it had changed, become more strident. To make matters worse, the coral filter made her suit look red, not pink – a direct no-no in our little book of colour rules. A blonde in a red suit carries certain meanings for me – and they weren't what I was aiming at. But time and money was limited, and we had to go for it. And given the fact that our poor actress was under-directed, five months pregnant and only had one take for her final scene as we were running out of stock, she did a great job.

What distribution did the film have?

We kept the production office running for six months after completion to set this up. Stella Nwimo, my producer, did some amazing work, and we got cinema releases with *Shine* (1996) and *Big Night* (1996). It also got reviews in *Time Out*, *The Guardian* and the *Daily Telegraph*. We entered it for loads of festivals, and it won three prizes, including the BBC Short Film Festival and the Palme d'Or at Cannes, which was completely unexpected. Jane Balfour handled the overseas television sales. Here it was shown on Channel 4, and more recently there's been interest from the Internet: so it's refusing to lay down and die. I still hear of it being seen on airlines and in countries where I didn't even know it was screening. God knows who does the subtitles and what they mean by now – it must be like Chinese whispers. But the humour seems to translate surprisingly well. Maybe the British don't have such a monopoly on irony as we like to think.

Do you think short film distribution could be improved?

I think there's a real problem in both production and distribution. Shorts of a certain style – strong narrative, fast moving and ten minutes or less – are easier to get screened now. But longer projects, non-narrative or contentious subjects are extremely difficult to get funded, let alone screened. That said, if you're prepared to shoot on DV and put a lot of work in, it's possible to make shorts more cheaply now than ever.

In terms of getting your film seen, TV slots have almost dried up in this country, but the Internet is opening up a new viewing audience. There are probably other possibilities that people don't consider, which could be exploited. Airlines already screen shorts, but why not stations, Post Offices, tube trains, bars, even shop windows? I think it's important just to get the films made and out there somehow, somewhere. Festivals are still the best way to reach a committed audience – and get a few days' holiday into the bargain. As for expecting the film to pay for itself, forget it. No-one pays for shorts.

What has happened for you since completion of Is it the Design on the Wrapper?

I was offered work on commercials very soon after – very useful if you don't let it take you over. It paid for me to spend six months drafting a feature film script. I've found myself working with people – in facilities houses, for instance – who might be prepared to do me a favour when I need it. And it's a way of paying back crews who've worked with me for nothing in the past – to hire them at full rate on a commercial. It's good for casting too: half London's actors seem to file before you in a day when you're directing a commercial, and I mentally note the good ones for other projects. I've also used commercials to try out a film stock or effect I'm unfamiliar with.

Winning the prize at Cannes was great, but it catapulted me into a very confusing time of meetings and feature offers. Eventually I realised that all I still wanted to do was write and direct my own stuff, and then I settled down to it again. Gerry, Stella and I set up our own production company, Riverchild Films, and we're developing several feature film projects including my own. As well as scripting, casting and preparing to shoot my first feature, *Blindfold*, I'm co-writing another film (*Sundew*) with an American screenwriter, and starting to collect ideas for a third. I've also written several more shorts, including a half-hour drama for Channel 4, *The Lizard Lover* (1998).

Lynne Ramsay

Lynne Ramsay moved from stills photographer to cinematographer in 1992 when she took a course at the National Film and Television School. She began directing films in 1995. Her work has received wide critical acclaim, especially her first feature film, *Ratcatcher* (1999). Her second feature, *Morvern Callar*, is due for release in 2002. We talked about *Gasman* (1997), the third short film she made.

Why did you move from cinematography to directing?

As a photographer you do your own work, so at film school it felt weird to be in this position where I was shooting other people's work. Although it was interesting, I started hating the formulaic structure of a lot of it. I was interested in film more as an art form, predominantely. I wanted to experiment with the form and not be tied down to the quirky ending.

It was a strange time because there weren't any feature films being made. It was before *Trainspotting* (1996). It was a precarious time for the film industry. I guess a lot of people were frightened of that and at the film school you felt the pressure. It had a style of making very slick, industry-standard films – a few films were absolutely fantastic, but quite a lot felt trite to me. The Department of Documentary was great at that time. People were working fast, intensely – they went out in twos making films. I thought about changing to documentary

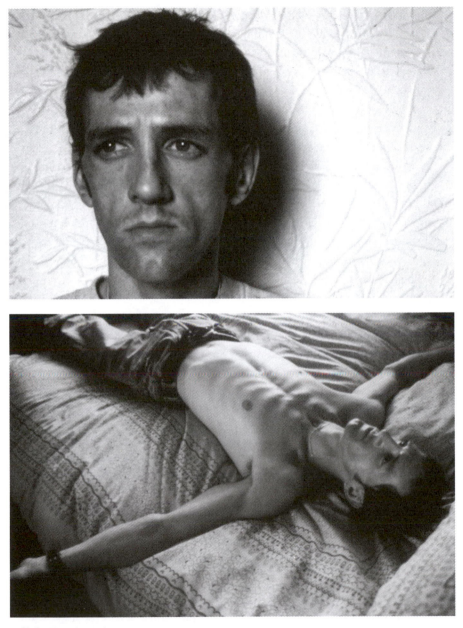

Kill the Day (1996)

but I would have had to leave and reapply, and I was like, 'Well I'm here, so I'll stay.'

Why did you decide to make Gasman?

At that point I'd made two short films – one was at college and one was through the BFI. I wanted to be a short film-maker – I was interested in the form, and I wanted to make a film completely from an articulate child's point of view. I wanted to play a bit with how to show this family, but in an interesting way. Also, I thought the child's realisation that her father's got another family was an interesting subject. I was in a pub one night and I wrote the story on a beer mat. I liked the idea of the young girl having this family secret – families always have secrets – and finding out under bizarre circumstances, being quite young but able to read that situation really clearly as well. And I liked the idea that you empathise with all the characters. You could read the father as this unsympathetic character, but I thought that by trying to bring the families together in some way – he probably naively doesn't think that they'll find out – but I think it's to do some good, and so I empathise with him. I empathise with the other girl as well, who gets her hair pulled. I think it's a no-win situation. It's an interesting, simple idea for a short, and simple ideas always work better for short films. Also there's as much emotional impact, maybe more sometimes, than in a longer film, because it is about concentrating on one thing.

Where did the idea come from?

In a way it was quite personal because I did meet my half-sister when I was older, but it didn't happen in that way. So it was actually quite a hard film to make in that respect. I was interested in the way that adults assume children are innocent, or that they won't recognise things, that they don't know. Also, the way kids deal with things can be really brutal. It has a kind of violence – it's much more direct. And I wanted to work with children and non-professional actors.

How did it develop?

It just came to me and I started writing. I liked the idea of the families meeting at a railway line, these crossing junctions, which was pretty symbolic, but I didn't want to shoot it in a heavy way. And at the end she throws a stone and that pathetic gesture was there – all this pent up anger that goes nowhere. It doesn't end with a conclusion at all, it never did. It was all sketched out – it didn't change that much.

I work in a pretty fluid way. One scene comes from another, or one character develops in a certain way because of meeting someone else, so a lot of the time it starts from either places or a single character.

What did you send to Tartan Shorts?

I sent a two-page treatment that was pretty sketchy really. I gave an outline about how I felt it should look, how I wanted to use these surreal images alongside a pure realism. I wrote pretty early on that in the first scene you don't see anybody's face, because everything was about the body language. From there I got shortlisted.

Do you think in images?

For me the narrative is inherent in the images. The writing and the images were quite mixed up, but I think that's a good thing. I'm quite glad I came from an arts and photography background because it probably suits film-making more. But my work is different now, I'm exploring things that are more led by the narrative, and other things that are much more led by atmosphere. At the very first stages it was definitely like writing the photograph you always wanted to take, the moment you always wanted to see or you did see in the street, and that felt really great.

Do you write about the characters during the development?

Yes, I do, but I don't think about them having a past. I start with them in my mind now. Everything is in the present tense and it never really changes, even though I'll have ideas in my head on what's going to happen to them or what's happened before. I love shooting in chronological order because of that, but I've not been able to do that all the time because it's just impossible unless you've got a lot of money. I treat actors reading that character in the present tense as well. So I try not to let them know too much about what's going to happen to them or what happened before, or let them read scripts necessarily. I might give them the script pages the night before.

Do you take photos if you're thinking of an environment or a certain sort of person?

I do more now. It's almost like when I went to film school, I wasn't a photographer any more. I can get inspired from a photograph really easily – to see all the narratives inherent in a picture. Sometimes a scene comes around an image, so I use photography as a reference like that. Then I'll see a photograph or I'll have an idea of an environment that I think is interesting. For instance, the canal in *Ratcatcher* – kids like to go somewhere that's beautiful but dangerous. I love those layers where something's really appealing but it's also really dangerous. I like the idea of the kid who's not innocent, so that went off and started developing into something else. It's not the kind of cuddly kid in the American movie at all, it's the complete antithesis of that. It's the same with the children in *Gasman*, she's quite aggressive. You don't necessarily like her.

The world these films describe is a pretty brutal world, and it's quite a brutal aesthetic as well.

I think childhood is brutal. I was fed up with seeing the sickly view of how we grew up in this country. I've had people in Glasgow come up to me and say 'I had the same background.' It's weird. Or even from quite different countries, it went down well in Russia, I thought that was strange. Films are about entertainment, sure, and so they should be and I don't have a problem with that, but I like going to see a film that maybe you'd relate to because it has a reality to it, or within the fantasy there's something you can relate to. I love film-makers like Terry Gilliam as well, which is totally opposite. I have both those things in my work. I'm not scared of something being tough, because a lot of things are tough and it's always glossed over. There's a big section of people making films that are glossing over stuff. I was never interested in that. I quite like hard reality sometimes.

So you got the treatment to Tartan Shorts, you were shortlisted, and what happened from there?

I was asked to change things about the script and I was pretty adamant that I wasn't going to change it too much. There was a little bit of pressure because I was using non-professional actors. I think the Tartan Shorts scheme is a lot to do with setting up people to be able to go from there to a feature. But I thought 'Well I've done it this way before. It works for me. I like working in this kind of way.'

When did they put this pressure on?

It was at the point we wrote a script. I don't remember it being intense. I was going to get to do what I wanted, but I think you've got to be up front, otherwise you can be manipulated into doing something that you don't want to do. People always think they know best for you or, 'We really like your work but can you make it into something else?' For me there was no point in that. The executive producers were quite good about it. I did some workshops with actors, did some of the scenes on video – I was casting through doing the scenes, and I proved it would work. I showed them that stuff and then they said okay. I stuck to my guns, and I think that's important.

Did you redraft that initial script?

Yes, I did, but I don't think I changed it that much from the beer mat idea. At that point I wasn't a believer in making a lot of drafts unless it really is going somewhere. I tried different things, but I felt the first idea – the clarity of it – would work. So from there I think I did two drafts.

What were the conditions of the commission?

The conditions were to get this accepted you have a delivery day, it's going to be fifteen minutes, executives come into the cutting room, stuff like that.

What was the budget?

It was £35,000 or £40,000, which was a lot at the time for me, but it was the first time I'd ever worked on the computer as well. I was always cutting film before then. In retrospect I thought I should have cut *Kill the Day* (1996) on computer rather than *Gasman*, as I was playing with the structure more.

It doesn't necessarily mean you'll make a better film because you've got more money. *Gasman* looked like 35mm but we shot it on Super 16. Other films I'd shot were much more rough and ready, but they had their own kind of aesthetic.

And the schedule?

They gave me a week to shoot, or five or six days, and of course I went over a bit, but we made it and we made it in time.

Did you have to show it in front of a group of people from Tartan Shorts?

Yes, first cuts. The executive producers came in, Barbara McKissick was working at the BBC at that time, and she was really good. Some things were a bit unbalanced, but it felt like I was lucky that time, it was pretty straightforward. If there was something that I felt I didn't want to change, I'd really stick to it. I remember there were problems in the party scene where one girl's pulling the other's hair, there were various options and when I look back it could have been cut slightly different, but every director does that.

Did they ask for any changes?

They came out of the cutting room making suggestions, but I felt if the work was powerful, it would speak for itself. So I listened to people and pretended to agree, but another part of me went off and did what I liked.

Then we presented it at a screening, with the two other Tartan Shorts. It seemed to get a really good response. Then it went to Cannes.

What did you hope to achieve with Gasman*?*

Well creatively, I guess to make a strong film that people related to, and also to make something interesting formally as well. Ultimately, to try and enjoy the process and learn something and take some risks. I feel more and more that it's a good thing to take risks instead of getting so scared that you don't do anything.

What sort of risks did you take?

Cutting their heads off for the first two minutes, that's kind of risky. Some people think 'What the hell is this?' but I was glad that I did that and was able to not get too scared about doing that. I think it was a really interesting beginning, one of the most interesting beginnings of a film I've made.

Do you usually work with the same people?

Yes, you need support around you. You can be egocentric about it and think 'This is mine and my piece of work' but basically you can't make a film on your own (unless it's video) and you can't make a film by committee, so it's finding the right balance. I want people I trust who tend to know what I'm talking about. It doesn't necessarily mean that you work with the same people all the time, but I think it becomes a shorthand. It gets better. The people I work with now will be working with other directors and I'll work with some other people sometimes. It kind of dictates how you work, probably if I worked with a different director of photography it would be slightly different, but I think whatever you're doing still stays there.

The soundtrack on Gasman *is really percussive. Who did the sound design?*

Lucia Zucchetti [Lynne's editor] and I did that. I was starting to get really interested in using single sounds in a scene, blank everything else out then use one sound. I love doing the sound though, it's sometimes more important than the visual. We just took things that had been recorded and heightened them. Like the train when they meet – I really like the sound. We didn't have enough money for the long track for this particular scene, and a friend of mine had this fantastic idea of using one of those hand-operated trolleys that run along railway lines, but annoyingly it was really noisy. It was quite hard to get clean dialogue with this noise – 'Ktsh ktsh'. But it was a fantastic sound, and I thought 'Oh, I want to use this sound somewhere.' When the mother and father meet we used part of that sound, and then it drops out, there's hardly anything, and then there's this strange sound that's nothing to do with the scene. So just playing about with a lot of the elements we had already fascinates me.

For me the editing and the dub are often the most enjoyable part of the film-making process. The shoot's about gathering the best material you can get, you have good shoots and bad shoots. You write this beautiful thing and then you see it crumble around you while you make it. It's where it all starts to fall apart, so I have a weird relationship with shoots.

It sounds as if you wanted complete control over the process on Gasman. *Do you think you were successful?*

Yes I was. Your attitude towards what you're making is really important, just stick to why you want to make it. I'm not saying that you shouldn't listen to people, but I think you should definitely have an attitude towards your own work, because there are points where you feel weak, you don't know whether it works. You have to try and keep some sort of vision of it. It isn't that I'm successful at it, because sometimes I'm not.

How do you feel about Gasman *now?*

I like films for different reasons and I don't ever love the films I make, but I see them as a process. It's a strong piece of work. At the time I probably hated it if I was honest, but I knew I'd achieved something. For me it's not that the whole thing completely works or it's a success, but I think it's achieving one of the things you set out to do. I set out to make a film about this girl that was emotionally powerful, and I think in places what I was trying to achieve was successful. Also I got some very, very raw performances out of these kids, and if you have one thing to build on for the next project, it's great. Certain sequences are too long, certain sequences could have been better, there are things in the script that we didn't quite get when we made it, there are things in the directing that are better than they were in the script. It's just the same with every film I've made.

Was there anything specific that you set out to achieve that you don't think you did achieve?

There were sequences in the party that I thought were more energetic and more alive in the script. Somehow the party went quite surreal. We set up a real party, these kids all went bananas and we filmed it. It wasn't even directed. The only part I directed was the bit between the two girls. What was really nice was that it was like a documentary, and they all went wild and had a really great time. Then they started getting really mad and all these fights broke out. We got it all on film, it was fantastic, and it's a way of working I've used subsequently.

What about distribution for Gasman?

They had a screening in London, it went onto TV eventually, and then it did the rounds of the festivals, so a lot of people got to see it. It's surprising how many people have seen it, so obviously being shown on TV was great. There have been all these things like Atom Films, Internet stuff, but basically short films don't get distributed. My films have had a bigger audience on TV than they've had at all the festivals, I know that. Only film industry people and film-makers will see it at festivals. The BFI short film that I did, *Kill the Day*, was shown on Channel 4 late at night, and Film Four have taken it up and shown it before a feature. I was always disappointed and sad that people didn't really want to see shorts, but I'd still like to make more shorts as a film-maker.

When you were developing the idea of Gasman *did you think about audience?*

No, never. I try to make a film in the way I would like it, and hope that other people like it, because I feel honest about what I'm doing. That tends to work so far.

What happened for you after the completion of Gasman?

Because it was successful on the festival circuit and won some prizes, I think it definitely helped me to make my first feature. It was up for a BAFTA and went to Cannes, and Cannes definitely gave it a nudge and helped me get finance. There's no doubt that if you want to make features, making shorts does help. Also I was lucky with timing, because it was after *Trainspotting*. That film started a lot of things happening in this country, whether you like it or not. It was a good time. I'm amazed that I got the money to make *Ratcatcher* to be honest, and also a great producer, Andrea Calderwood.

Do you think there's a connection between gender and narrative structures?

I don't know if it's gender or individuals, but we've been taught to tell a story in a certain way, and it's very rigid. Not everybody tells a story like that. You can see it's a gender issue because it's mostly men who have been making films, and it's a much more rigid form of cutting. I try to do things that are not that rigid, but I'm sure male film-makers have done that as well. The way we've told stories is very much like theatre in some ways – three acts. I don't make films like that nor do some other people, but we're used to seeing films like that. It's like a form of language and it feels like it's the only form being presented a lot of the time.

Are films with a clearer narrative direction easier to sell or get commissioned?

Probably. It's difficult to break out of the conventional structures but it's not impossible. It's quite interesting for me watching people looking at things I've done that they'd normally think they wouldn't like because it didn't present things on a plate, but then they liked it because they were given some room to come to their own conclusions. So I don't think there is one way. But because those are the kind of films which are given a lot of money, those are the kind of film-makers working in Hollywood, that's seen as the form of true entertainment. There is a kind of backlash to that as well. A mainstream film like *American Beauty* (2000) borrows from the cutting edge, the left field, and slightly subverts the conventional values. I think that it's become a wee bit more fluid now with the advent of DVD and stuff like that. I'm optimistic.

Damien O'Donnell

Damien O'Donnell is a partner in the Dublin-based production company, Clingfilms. He made five short films, three of which he wrote, before going on to direct his feature film, *East is East* (1999). Here we discuss his work on the website for Mike Figgis' latest film, *Hotel* (2002), and his contribution to the Beckett on Film project, *What Where?* (2000). The complete *Hotel* website may be viewed on *http://www.filmfour.com/hotel*.

How did your involvement with the website for Hotel *come about?*

Mike Figgis, the director, and the producer, Andrea Calderwood, got in touch with me and said they were shooting a film in Venice in February for about six weeks. They would have a bunch of actors living together in a hotel. He was going to shoot in a similar style to his film *Time Code* (2000) – which is multi-camera, three or four cameras, and in the final version the screen is divided into four. The plan was that you would be watching simultaneous action on four different screens from four different perspectives. For *Hotel* he also wanted to do a website – but he didn't want an ordinary, average website, just the usual one that has a lot of biographies, spiel and all of that – he wanted to do something different. He had the idea of putting short films on the website using the cast, because there were such a lot of people there and they weren't all going to be necessarily working at the same time. So he figured that they might do something creative for the Web which would both promote the film and also be an end in itself.

What's Hotel *about?*

It's about a bunch of actors who arrive in a hotel in Venice. Some of them are tourists, some of them are MTV-style journalists, and a bunch of them are actors, a director and a producer making a Dogma-style version of *The Duchess of Malfi*, a Jacobean play by John Webster.

My intention was to go over there and watch Mike Figgis at work, because there's no real apprenticeship for directors I feel, not for film. The irony is that the director is often the most inexperienced member of the crew in terms of experience on set. And cameramen and actors get to work with different directors but directors don't, unfortunately, so there are lots of ideas and skills that don't get shared. So I'm always curious if I'm given an opportunity to visit a set. I can watch a director at work to see what he does that is different to what I would do, or see if there were any clues as to how I might do the job of directing better.

So that's part of what drew you to the project, Mike Figgis himself?

Yes, I don't know whether I would have done it if it had been anyone else, I'm not sure. The second part of it was the fact that everything was shot on digital. I'd just done a commercial in Dublin which was shot entirely on digital, and I really liked the feel of it and the liberty of the process. You're working with a minimal crew, no make-up, no electricians, you operate the camera yourself. I really found that invigorating as a process.

If you work on a traditional film set, you have a lot of people there, all with their own individual responsibilities, and if you're shooting in sets or interiors a large amount of work has to go into setting up a single shot. On *East is East*, for example, the camera might be only running for 5 per cent of the total time spent, and I found that really a great pity. The whole point of making a film is to be committing performances onto celluloid, but that's only such a tiny part of the whole film-making procedure. So when I shot on digital, we decided to follow the Dogma rules to a degree; we had to find natural locations and people wore their own clothes, there's no make-up, no styling. Basically a lot of the fuss was taken out of it, particularly with lighting. We could use the light that was available, because these cameras are very sensitive to light. It meant that you could almost walk into a room and start rehearsing and then start filming. And on one day on that commercial I think I shot five hours of footage – which is probably a little excessive for a commercial – but we were just shooting alternatives to what we were doing. If I had a change of mind and I wanted to shoot in a different location we just walked across the road, walked into a place, give somebody £20 to stand in the corner for ten minutes, and I thought that was fantastic. It suits films about people, films that work on a personal level – personal dramas, where you're more interested in seeing people's faces rather than some epic landscapes or battle sequences or whatever, I don't think it's suited to that, but it's great for looking for some sort of humanity.

How was the website project first brought to your notice?

I'd been communicating with Mike, asking him for advice on his process because I was doing this commercial. And then I sent him an e-mail one day saying that it had worked out really well, and thanks for his help, and he said, 'Well we're doing this thing over in Venice. We want to make films on the website for this feature film I'm directing. Would you be interested in directing them?

Was there anything in writing? Did you actually see a brief?

Not for the website itself. Two people – Jonathan Green and Abby Williams – were already involved in developing the website, so they'd started to outline what the website might be. Then I went over and we had meetings, and we decided that as the film was going to be in quadrants we'd like to go with something like that, and have different activities in each one. Unfortunately with the Internet at this stage you can't run all four simultaneously, so all we could do was give a stylised impression of what the final film would look like. We decided to keep it very simple and keep the focus on whatever little animations or drama we had in the quadrants on each particular day. The idea was that we would refresh the website every day if we could. I didn't realise how big a challenge it was, because nothing ever works according to plan. If you wanted to get access to actors they might have been available from ten o'clock until twenty past ten but you might have been somewhere else, and then when you turn up to look for them they're back on set. So it became a bit of a hunt. But our real focus was that we'd have stuff up every day, it was almost like it was a little television station, just get out there and shoot it. Digital was the only way you could have done it. You couldn't have shot on film, and the format of the mini digital video cameras was just perfect for the website.

And were the other two people designing the website or were they out shooting or directing as well?

No, they were designing the website and organising the graphics and animation. I brought Enda Hughes with me, who's a brilliant short film-maker, and Lee Hickey as editor. We set up a sort of production line where myself and Enda would go out with two cameras and we'd film material – either background footage of what was happening during filming or our own little dramas. We set ourselves a rule for the website that we'd only represent the actors on screen in the characters they were playing in the film, just to give ourselves something to work within. We didn't want to replicate what they do in the film, but it's as if the film represented the lives of these characters at the hotel from Monday to Thursday and the website might represent what they did on Friday. Or if the film represented what they did in the afternoon then the website might give little dramas about what they did in the evening.

So that was the whole idea, to get something a little bit odd and entertaining hopefully, and funny if we could. We wanted it to spark an interest in the film, but it would also work in its own right as a place where you could go on the Internet just to watch, say, a three-minute film with David Schwimmer and Salma Hayek.

Was there anything on paper between the production team, or did you just have these discussions and go out and shoot?

We had proposals on paper for Channel 4 because they were financing the website. They wanted to know basically what we were going to do, but it was all very vague to be honest. We didn't tell them exactly what we were going to do, but we told them our intentions.

So they'd approved the budget before you came up with the detailed proposal?

Yes, because a lot of it was based on what we were going to do when we got to Venice, where we were looking for inspiration and what the actors wanted to do. So in that respect we couldn't tell them definitively – just like the film itself, which had no script. Mike had a treatment and he had ideas about how the story would go but it was a very improvised piece. We followed that same line for the website, improvising with the actors. It's a fascinating way to work, quite exhilarating. You can't really tell in advance what's going to happen, that's what's nice about it.

And also why it can go very wrong presumably, and that's what gives it an edge.

Yes, it can go wrong, that's true. But if you're lucky and things go wrong you can just do them again, especially with that process because the film's so easy to shoot on digital. I think Mike was very clever in picking Venice – it was a beautiful set, and it was all free.

And it's very theatrical in itself, particularly at that time of year.

Yes, we were filming during the Carnival. There was a quite chaotic evening where we – the website team – went out to film the main production unit, who were filming in the Carnival. They were filming all the actors ostensibly going round searching for the lead actress, Saffron Burrows, who's on the run from them. Mike said, 'Go up to anyone wearing a mask and see if it's her.' So you had these actors descending upon the actual revelers and tourists in St Mark's Square being pursued by four camera people being pursued by two more camera people. And at one stage the actors descended on these quite ornately dressed figures and we discovered they were being filmed for something else. It was like a media feeding frenzy. It was pretty odd.

And were you and Enda just going out with a camera or did you have any other people with you?

No, we'd just go out on our own, there was no crew. We had radio mikes or mikes on the camera.

And what sort of things were you looking for?

The intention was to make little dramas and sometimes we did spoof documentaries. For instance, there's a report on Mike's camera wheel, where we blur the lines between reality and fiction. Mike Figgis is talking about this wheel that he used – you mount the camera on the wheel and it helped operate these little cameras in a more efficient way. But we also had Rhys Ifans acting the director, and talking about the same wheel as if he'd invented it for his Dogma film, and we mixed them up. One of the opening pieces was Rhys being inspired by the ten rules of Dogma while he's on the toilet, and it's gently mocking the whole manifesto, which I do have great respect for, but I do believe a lot of it is not to be taken too seriously, everyone breaks the rules.

Do you know how many hours of material you shot?

We shot over 200 hours of material. We have a lot of material of behind the scenes that we never intended to shoot but I just thought was too much of an opportunity to miss. Our brief was to go out and make little dramas using the actors, but sometimes you might have a day when all the actors are being used, and what do you do then? We now have all this background footage of what was happening in the hotel, which will be useful for the DVD – behind the scenes activity.

Have you got any idea how many hours have been spent editing the website film?

We were editing as we went along, so we'd shoot something in an afternoon and Lee would start editing it that night and put it up the next day. So it was more or less the same amount of time – six weeks.

The website is very complex and varied isn't it? It uses every ability of the technology.

Yes. We wanted to give people something different to watch. You have actors of the quality of Mark Strong and Rhys Ifans, I don't think they've ever done stuff like this before, they've made these dramas specifically to be broadcast on the Web. And there's a limitation to the technology of the website as well. So, this is quite a unique format, I felt. You will be able to get films that have been made properly for cinemas and for television or short films that you can watch on the Web, that happens all the time. This was something that was made specifically for it, which I think is a first.

What do you see as the function of the website?

To create a world around the film, to develop people's interests in the characters and in this hotel and what's going on, and so almost to build up a taste for the film itself. When people see the film, they'll recognise all the characters but not the scenes. It's a trailer in a way, but it's my ideal form of trailer, because it shows nothing that's actually in the final film.

And is there going to be an interactive element to it?

Yes, I think the plan is to have a chat room and have people comment on it,

DAY 01

WELCOME TO VENICE
PIGEON CAM
THE RULES
QUADRANT IMAGES

?   FILMFOUR.COM

Hotel website (2001)

which is a bit scary. But another reason for being involved in this project was to
get myself brought up to speed about how a website worked, and how to make
films for a website. It's definitely something that's going to happen in a huge
way.

What do you think that you've got out of it? Do you think it will affect the way you
work? Did it make you think of specific projects that you'd like to do?

I'm hoping to do another short film this summer and I want to do it on digital
– I really like that process. What I got out of it personally was to work with
great actors – Rhys Ifans, Mark Strong, Heathcote Williams, Saffron Burrows,
and others. I'd like to work with virtually everybody who worked on that film.
Also the production process was very revealing about how you can do good
work simply and cheaply, because it's about the talents of the people operating
the equipment. It's not about having big cranes, huge scenes with hundreds of
extras and explosions. If you have a good group of people and a digital camera,
a decent microphone, you can do something really moving, funny, dramatic all
in a little room if you wanted to. They're merely tools and these tools are just a
way of recording, but it's what you're recording that's important and how you
edit it as well.

I'd love to take that medium and develop ideas with actors, because it's
amazing as a creative process. You have all these people and you can do something immediately, have a look back at it and refine it, and then go back again
and do it again, and look again and refine that. It's very, very liberating. You

don't have to wait overnight for rushes, by which stage if it hasn't worked the set's gone, you've moved on to another location, you have to go back. Because it's so instant we reshot a couple of things. We went out and shot something with the actors. If we came back and looked at the material and said, 'Well actually it could be better,' we'd go back and do it the next day. Because we'd had overnight to think about what worked about the piece and what didn't work about the piece and how to amend it, it was fantastic for us to do that.

What Where?, your Beckett project, must have been a totally different process. How did that project start?

Michael Colgan, the artistic director of the Gate, had the idea of filming all of Samuel Beckett's works. He'd toured the entire works of Samuel Beckett previously in Dublin, in London and I think in other places around the world. I think what he said was he was tired of touring the plays and it would be great to have something made that he could just hand people like a roll of film or a videotape and say 'There you go.' The Beckett estate has a lot of trust in him because of his previous associations with Beckett. Michael got involved with an Irish producer called Alan Maloney because he hadn't worked that much in film himself, and the two of them set about filming all the plays over the period of a year.

How did they fund the project?

I think some of it was private investment and then the whole thing started to take off and built up a head of steam. One of the first major monies in was from RTE, I think they put £1 million towards it. Ultimately the whole project ended up costing about £5 million. As it built up a head of steam and films started being made they could show them to other people and found more interest. Channel 4 invested money in it, and the Irish Film Board came in. So I think it was like that: some private investors, Irish national television, UK television and the Irish Film Board. I'd just finished *East is East* and I was in Edinburgh at the screening of the film when they approached me about it, and asked would I be interested? I didn't know much about Beckett's work. I knew his reputation but not that much about the material. They sent me a book of all the works and asked me to look through it, and to be honest through a combination of laziness and fear I said, 'Did you have anything in mind for me?' They pointed out one play at the end, which was the last play that Beckett had ever written, in 1983, called *What Where?* So I read it and I couldn't make head nor tail of it but I was curious about it, so I said 'Well OK, I'll give it a go, see what I can do.' It was a completely different experience from the website in that the website involved improvising and choosing and editing, and editing was a crucial part of it. Of course the major rule about the Beckett is that you can't cut a word, you have to reproduce what's on the page, which even Beckett himself didn't do. I learned that Beckett himself had directed that play and he'd made major edits to the text, or rearranged parts of what was happening, or re-interpreted himself, which he's entitled to do, but the word from the Estate was that nobody else could do that. And even if you came up with examples where Beckett himself had made changes they were only interested in you reproducing the published texts, the Faber & Faber edition. It was as much about studying the material and finding out what's in it, and for me it was a very, very pure directing experience, because we can't change anything, we can't have a better idea.

And you can't adapt it for the different medium either, or you can in the treatment and setting but not in the actual script itself.

Yes, I particularly wanted to put in a location that wasn't a void, because even though it was a void in the theatre, a theatrical void is very different from a cinematic one because cinema is much more literal than theatre. In a theatre, actors are standing in a blank space with a spotlight, it's not so important where it is. But because an audience is more used to seeing cinema as reality, or a reproduction of reality, I certainly feel that as an audience member I would like to know where this is all happening, even in the vaguest sense. So I suggested setting it in a library, because the whole work for me was about information – knowledge and power. I liked the symbolism of the library, about this being a huge collection of knowledge, and yet the lead character, Bam, is lacking that one piece that will satisfy him. Or maybe not, maybe he's being a lot more cruel. Beckett's work is so open to interpretation and he never spoke about it himself.

How did you set about deciding how to film it?

I read the script a few times and started looking for the four actors. I wanted to work with Peter Mullen and Gary Lewis – both Scottish actors, and an Irish actor called Sean McGinley. Peter wasn't available in the end, so we stopped looking for the third and fourth actors. I got this idea from what it says in the text – that all the actors should look as alike as possible – that maybe Gary Lewis could play three of the parts. Ultimately on reflection I should have taken that to its logical conclusion; I should have had one actor play all of the parts, but I made the distinction. That's one of the things I think was wrong in retrospect, but retrospect is a bit of a luxury isn't it?

Or an annoyance.

Well I'm not dwelling on it too much, it's something that's been done. I think it was great to actually film all the Becketts. It was a challenge. It would never be something that would universally satisfy either Beckett fans or an audience that was curious to find out more about Beckett. But what I loved about the whole project was that you found yourself in pubs talking about Beckett to people, and realising you've never had a conversation like that before in your life. The intention was to bring it into the mind of a contemporary audience, make them aware of that. It certainly has achieved that. When it is shown obviously there'll be some reaction to that; good, bad or indifferent, but at least if it's good or bad rather than indifferent that's an achievement in itself.

What was the budget on What Where?

There was no budget – that was such a liberating situation to be in, where the producer says 'What do you need? and we'll get it.' I said, 'Well, we need to build this set, and this has to look like a great library.' We wanted to have rows of old books but set in this really stylish futuristic environment so you don't know when or where it is, it could be all these old volumes resting on shelves somewhere in the future, for instance. That was quite an expensive set to build, but we built it on a sound stage in Dublin. They asked me how many days I would need to shoot it, and I cheekily asked for four days, which I got away with because we were the first production. We took our time, we shot it chronologically – which was great. The actors could build up on their performances as we went along. We were in that one environment and we were always lit. The set was still being built on the first day, I think we turned over at something like half four on the first day and we stopped at six. We got one shot done on the very first day, so it was more like three days shooting. It was very relaxed, very enjoyable.

The whole process sounds very artist-centred, in more of a theatrical way.

Yes, the pitch was that it was about nineteen directors filming nineteen of Beckett's plays and that was it. They said it wasn't about who was producing them, it was about directors and their interpretations of the work. I think the whole process was very supportive of directors and of the cast from the very beginning through to the end. I loved that, I would do that again at the drop of a hat.

Whatever I said about digital film-making earlier on, I'll still happily go out the next day onto a set which has a huge crane and a big 35mm camera standing on the top of it, and with lots of extras. I can enjoy both approaches of film-making equally. It's nice to be able to alternate, because you can pick up skills from one that you can use in the other.

It's about what the project needs, isn't it?

Yes, this wouldn't have suited digital video at all. The thing about digital cameras, especially the hand-held approach, is you're always aware that there's somebody filming because it's so close to news footage, you're more aware of the apparatus. Here you want to capture the performances in that environment and you want to be as clear about it as possible.

Did post-production go smoothly?

Yes. Because we were using the same actor in three different parts there were a couple of times when we needed them to be on the screen at the same time, so we had to do some very simple effects shots at a computer film-processing laboratory. We had to cut Gary Lewis out of one shot and then paste him into another so that he could look at himself, or he could walk past himself. That was a little bit tricky, but it wasn't so difficult. It was one of the more straightforward pieces of computer trickery you can do these days. We spent a lot of time at the edit honing it down. That was an unusual process because you can't cut out stuff, you can't re-order stuff, you have to reproduce what's on the page in the order that it's written – every word – in the final film.

How long did it take to edit?

I think the majority of the work was done in a week and a half. Then it was toying with the computer effects, trying to get them to work, and again it was very relaxed. I had to go away and I came back about a month later and sat down and worked on it at that stage.

Did the Beckett estate have any say about the final cut?

Not at all. Michael and Alan and Edward Beckett, Samuel Beckett's nephew, sat down and watched the final cut without the computer effects on it, and we discussed it and that was it. It was left the way it was. So it was very much what I'd done and how I'd envisaged it.

But at the same time I'm always open to debate. I think that work can only get better from it. There were several times on the website pieces, where we would sit down and have debates with people like Enda about something he'd done, if I thought that worked or not or whether it would be better to change it again. And he would come in and I'd show him something that I'd done and he would say 'Well, would you not think about this?' and a couple of pieces just changed radically because of it, some other pieces we just dropped because of it. You do sometimes need an outside perspective on something to engage with you or even vocalise what you might be thinking yourself, to hear in words what's being whispered at the back of your mind. 'This is not working as well as it should be, you need to either change it or drop it.' So I don't have a huge objection to people coming in. I'm not that precious about the final version. It is about whether the final film works for an audience rather than whether it works for you personally, that's the important thing. Because you know it's indulgent to spend all that money and use all this talent to end up with something that only works for yourself. You have to be aware that ultimately you're going to be showing this to people and they're going to come and they're going to be asking questions. People are asking questions in the edit suite, these are the same questions that will be repeated further down the line and you have to address them. It's an essential part of making a film. In *East is East*, there was quite a lot of discussion as we went through the cuts, some great ideas came up which might not have materialised if we hadn't been in the position to show it to other people and get an objective opinion. There are a lot of suggestions that we just chose to ignore as well, that's the beauty of it. You chose whether to run with it or not.

I think the problems arise when you feel they are unsympathetic suggestions coming from someone who's got power in the equation?

Yes, it's very frustrating if that happens, or people are making suggestions for the wrong reasons. Maybe people are saying 'Can't we put this back in because everyone wants to see more of this character? They're sexy or good looking' or whatever. You think, 'Well it's not what it's about.'

Are you happy with the distribution of the Beckett on Film work?

They've had a cinema premiere and have been on television. I think they'd like to tour them and have a Beckett festival rather than being part of another film festival. They have a longevity about them because there is so much interest in Beckett's work. But it's not going to multiplexes. It's not going to pack them in. Beckett was always testing his audience, and there are a lot of people who don't go to the cinema to be tested, they go there to be entertained and have the chance to switch off. They'll be on DVD and you'll be able to access all the films, but it may be another collection of short films that huge numbers of people will never see at the cinema.

Do you see this changing in future?

Well, what's interesting is that the whole nature of cinema is changing. We're having digital cinemas now and this may end the whole process of distribution of huge reels of film. You can get stuff on disks, or on little tapes, or beamed down by satellite, or being downloaded from the Internet – which will allow cinemas to be varied in their programming if they want to. It's up to the cinema, but that's the problem. It's not in the interests of people making major Hollywood movies that a cinema will reprogramme and drop one of their shows to show six or seven short films, so it's not going to be as clear cut and as easy as that. But as the technology becomes cheaper you might find that there will be a whole host of places that will open up, and there'll be little digital cinemas that really are specialist. Because it's so cheap to run they can take more chances and they can show short films.

It's nice to hear that you're thinking of making a short next.

I've read a short story in a collection edited by Nick Hornby called *Speaking with the Angel*, and there's one there I really liked and I know they were looking for directors. This one's a similar approach in that they're going to get different directors to shoot the films, again for Channel 4. I really like short films. It's refreshing in that you can go and take chances and make mistakes or whatever, and it hasn't taken two years of your life like a feature film would. I do like that immediacy about short film-making. There's not a huge amount of money at risk so you're able to take more chances.

Do you think that's the main difference as a director between shorts and features – the time that it takes up of your life?

I do think time is a huge factor. I haven't made another feature since *East is East* because I've been wary about getting involved in scripts that I didn't adore. They're a huge demand, and there must be something at the end of the day that's rewarding for me. If I don't think that, I'm a bit scared of investing that much time of my life into it. I'd rather do ten short films over that period of time than one feature film.

Anthony Minghella

Anthony Minghella lectured in Drama at the University of Hull until 1981. His writing for both theatre and television has been highly acclaimed. His stage plays are *Child's Play*, *Whale Music*, *A Little Like Drowning*, *Two Planks and a Passion*, *Made in Bangkok* and *Love Bites*. His writing for television includes the trilogy *What if it's Raining?*, regular contributions to the series *Inspector Morse*, and *The Storyteller* series. In April 2000 he and Sydney Pollack set up the production company Mirage Enterprises, which has been involved in such films as *Sense and Sensibility* (1995) and *The Fabulous Baker Boys* (1989), as well as *The Talented Mr Ripley* (1999). He is now working on his next feature film, *Cold Mountain*. We discuss his short for the Beckett on Film project, *Play* (2000).

How did you get involved with the Beckett project?

The Beckett film happened in the most odd way. I was coming back from Australia, where I'd been promoting *Ripley*. In the airport lounge in Sydney I read this article saying that the Gate Theatre in Dublin were going to film all of Beckett's plays. Beckett had been my post-graduate subject and there was a time in my life when there was no question on his work I couldn't have answered, and *Play* was the very first play I ever directed, and so I was very jealous of this project. When I got back to Heathrow I called my agent and said 'They're doing these Beckett films and I want to do one please,' and by the time I'd got my bags I'd spoken to Michael Colgan, who's the producer, and I was doing *Play*. By the time I was into London I was already trying to set it up, so I very much volunteered to do one of the films.

And how did you decide on your approach to it?

I've come to trust almost instinctively in the first things I think about, and they tend to always remain. Built into the theatre version of *Play* is an attempt for an audience to understand a conceptual idea much more than a content idea. The idea that I immediately had was that, in a typically iconoclastic style for Beckett,

Play didn't rely on your being there as an audience. *Play* was happening and you visited it – it didn't start for you and it didn't finish for you. If Beckett had been writing that play for the theatre now, I'm sure it would have been like a video installation: you could walk in at nine o'clock in the morning, come back at one and it would still be playing, and you could sit for ten minutes and go. What you have to understand about it is its form, the form is everything. The central idea is that people would be punished into speaking, punished by language, that the provocation of language would be unwilling in the sense that most of us generate our stories willingly and we volunteer our information, and in plays people volunteer to speak. In this particular play they're trying not to speak; they're exhausted by their speaking, they're not attached any longer to what they're saying and their aspiration is to silence. Their aspiration is to be relieved of the burden of having to repeat for the thousandth, ten thousandth, ten millionth time the banalities of their domestic irregularities.

What instantly occurred to me was that movies replicate part of this in the most prosaic way, because if we were doing this for a movie, you would say 'Cut'. Then you'd say 'Next time can you not move your hands so much but just try and keep them down' and I'd try and do it again. And you'd say 'It's good, but now I've told you not to move your hands you've got rather static vocally. Can you try and keep the energy in the dialogue but not using your hands to engender it?' And we would start to try and refine a piece of dialogue until we felt it was giving us everything we wanted. So having just come off a film set where I'd been working – sometimes doing twenty or thirty takes of a look or a turn – it occurred to me that *Play* anticipated this process in its structure. Whereas in the theatre the only way you could suggest repetition is over time, the only way I can tell you I have repeated something is to do it twice in front of you, on film there's the possibility of inferring from what you're seeing that one line is the product of more than one take. You can verticalise repetition by quite aggressive cutting. You can say 'This is not just one take.'

I had this idea of a Dadaist text. If I got you to say 'Hello, I've just come to Hampstead and it's rather hot today,' and I shot you on a 50mm lens, on a 28mm lens, on a 300mm lens doing that, then I shot you hand-held doing the same text. Then I lay all the texts on top of each other and just splice between them, all that would be changing would be the take and the size, I wouldn't be having to take frames out, I wouldn't be trying to accelerate the language. It would be as if it was in real time, but the implication would be of ten or eleven takes. So that I could not only just do the repetition inside the text, but I could also suggest and make you conscious of the number of times the actors had done each take. So that was the very first idea, it was like a flash, and from that came the whole idea of the film.

The other thing that occurred to me was that film is literal in a way that theatre is an imaginative space. If I'm in the theatre it's essentially metonymic, isn't it? If you see a chair and a man comes and sits in it and puts a crown on his head, you are persuaded he's a king.

Or you know you're supposed to believe he's a king.

And you do, you don't question he's a king. If I made a film and a guy came in and sat down in a chair and put a crown on his head I'd think, 'He's a madman, this is about someone who's a bit bonkers.' In the theatre, if he said 'Where are all my subjects?' and an actor came and said 'They're here my lord,' you start to go on an imaginative journey. As the prologue of *Henry V* says, 'Piece out our imperfections with your thoughts' – that's the contract between the theatre audience and the theatre. It's a wonderful contract. Film has no such contract.

Quite the opposite.

Yes, quite the opposite. If we don't see that we're in Paris we don't believe that we're there. We're very literal as film audiences. We're always questioning the credulity of every moment that we're shown, not withstanding the fact that simultaneously we understand that it's not real. This is what the bizarre thing is, we insist on a kind of social realism of our images while knowing always that they're not real images. We see a love scene and we see two people in an intimate relationship with each other. We want to believe that there's a real activity going on, but we also know that there was a sound recordist and a lighting cameraman and a director … there were forty people in the bedroom, but the request that we have of the film is that it denies the presence of those people. It's a very complex convention that relies on verisimilitude. The camera only sees what it sees, and so you're always having to give information in an extremely prosaic way.

Play on the stage has only three urns, and trying to decode that signal we understand that there are thousands of urns, everybody is in an urn. None of the three characters know that the other is there, so that must be a message to say that there could be a thousand more urns. It's an implicit way of assimilating the text. But if I made the movie with three urns there'd only be three urns. It would be about three people in three urns in a world of three urns. The first thing I had to say was, 'We have to show that there are thousands of urns.'

When working on an adaptation, I feel passionately devoted to the source material. I've a quite developed if not very original idea about adaptation, which is that you shouldn't be genuflecting to a novel, you should be trying to find some way of creating a movie. Your devotion has to be to the movie and not to the source material, but can only be informed by the source material. So you are trying to find correlatives, that's why I'm always thinking 'What is the experience I have as a reader? How do I replicate that as a film-maker? What is the experience I had as a playgoer? How can I replicate that so that I have a film experience which has the same value and intensity and meaning?' And often that means going in a completely different direction from the architecture of the novel or from the play. Here I've maintained everything, every single word that's printed in the text is in the film. The most radical notion is to piece out the imperfections myself rather than letting an audience do it.

And the correlation between the camera as interrogator rather than the light?

That's the other idea I had – that the camera is much more literally provocative in a way that light can never be, because if you're not on camera you don't exist. Film is fascist in that way. The tyranny of the camera is that you can talk as much as you like, but if my camera is not pointing at you, you're not there. I have to pan onto you to find you. Everybody who's ever stood in front of a camera – even being photographed – knows the tyranny of the lens coming on you and how everybody suddenly changes their position, can't smile any more, doesn't know where their hands should be. It seemed to me that exactly the correlative was to use the camera as a provocative, invasive, tyrannical verb as it were. It was going to be the fourth character, which meant that rather than disguising its presence, I wanted to draw attention to the fact that there was a fourth character.

In the play the fourth character is the lighting operator, and Beckett's very clear that there are four people in the play. I wanted the film-maker – not me as film-maker but a sort of idea of a film-maker – to be visible by making the audience aware of the things you normally try and hide. So I recorded camera noise and the focus gun and exacerbated it in the mix. I did the focus myself in the film so that it's searching all the time for focus. We swung the camera. We did lots of things to draw attention to the camera searching for a face because I wanted to dislocate this contract of 'Don't let me know that you are here.' I wanted people to go 'Oh there's a camera, there's the film's leader' – all the things we try and hide. I just wanted to, as it were, lift up the skirts of the film-making technique, not because I wanted to write my name on the film, but because I wanted the audience to be aware of the fact that these three characters were in thrall to somebody else. They were being forced to say what they were saying.

Another quite shocking shot in terms of the stage play, is where you have a three-shot profile and you're pulling focus between them, because on the stage you only see one at a time.

I just thought that again the camera can move. This is one of the things that we really discussed a lot. Somebody said, 'You can't go behind Alan Rickman's head.' And I said, 'But the cameras can.'

And you did, wandered off and back, and wide as well.

Cameras can do that. When I was directing the three actors I would do all the things I don't normally do. My whole theory of working with an actor would be to give them emotional space, if I invade their space then they retreat. So I try and find a place intellectually and physically with them where they feel they're supported but they're free. I try not to make them feel like the shot can only allow them to do one thing, even if it's true, because I'm hoping that they will generate the same condition that I require, only self-managed. Then people feel incredibly empowered and free. Here I did exactly the reverse; as soon as somebody was settled I unsettled them. As soon as they got into the urn I turned over, so they were flustered and the head movements were not oiled or easy. I was constantly provoking Alan Rickman to go faster, because his natural metabolism is much slower than that. I was holding the camera very close, because I wanted them to feel the same circumstances the characters are feeling. I also realised that I didn't require any fluidity, because the stage directions said 'As fast as possible and with as little inflection as possible'. In a sense I wanted them to lose contact with the emotion, because the writing is so beautiful.

Is the pace of the second half faster than the first?

Yes, it is slightly faster, but it's not only faster – it has probably 50 per cent more cuts in it. We found we had to build up to that pace, because originally when we started it was just so disorienting that you had to acclimatise to this gradual fragmentation, and then it really goes wilder and wilder and it's slightly exhausting. I mean it's only sixteen minutes long and it's exhausting to watch it, particularly on the big screen. It's amazing to see it on that, and really tough to watch. It couldn't be twenty minutes long. When I did it in the theatre I think it was nearly thirty minutes, because what you can do in film is drop frames between the lines, not of the text but in the pans and the cranes. It's very aggressively edited in a way that's totally contrary to my usual approach. I am obsessed with oiled, invisible technique: I spend hours trying to refine moves or cut out tiny imperfections of sound. Here it's all the opposite, it's about drawing attention to those things. In that sense it was a hugely, hugely liberating experience.

When you undertook the project was there something specific you wanted to get out of it?

There's a slightly evangelical element in me, and I think that Beckett is the most significant writer that I've ever encountered in terms of my own work, in my own thinking. So what I wanted to do was contribute to what seemed to me to be an extremely important series of documents which might be the first time that people had encountered him. My son's first encounter with Beckett was watching that film. I wanted it to be a sufficiently vivid experience that he might be attracted to see something else. I wanted him to discover it, not just him but the people who might find themselves looking at this film and not knowing Samuel Beckett. I wanted them to know more about him. The thing about Beckett which most identifies him in my own mind is the modernity. What he was doing was so modern – almost too modern now – and so I felt that to do a kind of classical film based on his plays completely defeats the object. If you use the conventions of contemporary cinema to bring Beckett to people, why do it?

Are you concerned about the distribution of the Beckett project?

No, process is the only thing that interests me in any work. I've never seen a film I've made after I've finished it. I have no interest in the result. I have no connection to the result because the result has nothing to do with me. The result is about some other people, and the process is about me. Although I have seen the Beckett film, partly because it's only sixteen minutes long, partly because I didn't write it – which makes a big difference to me, I don't feel quite so exposed. But if you said to me, 'We're now going to sit and watch *The English Patient* (1996) and talk about it,' I would have to leave you, because I couldn't subject myself to that and I wouldn't want to subject you to it.

Why is that?

Because I'm thoroughly exercised and gratified and nurtured by making movies. I think it's a fantastic privilege and gift and I don't like results particularly. I know I wouldn't like the film if I saw it, and I'd be aware of all my faults, it would turn to ashes so quickly for me.

When I'm working on the film, I'm obsessed. I'm there all the time, I never leave the cutting room, I go all the way through the process. But once I've delivered the movie, the process is finished. Actually now there's a sort of strange coda which is the DVD commentary. I'm going out to LA next week and I'm doing a commentary for *Truly, Madly, Deeply* (1991) so I have to watch the movie then, but I'm by myself in a studio, so it feels like I'm continuing a process.

What are the main differences between working on shorts and features for you?

On a short, by definition, the crew list is on one A4 sheet and not a book or a manual. Everybody making the movie is in the room together. When I made *Truly, Madly, Deeply* it had the characteristics of a short film in so far as we only had twenty-eight days of shooting, the whole crew could fit in this room, we had no money, we travelled everywhere together and the process was so undiluted. I wrote it, I directed it, I cut it and it was done in a matter of weeks. Then you go from that to *The English Patient* where you're on year five and you don't know really where it's going or what it is you've done, and the actual shooting seems to be a lifetime. You go into a tunnel and you don't think you're ever going to emerge from it. You can't think about anything else.

That's a very, very weird process. So part of me longs for the freedom of doing something simpler.

I'm conscious of not wanting to suggest that if you said to me 'Okay you can stop making *Cold Mountain*, you can make twenty-five short movies with three people,' I wouldn't want to do that. However, I do know that part of me – coming off the back of films like the Beckett film – wants to see if I can go back after *Cold Mountain* to a movie that I would make instantly if I could. If I could just shoot in London a contemporary film instantly, that would hold an enormous appeal to me.

John Smith

John Smith works within the area variously termed experimental, artists' film and video or avant-garde, and has been doing so since 1972. He makes pieces for art gallery installations, cinema and television, and has had retrospectives in Cork, Brussels, Vienna, Tokyo, Leeds, Bristol and London. Here we discuss his film *Blight* (1996), on which he collaborated with the composer, Jocelyn Pook.

Where did the initial idea for Blight *come from?*
Around the time that I knew that my house was going to be demolished, I applied for a grant from the Arts Council to make a film which revolved around the demolition of the houses where I lived and the building of the M11 motorway extension. The idea for the film was quite vague at first, to do with recording documentary material and creating stories from it, and it evolved gradually. One of the good things about getting a grant from the Arts Council's Artists' Film and Video Committee was that they didn't require a script. I'd have serious problems with applying for money with a script, that's not the way I work at all. I have ideas which are quite concrete but they're to do with the individual elements that might come together in a film. The structure comes later. The process is to do with responding to material I gather of different events.
Do you start making notes or taking stills when you think something might turn into a project?
I don't often take stills. I make notes, yes, but what I write is pretty minimal to begin with, to do with a core idea. The original idea I had for *Blight* was to do with a sense of a house as a living entity, of it having a consciousness.

I started work by filming the demolition that was going on in my street. I got a fair bit of stuff together without really knowing what I was going to do with it, because at the time I was being evicted from my house and I didn't have time to start editing. I had to find somewhere to live, but I knew it was the only opportunity to film, so I shot quite a lot of material. Some ideas

Blight (1996)

started to emerge as I filmed the demolition. A lot of the shots of the house next door being demolished were shot from my bathroom window, so I was able to film a lot of close ups. One was of the elbow of this demolition worker with a spiderweb tattoo on it. I thought 'That's interesting, that looks really sinister.' The tattoo also reminded me of the motorway network around London, so I knew from the start that I wanted to develop ideas around this image. Later on I did interviews with people about their memories of the places where they had lived and a woman started talking about how, as a child, she always had to get her father to kill the spiders in their outside toilet. This coincidence was developed into a central theme of the film. I'm a great believer in serendipity.

The first image I shot was the one where you see the poster for *The Exorcist* (1973). I came home one night and went out to the back garden to find that the house next door was half demolished. Suddenly this house I'd lived next to for twelve years – knowing the family but never having been inside the house, nor been on particularly friendly terms with them – was exposed, and there was this obscene feeling of looking into somebody else's house, this stripping away of their privacy. But also a feeling of fascination – a teenage boy had lived in this room who'd painted a mural copying the poster for *The Exorcist*, and I thought this was so sinister. I came home just as it was getting dark and I went into the back garden, and over the course of the day they'd knocked down the walls of the house. I could see this poster looming. I thought, 'That's so poignant as an image', so I shot that the next day and thought, as with the spider web tattoo, 'How might that influence the film?' As a result I decided to film the opening sequence in such a way that you don't see any people. There's the sequence of close-up shots where you just see the bits of the house, joists and bricks falling, as if there's a kind of poltergeist in the house, some unseen force which is making the house destroy itself. And the silhouetted image of the exorcist on the mural came to represent the man from the Department of Transport, the faceless bureaucrat who had ordered the demolition.

Do you tend to shoot in order?

No, very often a film will start in the middle and then things will build around it. The shape of the film usually emerges in the editing. I don't storyboard, I produce masses of notes, but nothing that would communicate anything to anybody else. I nearly always work on my own so it's not really necessary.

I don't like to work with a crew. Every now and again I'll reluctantly create work in a situation where I need other people, but I usually try to do the whole process myself, partly because I work very slowly and I feel embarrassed keeping other people waiting around. I can spend half an hour framing one shot! Also economically it's a problem, if you're paying somebody for a day's work you want to get something for it. For me it's very important to have time to look at what's in front of the camera and consider it, to think of all the possibilities it might have; not be rushed into decisions by deadlines. *Blight* was originally budgeted with a crew, and I said to the producer that I wanted four weeks shooting. He said, 'You must be joking, it's a fifteen-minute film, you can't ask for that.' So we got it down to two weeks, and he said, 'Alright, I suppose we could try it on.' In the end I think we got the money for a week's shooting with a crew, but we did a one-day shoot and I carried on filming for six months on my own.

How did you become involved in the Sound on Film scheme?

Having had this grant to make the film, and having gathered some of the material and not started editing, the composer Joss Pook, who's a friend of mine, phoned me up and said 'Do you fancy applying for one of these Sound on Film things?' And I thought, 'Yes, I would.' I really liked her music and I thought it would be nice to work together, so I agreed. We got together and talked about some possible ideas. Ultimately, we decided that nothing was developed enough to be able to put a proposal together in time for the deadline. So we decided to go with turning *Blight* into the film that we made together.

Was the proposal shortlisted?

Yes, and we got £2,000 and three months to do a pilot. I'm not sure that the pilot would have been commissioned if it wasn't for the fact that Rodney Wilson at the Arts Council knew my other work. After we were shortlisted Rodney told us that the committee had thought the idea was pretentious and hadn't liked it very much, hadn't really understood the idea. Then he'd showed them another film of mine – *The Black Tower* (1987). He said that having shown them that, people had tuned in, understood the proposal a bit more clearly. So there's a real difficulty I think in applying for funding, if you don't have a concrete script in which you describe the objectives precisely.

How did you go about making a pilot?

Because a lot of material had already been shot there were several different possibilities. We did shoot new material for the pilot but in the end I junked it all and used the stuff that I'd shot already. The pilot was basically the opening scene of the film with the 'Kill the spiders' voiceover. Those three minutes became the pilot. We felt the music was incredibly sparse and, given that it was Sound on Film, specifically composers working with film-makers, we were slightly worried that there wasn't enough body there. Joss had recorded some musical sketches for other parts of the film, so we submitted them as well.

Did you collaborate closely through the process?

On and off. Joss had other work on. All I was doing was working on the film, so there were periods of time when we didn't get together. A lot of the time we worked on our own, but tried to meet up as regularly as possible to show each other what we were doing. It was a reflexive process, with each of us responding to what the other had done.

What were the conditions of the commission?

We had to have a producer – a new experience for me. I had to sign a contract with the producer's production company, who in turn had to sign his contract with the Arts Council and BBC. So, on paper, the Arts Council and BBC had control of the final cut. And the deadline was only about nine months after being given the money which, for me, is a very short period of time to make a film in.

How did you feel about signing over control of the final cut?

I didn't like it. Especially when we had a meeting to show the rough cut to the Arts Council and BBC, and Rodney from the Arts Council had some reservations about the end of the film.

Why?

He felt that the ending of the film was too literal, that it was too verbally oriented. Although I reacted against this at the time, having got away from the situation and calmed down, I realised that I agreed with a lot of what he'd said and made some changes. Originally the sign at the end which says 'New Motorway Opening 1997' was a much wider shot, very descriptive. Now it's a close shot of the sign with lorries moving in front of it, so it relates to the scene with the cars moving across the corrugated iron fence. It has a more abstract quality. You barely have time to read it, it's just these glimpses.

Did you record the sound yourself?

Yes, the sound is all post-sync, it's all recorded later. The interviews were done separately, and I simulated all the sounds of breaking pieces of wood and bricks falling and things like that. But also I went out with the composer to record some of the sounds like the corrugated iron sound, which is a recurring theme. She did the percussion, she hit the fence and dragged sticks across the fence, and I recorded it.

In terms of things that are said, the central part of the film is the most emotive bit I suppose, the 'Don't really remember' song. (I call it a song because it does really sound like a woman singing, and the bit where she's saying 'Don't really remember' in isolation sounds as though it's sung until you hear the whole statement.) That was very much from Jocelyn, the composer's perspective, that she noticed musical qualities in voices that I would have been completely oblivious to. Lots of the fragments of speech were chosen for their musical qualities, for example, the repeating phrase that you hear throughout the film – a woman calling to her children in the street, saying 'Jordan and

Kim, Jordan and Kim, come on, Kim, come on.' Again it works in a very musical way, though what's said is important too.

The use of repetition, the pace and the shape of the film seem to be musical.

I would like to think that all of my films are structured musically – I pay a lot of attention to pace and rhythm and am just as concerned with the abstract properties of the films as their literal meanings. In *Blight* the different parts were edited and put together in quite different ways and although there was a lot of to-ing and fro-ing with rough edits of the visual material and the sound that I was working with, and the music from Jocelyn, there came a point where we had to decide that one element was going to be more or less fixed and we'd work around that. Most of the film editing was done before the music was finalised – apart from the middle section, the 'Don't really remember' piece, which was the opposite way round, the images were cut to the music. The corrugated iron stuff, for example, was edited just with the sounds of cars and lorries, and the music was added later. But there's the amazing thing with music of course, that whenever you put it together with footage where there are cutting points that are very obvious – like the movements of the cars across the frame – things always synchronise. That scene was only tweaked a little bit after the music was added. But having said that, Joss had the images in her head when she was writing the music and I had the music in mind when I was editing the images.

It must be one of the most subtle protest films.

I hope so. It's actually more didactic than I expected it to be though. The pieces were edited as separate sections and then I joined the bits up together. The first time we saw it as a continuous piece it looked in some ways subtle, but also ultimately direct, incredibly agit prop in its resolution. In some ways, looking back at it now, it would have been quite nice to have had another shot at the end, which actually let everything level out again after the climax. Something really unexplained – I suppose I do worry about the punchline thing a bit.

Why do you worry about it?

Because it can seem like a resolution, too much of a closure. I don't think that a film should pretend that it's given the viewer everything. I feel that it should stimulate imagination, it should make you do work on it – that's without it sounding like hard, unpleasant work – the pleasurable work of looking at something and making sense of it. I like to see a film or look at any piece of art and walk out wondering, still having questions and not wanting those questions to be answered for me.

Do you prefer to make short films than longer ones? Have you got a preferred length of film?

Not at all. It's completely in relation to an idea, however long an idea takes. A film can be any length. Artists have always made films of all sorts of lengths but the mainstream is still ruled by duration, by fitting into slots. The curious thing to me is this distinction between short films and long films. Why aren't there more medium films? The problem is the difficulty of screening films of that kind of duration. Certainly in a film festival context – which is one of the main ways one gets things seen initially – there is a pressure to make things which are either under thirty minutes or an hour and a half long.

In what ways do you feel you've developed as a film-maker?

My films now do use editing conventions, and that's something I never learnt at college. With the first films that I made, there was no need to know about those sorts of things. They were very often visual ideas, formal constructions which had no ambition to create a sense of narrative continuity or anything like that. Although they subvert it, the later films play much more on conventional narrative construction. And I think I've refined the ways in which I combine a range of interests in my work, creating dialogues between formal manipulation and subject matter.

And what about the future?

It's hard to know. With the shift to digital media now, the things that I've done most recently have been shot on a mini DV camera. Now on my computer at home I can do things I would have had to pay £300 a day for a year ago. There's a self-sufficiency now which makes me much less dependent on external funding.

Do you think that's all good?

I have mixed feelings about it. I like video on a monitor but, although it's improving all the time, most video projection is still vastly inferior to film. I went through a period of being very depressed over the demise of 16mm as a theatrical medium. 16mm's been on the way out in this country for ten years now, and there are very few laboratories left that even make release prints. 16mm is still fairly alive and well in terms of television, for how long I don't know, but really that's just in terms of negative processing and then immediately going to telecine, and everything being digital after that. For instance, I think there are only two people in the country who make optical soundtracks now, and in my experience they've deteriorated quite a lot. The wonderful tracks you could get fifteen years ago are now very hard to achieve.

I'm in a transitional phase at the moment, because I'm starting to think much more positively about digital media. I've started editing on a computer recently and much to my surprise I'm really enjoying it, it feels much more tactile than I expected. The technology offers a lot of new creative possibilities to someone who is used to editing on film. For example, there's a film I'm planning at the moment, which will be composed of still images that break out into live action very briefly and then freeze again. It's now possible for me to shoot that on film and then work on it on a computer without having to go to the expense of optical printing and laboratories and things like that. I can just do that at home and then ultimately get a transfer to film back from video. Another piece I'm working on is to do with changing speed and reversing action. They're very simple effects, but in the past it would have been quite prohibitive for people working on film on a low budget.

Have you collaborated with a composer since Blight?

No, for me it was a bit of a one-off working with music. I would like to do it again, but there are some things about music in film that I'm apprehensive about, because it's so emotionally manipulative. There is a danger that people will look at things on one level because they're being told how to respond emotionally, whereas most of my stuff is really much more open than that. It can be looked at in one way or maybe in another. I think that the main reason that *Blight* is so popular is because of the music, because it makes it instantly accessible and in a way directs you how to look at it. I'm in two minds about that. I was very pleased with it but it's not something that I would do immediately again.

What do you feel you're aiming to do in your work?

I could give you lots of answers to that one. I want to communicate things that I can't express in any other way. I'm really interested in the ways in which we communicate outside of the spoken word. Although I use text a lot in my work, very often the words are to do with confusing any specific literal meanings. There's a kind of love/hate relationship with the power of language, and a frustration with its incapacity to truly describe experience. Most of my work is to do with the many different ways in which we can look at the world, and communicating things in a way which isn't a slave to the objectifying claims of the word. I'm very interested in ambiguity and how everybody sees everything in different ways, and that we can have an entirely different perception of an identical event; in playing with those things and giving very ordinary things new meanings through how they're put together.

What sort of budget do you normally work with and where do you get funding?

It varies because some of the video pieces are shot for next to nothing, and the cost in video for me has always been in post-production. Recently I've got my own editing software on the computer – it means that now it can cost almost nothing to make a video piece. So some of the video pieces have been unfunded, but all of the films and some of the video pieces have been funded or part-funded by the Arts Council. These were basically materials-only grants, where you could include paying for other personnel if you needed to. The grants I've had have been between £1,500 when I first left college up to the one I'm working on at the moment, which is £12,000. But there have been

Arts Council/TV projects, which have been higher budgets. *Gargantuan* (1992), a one-minute film for BBC2, was about £2,000. *Slow Glass*, which is forty minutes long, was a £20,000 Channel 4 budget in 1991, so that wasn't a bad amount. And then *Blight* – because it was mainly funded by the BBC and not the Arts Council – was a much higher budget of about £72,000. So it's phenomenally different in terms of resources.

What would you like to see in place around funding?

I certainly think that there should be more of it, but also I think it should be allocated more broadly and adventurously. There is a lot of money for film from the National Lottery at the moment but 99 per cent of it is going into mainstream cinema. And it seems that government policy-makers see short films solely as a training ground for the features industry. The Arts Council's Artists' Film and Video Committee has been disbanded now, but even when it existed it only had a national budget of about £100,000 a year for production. So I would like to see more state funding put into a film culture that was valued for itself and not just its business potential. And that doesn't mean that I think radical and challenging work can't be popular and entertaining too.

Have you any thoughts about what you'd like to see in terms of a sustainable way of production and distribution of the kind of work that you do?

Yes. I think a lot more short films could be screened in art cinemas alongside feature films, although that does emphasise the feature film as being the main thing. Inevitably there's a value judgment made between the two which I personally don't see. But the most exciting opportunity for artists working with film at the moment is in gallery exhibition. The biggest advantage of gallery exhibition is that it allows people to hear about something, by word of mouth or reviews, and get to see it while it's still showing. One of the main problems with getting to see artists' film and video work in the cinema is that it's very rarely shown for more than one screening – it gets no critical attention and you often only hear about it after the event.

Do you think distribution could be improved?

Maybe it's idealistic, but I think that there could be more confident and ambitious programming in the art cinemas. Where someone's programming something and decides, 'Yes, I really like this work. We're going to give it a lot of publicity and show it for two weeks.' Or every Wednesday for a month. I think that's the way to expand audiences. It could be one person's work or a mixed programme of short films. At the moment people haven't got the opportunity to find out what's going on and go and see it while it's still showing, so the seats for one-off screenings are often empty. I'm as guilty as anybody – I'm not prepared to go and take a risk on seeing a film by someone I don't know unless I've read or heard something which makes it sound interesting. So much publicity is superficial as well. There may be one or two sentences, saying the work is hip, stylish or whatever. There's not enough critical writing, not enough information available.

How do you see your own future as a film-maker?

I can see myself doing more video installation work, like *The Kiss* (1999) that I made in collaboration with Ian Bourn, which is concerned with a repetitive mechanical process. It involves a five-minute loop cycle and benefits from being seen several times. I think my work has started to change recently, I seem to be having ideas that are more circular, less to do with beginnings and endings. I'm sure that this is to do with the recent developments in gallery exhibition. The film that I'm working on at the moment may end up being two different pieces – one for the gallery and one for the cinema. But I'm still mainly concerned with the cinema, I see the gallery as an additional means of exhibition, not as a substitute.

Jonathan Glazer

Jonathan Glazer worked initially as a theatre director before becoming a film producer and director in 1988. He made award-winning trailers and promotional material and then became a writer/director. Since joining Academy Films in 1993, he has made a number of commercials and music videos, many of which have won awards. His first feature film, *Sexy Beast*, was released in January 2001. Here we discuss the Guinness *Surfer* commercial – which has won many awards including the Channel 4 audience award for Best Advertisement Ever.

How did your work on the Surfer *commercial start?*

It was already a favourable situation for me, because I'd done *Swimblack* with the same creative team and the same clients. My relationship with the creative team – Tom Carty and Walter Campbell – was already good. I guess because of that, and maybe because the first one did very well for them, it gave us a little more freedom to move the idea where we wanted it than we would perhaps otherwise have had the freedom to do. They approached me with an idea about a surfer waiting for a wave, the biggest wave of his life.

Did they bring a storyboard? Had the client approved the idea?

No, I don't work in the traditional way of being given a script and a storyboard. The only things I ever do are the ones that I can develop myself from the germ of an idea.

Is the way you work more collaborative now?

Yes, it's more the way films should work as opposed to advertising – which at its heart is, I suppose, very regimented and manufactured. The way I try to do things is a bit more organic than that.

So for *Surfer* the idea came as just three lines. I was shooting something else at the time and we just started talking about it and started looking at certain references. For some reason I was looking at Eugène Delacroix – I was looking at painters more than anything else. I thought there was something there which was more poetic potentially, that I could get something more surrealistic, unusual out of it. Then my assistant found an image on the Internet, and we started talking about horses, and it just evolved. It was a Greek painting, I think a mythological idea and image, to do with Neptune or something like that. I thought it was a wonderful image and I said to the two guys, 'Why don't we do it like that?' And the more we talked about it the more we realised that it would be quite exciting and an unusual way to do something.

I remember them suggesting that it open with the camera on this guy's face for as long as possible, and of course in a commercial a long shot is like six or seven seconds. That has tremendous impact because you're used to a quick-fire series of images and manipulations, and I liked that straight away. It's trying to set up a cinematic atmosphere that the format on the whole won't allow, which is spending time on something and having ambiguity through the length of a shot. Seven seconds in a commercial could be equivalent to ten minutes in a film.

And then, of course, we go through the whole process. You write the script, take the script to the advertiser or the agency and try and get them to agree to make it.

Do you propose a budget or do they tell you how much there is?

Both actually. We agreed a budget of something like £700,000. It's a lot of money for one and a half minutes.

Do you produce a detailed script and a storyboard to get that budget?

Yes, you have to dress it up more. We did a rough animatic on tape, we put some storyboards under caption cameras and moved horses around and things like that, put some pieces of terrible music with it and showed it to the client. It was never something that was going to work on a basic narrative level. There was always going to be that ambiguity, and it's a hard thing to sell to anybody. In my experience of doing adverts, the best ones I've made have been with people who have power in the agency themselves. With unusual ideas you need a good benefactor, someone who's going to trust the process and know that you won't get there straight away, but that's alright.

What's the next step?

We got the budget and then with my producer at Academy Films we started the process of working out where we were going to shoot it. What was particularly difficult about this was that it was weather dependent. We went to Hawaii, the capital of surfing, but we had to go in the month when we were most likely to get the size of waves that we needed to make the story work, which was January. So we waited a couple of months before we shot it for that reason. Then we established a production base on the island and started the casting process, which goes on forever – it does with me anyway, trying to find the right people and faces.

And you found them on location?

Yes. I found the main guy on Kauai, which is the northern-most island in Hawaii, and then we looked at loads of surfers. I wanted the whole thing to be very pure and uncosmetic, because sports now are covered in logos and sponsorships and all the surfers have gym-buffed bodies and long sun-kissed blond hair, and there's very little surprise in those kind of images of people. I started looking at the fifties and sixties surfers with people like Buffalo Kilano, a leading surfer at that time. They were surfing with these very basic long boards. The romance of it all was much more intact, and the imagery was pure and more aesthetic. I wanted to find those kinds of people, and they're hard to find because the world's changed. So we looked at all sorts of people – champions and ordinary guys. The main guy, Dino, was a surfer, but he surfs the way anybody on the islands surfs, the way that if you lived in the Alps you'd ski – but you're not necessarily going to be able to do the most dangerous mountain. He was an out of shape, forty-something beach bum who picked up German tourists, and lived under a palm tree, literally; but he just had this extraordinary Rock Hudson sort of face to me. He looked slightly nostalgic and wonderfully weatherbeaten, very soulful, very real and intriguing. He had this really long hair and he wouldn't cut it. We offered him more money to cut his hair and ultimately, of course, he did.

There were two days out of the seven-day shoot where the waves were forty feet, and they measure them from the back, so the face of the wave was sixty feet. It's extraordinary. Dino had never surfed waves that big, he looked terrified.

How long were you on location?

I was there for about three weeks.

What did you do about planning the shoot for the special effects?

What we worked out with the special effects company was that we should just go and shoot it. Because it's all so unpredictable, our best laid plans would come to nothing. They were developing software at the time that would create the correct compositing of horse and wave and so on, and doing lighting tests and things. They talked about doing CG [computer graphics] horses, which I always resisted because in 1999 it wasn't anywhere near good enough. So I insisted that we used real horses and real waves. That required a lot of testing, a lot of new software had to be written just to see how well they could composite those things, because you're compositing something muscular and

Surfer (1999)

something liquid and it's a very tricky blend, and for a long time all the special
effects looked dreadful. Right up until the end there were a lot of wobbly
knees over it, and they were thinking, 'My God, we'd better drop the horses,
we shouldn't have them.' But the computer film company that did all the
effects was pretty amazing.

The special effects people didn't ask you to shoot anything particular for them?

On the horses, yes. But only once we'd come back from Hawaii. We knew we
needed to do two days in a blue screen studio to shoot horses, Lipizzaners, so
we did some tests when we got back. I was cutting the location footage and
imagining the footage with the horses. The shots I was choosing, I was allowing
space. It's kind of difficult because as you're cutting you're only working with
half the image you'll get – more so in a sense than a much more controlled
special effects thing. If you're doing some special effects movie and a guy
walks into a room and shoots, you know there's going to be a window blowing
out or something – it's not a difficult thing to put your mind around, when you
cut you're only cutting in one element. But to cut this was like imagining a
painting finished with only half the brushstrokes on it, and that was more difficult. So we ended up in a big blue screen studio for two days, with two horses
that could jump and do these things, and shot them in wet conditions and dry
conditions doing different things using specific lenses and logging everything. I
only used the stuff we did in the water for two of the shots, the rest were dry –
the horses were wet but they weren't in water. We defined their muscle tone
with make-up, dark, low lights to make them register as much more visceral
muscular forms on film.

All I could do on the Hawaii shoot was keep records of lens height and lens
width every time we shot something. But when you're throwing cameras
around with sixty feet of water coming towards you it's not very easily done, so
a lot of our mathematics were way off, and in the end you do a lot of it by eye.
They could analyse the footage once we'd cut the first element, which was just
the surfers on the waves, and then work out to the nearest five millimetres
what the correct lens was to shoot the horses and from which specific position,
so the perspectives were the same. The lighting was the next task – to make
the lighting the same, and then you'd have a chance of compositing them
seamlessly, or near as dammit.

*Was there any moment in this process when you got scared that it wasn't going to come
together?*

Every single time I've done anything I've never thought it would come
together, but it's worth taking the risk.

At what point did you know it was going to work?

On the last day, genuinely, and it went through six weeks of horse work. The difference between things that don't work and things that work wonderfully well is fractional. I think that ingredient in film-making – whether it's having charging stallions on a sixty-foot wave or the most intimate moment in the performance of a straight narrative – creating the greatest impact involves fractional decisions. I'm not talking about being pedantic, I mean making those very simple choices about why something works on a more coruscating level than something else. In the example with the horses, they needed positioning, blending and sizing in a way that if they were 2 per cent different they wouldn't work at all – and they didn't work for weeks. So it only came together right at the end.

And then did you take that to the client for approval?

Because post-production was so long, the client had to be kept in the loop for most of the process.

You showed them rough cuts?

Yes, and they were scared – they thought it was terrible.

Why?

Because it's in your head, not theirs, and you have to tell them what is in your head, but all they're seeing is what's there. So they were reluctant to let the work continue, they were thinking of trying to get out and cut their losses by not having the horses.

When you showed the final cut of Surfer, *what was the response?*

I think they liked it. You never know. They don't say anything. It's only when others see it for the first time who aren't anything to do with the process that they truly judge it.

They did ask for some changes on the soundtrack.

What did you hope to achieve creatively?

I always want to do something that I think is distinctive and good and where I can grow each time. I try not to repeat myself, I'm sure I do repeat myself, I just try not to. I'm not one of these people who thinks that if you're in advertising then you're some kind of philosopher who can seduce the nation with a kind of miniature philosophy. It just appealed to me and I thought it had something which was involving, I thought it would be an extreme experience on film. It would be classical, it would have parable and mythology, and it would also be very modern. Why do you do anything? You hope it will be good.

Do you feel in this particular case that you kept control of the project?

As much as you can, yes. And my music videos are the same. You work with an artist – or an artist wants to work with you – because you share some sensibility or other that's going to push the work through. If I get sent a piece of music by Westlife or Boyzone, I'm not going to do it, because the record company would be all over it. And it's the same with commercials. There's no difference between ... well, there are huge political differences but I think to an extent everything is the same: music videos, commercials and now – having just done one feature film – film is just an expanded version of the other two things. You still meet idiots and you still meet clever people, you still meet insightful people, and you meet passengers, and the principle is the same.

What do you mean by 'political differences'?

There are politics in anything, any creative pursuit. Advertising is the closest craft or filmic form to selling something directly, and so everybody involved in the process apart from the creative people have a different agenda to you. But if you can convince them that your agenda is serving their agenda then you're closer to achieving something good. I don't want to make a film that plays to three people, but I want it to be as strong and as uncompromised and undiluted as possible in whatever I work in.

You're also known for your music video work. Do you feel you have more control over music videos than the commercials?

Yes, and I've had an awful experience on my first feature film – *Sexy Beast*. If I could get the freedom that I've had in music videos on a feature I'd be very happy.

What was awful about it?

Just bad karma on the whole thing – it's just a fraction of what I wanted to do. I think a lot of it, to be fair, came from my own inexperience of doing a film, and thinking that I would be surrounded by the same kind of trust and common concern that I've had in my company, by the people I've worked with.

Did you take the same people with you, the people you're used to collaborating with?

Very few. I had to kick and scream to get a couple, but actually they were the best ones in it. I was scared of it. Ever since I was a kid I wanted to make films and I resisted making certain films until this one, and there's a lot of emotional investment in it. I think it just didn't come off the way I anticipated. I was putting my finger in holes in dams every day in much more of a way than I think would normally be the case. I know from conversations I've had with other people who've made first films and the people who financed the film that it was an extreme example.

It sounds as if you broke your own rule on keeping with people of a similar sensibility.

I did, and I'll never do it again. And I can only look at that with hindsight and realise that I made a big mistake. I'm pleased the film was well received, but it's not what I wanted to do. I don't mean that with sour grapes, I just mean it should have been more than that.

Will you carry on with your other work – commercials and music videos?

Yes, I'll do it again when the right collaborators are there. I've done another Guinness commercial with the same guys, and we're in hell with that right now because the client wants x and we want y. So despite the fact that we've sold them a lot of pints of beer they're still telling us they know best – and to a certain extent they do. But you want it to communicate properly, I'd be the first person to throw away something beautiful if it doesn't communicate.

John Hardwick

In the 1990s John Hardwick became involved with conceptual art group FAT (Fashion, Architecture, Taste) and performance company Blast Theory as artist and performer. Increasingly drawn to film and video work, his no-budget shorts became a regular contribution to the Exploding Cinema shows, a film club in London. His first funded film was made in 1997 and he now works with Helen Langridge Associates. The films we discuss here are *The Sweetness Lies Within*, a music video made for Hefner in 1998, and *To Have and to Hold* (2000).

What was the first film you made with a budget?

It was a film called *Glottis* in 1997. Up till then, I would apply for every incentive I knew about – like the BFI New Directors. My showreel consisted of Super 8 work, which I'd projected onto my bedroom wall, shot on a VHS camera and edited with two VCRs. It was very low key and very rough. It took me six years to get money to do anything remotely official, but I was always trying to get money to make films. The Exploding Cinema took quite a big part of my life at that point. It was a very lively period.

Then I got the money to make *Glottis* and I thought 'What do I do?' This is a £10,000 or £15,000 budget, and everything I'd done had been with a Super 8, cutting it with scissors and stuff like that, but this had to be 35mm. I did briefly have a job for six months when I first got to London, as a runner at an animation studio, and I met a woman called Jane Harrison. Since then I'd been working very much in the underground, squatty, anarcho sort of area. I heard she'd started producing pop videos, and eventually tracked her down and said, 'You've got to help me. I've got this money and don't know how to spend it.' So she produced that, and she is now the rep at Helen Langridge Associates, my producers, so we're still working together.

Can you tell me about the development of The Sweetness Lies Within? *There's something about the way it mixes a documentary and music video approach with something else, which is very touching.*

It changed radically during the shoot, and it's interesting that you say it combines documentary with something else that you can't quite define, and I can't quite define it either. It's really the documentary of a pop video going wrong, and I really like that bit of work.

How did you get the commission?

The guy in charge of video commissioning at Too Pure Records sent me the details. They'll send it out to on average five directors or director teams. You get the music, photographs of the band, and you might get a brief. If there isn't a brief they say what they would like: upbeat, downbeat, whatever. It's always the same thing, it's always upbeat, pop, must appeal and sell records. Then you spend however long you spend on the idea. Sometimes it comes like that [clicks fingers], sometimes you can spend weeks on it. And it's frustrating because it's work you never get paid for if you don't get the job. I sent back a treatment and a showreel and I got the job. A treatment will consist of two sides of A4, though some people put visual references in.

That was the first treatment where I just wrote it really instinctively. I had no idea why certain images were there. For instance, I saw a girl cycling at some point and that seemed to fit, slow motion and fast motion seemed to fit. Normally I pick up on a certain sound in the music or a lyric that will give me an idea. For instance, in one of the Travis videos there's a pastiche of Hitchcock's film *North By Northwest* where a plane attacks the singer, and that is because there's a guitar sound that sounds like a plane engine roaring. So often there's a very clear correlation. But mostly it's a lyrical connection. But in that one (Hefner) the ideas didn't make too much sense. I wanted to have some sort of choreographic element in it because the band's quite interesting looking, and I wanted to work with some mates. It was incredibly low budget, I think it was £4,000–£5,000.

I didn't really have a plan for a story at all. There are three strands to the story: there's the guy who's the jogger, there's the arguing couple, and there's the band who were just sort of dancing really. And what was going to happen was you followed this jogger until he sat down on a bench with these people and then they all break out into dancing. But because he twisted his ankle on the third or fourth take and went off to hospital, we had to amplify other stories and downplay his. I remember thinking, 'Well everything's gone wrong on this. I'm going to keep this going and incorporate every mistake in the edit, try and make a virtue of that.' And we did certain things where we'd turn over before we said, we'd keep it rolling after 'Cut' was said, and things like that. Because personally I really like that moment in films where you see a performer go 'Right, I'm on' [stands up], and there's a lot of that in there, particularly with them waiting for the cue to dance and stuff like that. To see a performer switch is an exciting thing, it really can be. Some actor said, 'Just because they call Action, it doesn't mean you have to do anything.' But everybody's instinct is to go 'Bang, I'm off.' So if you're rolling before that you get a bit of that.

Who did you work with?

At that point I was working with Derrin Schlesinger, a producer, who I continue to work with. The cast – Rachel Harrison, Sean McDermott and Danny Salmon – are pals, Quinn, the editor, I've worked with for years. I've never really settled on a director of photography (DoP); the fellow who did that was somebody who'd done the focus pulling for a guy I'd worked with previously, and he was starting to make that jump across to being a DoP and did a fabulous job, I think.

Did you go into the shoot with a tightly worked out idea?

No, it was the first shoot where I decided to be a bit more prepared to improvise. Because if a situation's interesting, or a location is interesting, or a character's face is interesting you can actually stay with it quite a lot, and I think the stuff I'd done prior to that suffered from too much event. There's actually quite a lot of event in that as well, but the areas that are interesting are the areas that are just down time between events really; someone just standing there before they set off and run, things like that, are interesting moments I think. But we did have total creative freedom on that because the fellow who runs the record company is the elder brother of a school friend, so he trusted us to come up with something.

What documentation did you produce for the shoot?

I give everyone involved in the shoot an A5 photocopied booklet. And that has in it related visuals, storyline, lyrics, a diagram of the structure of the piece, location map, storyboard, and production details, contacts, etc. Everyone feels they know what they're a part of then, which is the most important thing, I think.

How long did you have in preparation, shooting and post-production?

A one-day shoot takes about a week to prepare, but if you can you like to think about it longer than that. I worked out the choreography with Danny and Sean one evening, one hour is all it would take. So in terms of my work a couple of weeks beforehand, actual production office work a week beforehand, a one-day shoot and a three-day edit, with half a day on-line.

Has it been shown widely?

I think it was popular and people liked it, but because the band were not so well known I don't think it's been widely seen. It was on MTV a couple of times, because they have certain programmes where they show the more obscure stuff.

What do you feel when you see it now?

I think it has a charm to it. It's very loose limbed and I like that about it and I haven't really been able to achieve that subsequently – I think there's an incredible freedom to it. I think it has almost a New Wave looseness, doesn't it? Film can be anything; you can film the mistakes, film somebody having a laugh during the catering break or whatever, without being too indulgent, because I think there is a structure there. I think there's a joy to it. It was a hideous shoot actually, there were lots of arguments, but as a piece of finished film it conveys a sense of freedom. It's quite romantic and I have a tremendous amount of affection for it. I wish I could repeat it really.

Sometimes when plans go awry, the shoot stops being target-driven, you stop ticking the shots off on the storyboard, and it becomes more exploratory. The camera is very exploratory there. Rachel has a vulnerable quality to her and you give yourself time to explore that, which goes perfectly with the lyric.

Yes, I think you're right, if your targets are smashed you indulge something else maybe.

Did that film change things for you?

It didn't change my career, but it opened up something for me creatively and that's the most important change really, isn't it? From that point on it started to solidify for me the notion that I was never going to make popular work – not trying to be obscure, it's just that what I personally like to make isn't that much of a crowd pleaser. The constituency for that kind of work is never going to be great. I'm probably making it sound like it's very obscure and inaccessible and it's not of course, but neither is it a shiny, easily digested pop video. So yes, creatively and for my own self-perception it had quite an effect. But it's not a piece of work that made people go 'Wow, we're going to give you lots of money.'

You don't think that certain types of group are now seeking you out because of it?

That's an interesting point because when that came out and I was happy with it, I thought 'Now I can get hold of the groups I really would like to make work for, like Stereo Lab or Pavement or whoever.' I think this is much more a reflection of what I like to do than Orbital or Blur or any of that stuff which is much more generic. But that hasn't happened either. When I saw that I thought 'Oh yes, that's my signature', I had a sense of recognition there. But I haven't drawn it as well since, and that's a frustrating thing.

To Have and to Hold *was a very different process presumably. How did that idea originate?*

I was thinking about love stories and the psychodrama and melodrama of love stories, and how they're often about people splitting up. But what if there's a physical impediment to people leaving? I started to think what that might be, what if you had this ludicrous physical obstacle?

It just came up?

Yes. Like a lot of people, I read stories about this logger in Canada who was fixing a tyre on his truck in winter and a wheel rolled and he had to cut his own fingers off to escape. I've never read the exact story of To Have and to Hold, but there are ones like it, where people have to self-mutilate, or about the strength people can gather in terrible situations, the things people can do

To Have and to Hold (2000)

to each other and themselves in order to survive. I was thinking, 'What if you were trapped in a car and you had to do something obscene to get away from that?' I suppose it was a combination of those two things. There's a fascination in all the newspapers – whether tabloid or broadsheet – with this sort of subject. Like in *The Guardian* News in Brief you get those little things, 'And in Sri Lanka last week a man severed his own head in order to get out of a park railing. He's since been stitched up in Kandy and he's now okay.' Just weird, weird stuff like that.

I'm not really that fond of the film because to me it was like a task, like a crossword puzzle. The idea was developed not in a cynical way, but not a warm way. It's a 'what if' kind of thing, and I think the whole project reflects that. It was a deliberate artistic decision to be physically and metaphorically cold with the whole thing, the blue tint to it, for example. Maybe I've gone a bit too far to compensate for the fact that although it was exceptionally cold it's hard to film the cold, it doesn't show, so maybe it's a bit too blue. And because it's about somebody trapped in a car, there's absolutely no movement – the woman can't move so the camera doesn't move. There's only one camera move at the end when she's walking up the road and it slightly dollies back. I like the fact that that's quite buried and missable, because it's obviously a right way of dealing with that subject matter. It's sympathetic in that sense with the subject matter, isn't it? The camera's fixed because she's fixed.

A claustrophobic feel.

Yes, and all that conspires to make the film feel cold, which I think is right for what it is, but you could have a sort of warmth behind that. I don't know how best to express that. It plays well with cinema audiences here because it's a really manipulative film. It's a strange piece of work.

Who funded it?

The BFI, Film Four Lab and the Arts Council. It was the last time the BFI ran the New Directors Scheme and they were doing it in conjunction with Film Four. I sent in a script, director's notes and a breakdown about the look of the film, the use of sound, the photography, the editing rhythms – that sort of thing, which is good, because it does give people a sense of how you will approach the script. There was also my CV and showreel. And I got an interview.

Who was at the interview?

There was myself and Derrin Schlesinger my producer, there was Kate Ogborn at the BFI, Roger Shannon at the BFI and Robin Gutch from Film Four Lab.

What was the commission?

To make an eleven-minute film and to not go over budget, which was £40,000. But then we got another £30,000 from the Arts Council through the Lottery. It was expensive, there was a lot of film shot and the locations were difficult. We shot it in March last year in the middle of a pine forest. We shot for six days, because you only had usable light from ten in the morning to about three or four in the afternoon, so it was really tricky. We needed a lot of quad bikes to get people in and out of the wood, we destroyed a car, so yes it was pricey.

After getting the commission, how did you develop the idea?

I researched crashes an awful lot, and I discovered this really bizarre thing. You know the plane tree avenues in France that are a real feature of the land-scape? There are all these different lobbies – some saying 'We should keep them,' some saying 'No, they're killers, we should get rid of them.' That's because joyriders or drunk drivers hit a bump in the road, hit a plane tree, and die. Their argument is that if the plane trees aren't there they go into a ploughed field and a lot more people would be alive now. So you've got the Heritage lobby and the Let's Not Have Any More Deaths lobby. One thing that interested me was that the French paramedics talk about this phenom-enon called 'clean deaths', where they get to a car and there's no exterior problem with the dead people in the car. Car protection systems are so good now – air bags, seat belts, roll bars, shatterproof glass, everything's good about

To Have and to Hold (2000)

the architecture of the car. The body goes from sixty miles an hour to nought in a second; the exterior's completely protected by all these things, but the inside just smashes to pieces, like the heart is still going and will sometimes rip off it's stem. The internal organs smash against the rib cage, so everything's broken inside basically even though it's clean on the outside. Which is why the damage to the man in the car is so slight, but hopefully consistent with a side impact. I also researched an awful lot with a doctor and various pathologists; I wanted to know whether rigor mortis could do this and they all said 'Yes, at sub-zero temperatures rigor mortis could last forever.' It goes off after thirty-six hours if you're above zero. They said 'The surviving character who's trying to prize these fingers off you might want to slightly damage her good hand so there's an added difficulty, but essentially if a person's weakened through lack of food or whatever then yes, that absolutely would happen.'

The location took me a long time to find. I went down to Devon and Corn-wall, I went up to north Wales, mid-Wales, Norfolk, the New Forest, just everywhere looking for the right place. I didn't approach it in the right way at all. In the end we filmed outside Oxford, near where a friend of mine lives, and I should have been more thorough in individual places instead of panick-ing, you know. I spent three months in pre-production.

And did you choose all the crew and cast?

Yes, I did. The male lead – Paul Davies – is a mate of mine from Volcano

Theatre Company in Wales, and the woman, Suzanne Lothar, I saw in a film called *Funny Games* (1997) by Michael Haneke. I asked her and she came over and did it. She's really big in Germany and kept telling us that as well. It wasn't a great experience really from a director-actor point of view. I don't think she was happy, and I wasn't, but I think she delivered. I think she's a really good actress, but there could have been a lot more done in terms of the performance there.

But then it's incredibly constrictive to spend six days – or as a viewer thirteen minutes – in a car. That was another challenge – there was this whole series of challenges. Could I pull this off? How do you make a film spent inside a car for thirteen minutes watchable? There are almost no camera moves. And also when there are only two people and one of them is dead, you can't have conversations, you don't get outside the car, what do you do? There are a lot of obstacles to achieving something that someone's going to want to watch.

It's quite a big and complex production, with a relatively big budget. Did you find that difficult?

I've much preferred working with lower budgets definitely; much smaller crews. But if my idea necessitates that, and it did, it's my responsibility, and you have to accept that and get on with it. We had a talented crew who worked really hard on it, but I personally get intimidated with crews that size. It's hard to be happy in that situation.

How long did post-production take?

We were editing for about two weeks, and we had a rough cut in five days. We showed that to the people from the BFI and Film Four, and they had real problems with certain parts of the edit. The film's almost two minutes longer than it should be because I thought it played right at that kind of duration, and there were certain sections that some of the commissioning panel felt didn't work. A lot of what they had to say was really helpful, and I would count some of those people as pals now because they really do know what they're talking about. Other bits you would have to fight for. I wouldn't just capitulate and say, 'Oh, you've been in this game a lot longer than me. Right, you can have it – there you go, the commissioner's edit.'

How do you tell when you're so close to the project the difference between what's right and what you should fight for?

I don't know. Sometimes you can be seduced by good debating rather than a good argument, and you have to be careful to avoid that. It was the knottiest edit I've ever had. There were certain things that some people wanted that I just didn't want, and in the end we got away with it. For instance, there's a montage sequence that goes from the skid marks in the ground, to the damage on the tree, to the damage at the front of the car, to the damage on the window. That was deemed far too long and unnecessary. The sound goes mute at that point as well, and pace was really slowing down there. They felt it needed to move on to see how the woman was going to react, and stuff like that. So I had to fight hard for that, and it stayed.

Why did you feel it should be there?

For the rhythm of it – those shots were composed so still because they were almost like forensic police photography. This is where the car came from, this is what it hit, this is what happened to the car, and this is where the man's head hit the window. Then you're back into the story. I felt the pace of that was right.

And what was the sort of thing you did give way on?

We had this long final shot where Suzanne walks up the hill, tracks past us, looks down the hill and then walks off again, and it just went on too long, the film was already running over time. I said we could dissolve from Suzanne looking down the road to her walking away, and it wasn't quite working. So Kate Ogborn from the BFI suggested having a really long dissolve. It works, and I like it.

So was it one rough cut, some changes and then was it approved?

No, the wrangling went on for a while. There were still misgivings about it, but then there was a screening of all the films at the Edinburgh Film Festival, which neither I nor Derrin could attend. The film got a good reception and both Kate and Robin called to say, 'The film went down well, it works how I think you wanted it to work, so you're right,' which was brilliant of them to do that.

What do you think you got out of that process?

I kick myself in the pants for completely losing track of how to work with actors. On this next film that we've done, *Mule* (2001), I did a lot of preparation on working with actors, reminding myself how to do workshops, rehearse, build new ideas. I really enjoyed working on performances with those people. So through missing opportunities on *To Have and to Hold* I realised what I wanted to do next.

How do you decide on length? You said initially eleven minutes and it was thirteen.

The commission for a film like that dictates the time, although they gave us some leeway because they saw the film benefited from being longer. The one problem with short films is that, in Britain anyway, they do seem to be fifteen minutes or less and so you can only say a certain amount of things in that. Also with broadcasts, a half-hour of TV needs to be something like twenty-four and a half minutes long, and you have to make it exactly that. You can't let the film find it's own length. They're not going to shift and shunt adverts for you because you want it to be thirty seconds shorter. I would make *To Have and to*

Hold longer, personally. Duration should be organic, but with a lot of these schemes you can't be that organic. Quite a few short films are incredibly busy, with a lot going on in them. So with something like that, although three days passes in that film, it does feel fairly languorous in places. Again that's something I would extend if I could.

What's next for you?

Ideally I would like to make something longer. At the same time I don't genuflect in front of feature films like certain people do, because I think there's a number of great film-makers who have made short films and medium-length films only. I like the short film form and I like pop videos – I think there's great stuff you can do in them. There's an inherent snobbery in the British film industry, 'Oh you're not really a film-maker are you? You haven't made a feature film'. And I don't think I speak from bitterness, I speak in a fairly clear-eyed way.

How do you see your future? Have you got a direction you want to go in?

I'd like to do more documentary work; film essays really interest me. Straightforward narrative isn't particularly exciting to me. I often go to the movies and watch a lot of those movies, but I wouldn't want to spend two years making *Con Air* (1997) or even *Secrets and Lies* (1998). The sort of film-makers who interest me are chaotic. Herzog is one of my favourites – there's an incredible chaos and anarchy to his films. Harmony Korine – some of his stuff looks a bit like a fashion shoot sometimes, but he's so imaginative. Von Trier's work is very exciting.

Are you interested in doing commercials?

Not really, no. I foresee a point where I'll probably do a few to make some money, but I don't need a lot of money, and I do think psychically if you do that there's another cost. Somebody's going to pay you £10,000 to do that but what's it costing you? I don't want to do pack shots of toilet paper.

What is it costing you?

I don't think it's anything like artistic integrity. It's just time spent doing the wrong thing. In the couple of months it takes to do an advert I could read a couple of good books. What would I prefer on my gravestone – 'This man made lots of money' or 'This man read some good books'?

Winta Yohannes

Winta Yohannes was born in Eritrea and moved to Germany with her mother to escape the effects of war. A short course at the New York Film Academy in 1995 confirmed the direction she wanted to take, and she stayed on to gain professional production experience. She then took up a place at the London International Film School (LIFS) graduating in 2000. She is now writing a feature-length script and making music videos. We discussed her graduation short, *Cherish* (2000).

How did you become a film-maker?

I grew up in Germany. After school I wanted to go to New York because I'd been there on vacation twice and I just wanted to get out and see a bit of a different world. New York is very energetic and it completely hypnotised me as a city. I always wanted to make films, but I wanted to get an experience of doing it and see if film-making was really for me, because it's so easy to fall in love with an idea of what you want to do just because you like films. I did a two-month course at the New York Film Academy, where you do a couple of really little films like one minute, three minutes, and then you end up with a ten-minute film. And then I worked on low-budget sets, music videos, things like that.

Why did you decide to make Cherish?

It was my graduation film from LIFS. I could have done a documentary, I could have done something longer, but I want to direct drama so I wanted to do something that could be a showcase but also to develop my skills as a writer/director. Film is very expensive, so it's better to do a short with your own money, on your own terms. I thought that if I do a couple of shorts I'll be more ready for what I eventually want to do, which are feature films. Every film you learn something, and every film I've done I've taken one thing that I want to improve on. Plus I've seen friends of mine doing features, and even getting funding, private funding, and their films are still on the shelves, so I'm trying to think more in terms of doing a couple of little things that will take me one step at a time. It's such a disheartening process to make a film – and a feature as well takes so much time and effort – and then for it not to be distributed. I'd rather wait than rush into it. When you make a feature you have to be ready for it, because if it's not good it's very unlikely that you will get an opportunity to make a second one, especially if you're a woman and on top of that a minority.

Could you describe Cherish *for us?*

It's a portrait of this girl whose parents are separated and she has an idyllic idea of what love is and what her parents used to be like. She doesn't actually know much about it, but she idealises love. Then all of a sudden her dad pops up into her life and makes her confront certain aspects of her life. What does she really know? How she sees things, is that really how it is? When I was young I had an idea of love, and when I grew up it was just a whole other ball game. So it's a kind of coming-of-age story. But at the end of the film it's not like she's realised how it is, it's that she's at the beginning of realising that there's a lot out there that she doesn't know and that things don't work as easily as you think they do when you're a teenager.

How did you first get the idea for it?

I had a different script at first that I adapted from a short story by an American writer, J. California Cooper, which was brilliant, but it would have been very expensive and difficult to make, so then I thought that I'd rather do my own story. I was trying to find a story. I took my time to find it, and I think it's inspired by the fact that I met my dad quite late. I think it was inspired by a visit to him. I don't know why because I was writing about other stuff, but I suddenly thought, 'This is something real, this is something that I can relate to.' A lot of friends, and people that I've met, can relate to this, because even people who are twenty-six/twenty-seven have issues in understanding why their parents are not together or why things are the way they are. I thought, 'That's quite universal.' It's not especially a black story. It's a story anybody can relate to if you're interested in it or if you have similar situations. I like stories where you can involve all kinds of backgrounds.

Was it a personal experience that started the idea?

It was the trigger, yes. It made me reflect on certain things. The story is not my story, but the idea behind it is quite close to my heart. I went to my dad, who lives in New Haven, Connecticut, in the States. I actually went there to write. It was really quiet, and I was sitting in front of my computer thinking 'There must be a story, there must be a story,' and then it sort of sunk in that there's a story right there where I was. I developed different approaches to the story, and then I went completely away from being right there and took a more universal setting of the dad coming to meet his daughter that he's never really known.

You wrote different versions of it?

Yes I did, I started immediately writing scenes, dialogue, in order. But then I would change things around. I always want to force myself to write a story-line first and then a treatment, but that really blocks my writing because then I tend to analyse it straight away and think, 'Oh no, this is really clichéd,' so I write the treatment afterwards. For a feature, that will be a little bit different I think, so I'm struggling with that as I'm trying to put a feature idea on paper right now, and my old way of working on shorts doesn't really apply to that.

So you wrote it all out and then played around with the structure of it?

Yes, I wrote one scene not knowing what the next scene was, and then maybe later I'd go back and think 'I need a transition scene here.' But I guess it depends on the story. If I would write a story that's completely outside of myself, I think it would be easier for me to make a structure first. If something's close to you I think it's sometimes very hard to judge it right, and you can block yourself by thinking about that constantly while you're trying to make the structure and the treatment work. So I thought it best to get it out first and then rewrite it.

Cherish (2000)

How long did it take you to write the script?

About two weeks just to get the idea of the story I'm doing, and then I kept rewriting it.

When did you get the idea that the gift from the father to his daughter would be the traditional Eritrean dress?

That was in there from the beginning, because it's a quite typical thing to do. Not the dress necessarily, but in Eritrea if somebody comes they will bring you a present and most likely they will bring you something connected to home, and if you hadn't grown up there it would be a little bit alien. So it could be jewellery, it could be anything, but I thought a dress would be so obvious for her to think 'What's that?' or for her boyfriend to say 'What are you wearing?' At first, we didn't plan for her to wear it at the end, but then we thought it was nice because it's almost like the dad is there. She's wearing it and doing the opposite of what she should be doing in that dress, and it added to the meaning.

What would you say Cherish *means?*

What it means to me is that a lot of things are really mysterious to you and that you'll never really understand them. You can understand them logically, but that's a very different thing to understanding them emotionally. There's also something going on around tradition, the old life and the new life. Her father bringing her the dress is trying to tell her, 'Don't forget where you're from.'

What was the next step after you had finished the script?

Then I had to find people to produce it, which is usually the biggest problem. I was looking for people in my school, but there were not many people around who really wanted to produce. And the few people who do want to produce, and are good at it, have been doing it for so long for everybody that after a while they think 'Now I'll get a real job, get paid. I can't keep doing graduation films for the rest of my life.' So it's very hard. I found two people two terms below me. I sent them the script and they wanted to do it. I had the camera operator who worked on my previous short, who was also from my school, and he introduced me to the cinematographer who was from the National Film School, and then we crewed up and started on the production, which took longer than we expected. We postponed once because we didn't have enough money. It took us half a year, whereas usually in our school we turn things over in three months from writing the script to final dub. So I was quite used to a different pace, but when you're all alone it's very different, and as a director/writer you're always the one who always has to push people, especially if they're not getting paid. It gets really painful at times – you have to always motivate people.

Did the script go through an approval process at the school?

Yes and my tutor suggested a couple of changes. I had a couple of things happening that time-wise weren't really in a logical order, so I changed them. And we had a scriptwriting teacher, an American writer called Pat Silverlaski, she helped me. But at the end of the day what you change is really up to you. I think our school's quite free in that way.

Did your script change much during production?

No – maybe a line or word, but no major changes.

What was your budget?

For your graduation film you get £2,000 back from the school from your tuition fees, which is not enough to make a film. Then the camera operator put half of his graduation budget into mine, £1,000, because he wanted to shoot 35mm, and we did get some free film stock. I got £2,000 from family and friends, so we had £5,000. But it ended up being £6,000 as we did go over budget. On our last weekend we were shooting in Richmond Park by the river and we got flooded. We lost the weekend's work, and then we had to reshoot the end of the film, which meant new insurance for another week, everything. That was really difficult. It was like, 'Why?' – but it happens. And then we had to wait because the actress was doing something on *Casualty*. That all took us over budget.

How did you find your cast?

I found Verona Joseph through *Spotlight* and the boyfriend through *PCR* (a weekly casting publication). He didn't have an agent at the time but he got an agent after *Cherish*. The older people were really hard to find – that was actually the reason why it took us so long to make the film. Most black actors are either busy, or they've given up acting because it hasn't gotten them anywhere, or they're quite well known and not interested in student films any more. Hubbard Casting were really nice. I faxed them a synopsis and then they suggested names. Then I'd call and say 'Hubbard Casting recommended I speak to you.' You can make a stronger approach this way.

And were you happy with the way casting turned out? Did you have any reservations?

I think it was definitely difficult in terms of the older actors that we had. All three of them were already known TV actors, so they're obviously used to professional shoots, and our film was quite well organised considering, but it was still a student film. It's not easy to work with people who are older than you are, because they have a way of doing it and then you come and you want to do it all different. I think it did work in the end, but it was harder work than with the younger people.

What did you hope to achieve by making Cherish?

My biggest goal was to make a short work and say, 'I'm really happy with it,' but it never happens like that. I wanted to make progress as a film-maker and work more with actors. Before I've been more into how it looks, what the feel is, and I've seen that there was a hole there around directing actors. Now I've concentrated on that. And I've learned that I'd love to do a storyline that I haven't written myself. It seems clearer to me when I read something that somebody else has written. You see more potential in it.

Do you see your cultural identity as an important part of what you want to do? Do you want to continue making things that say something about the black experience?
I definitely want to do that, but not only that. I'm kind of all over the place – I'm Eritrean but I didn't grow up there, I grew up in Germany. I live in London. So I'm actually interested in anything that is a good story, it doesn't have to be black but it doesn't have not to be black. I don't really want to restrict myself into anything specific because I think I'm quite young still. Of course this background is part of me. My first feature that I'm writing will deal with it, but in a very different way to people's perceptions of a black film. Everything that's in the cinema that's black comes from America. We don't really have anything here to say that we exist, we have a different culture that might be interesting, and maybe we would like to see that as well. In the States black films are just money-making entertainment, except for Spike Lee, and I'm not interested in them.

Do you feel your gender is important as well?
Definitely. So far all my main characters have been women, and not out of a conscious choice, it's just natural to me. When you look at most of the big films it's just the girlfriend, the supporting lead, it's a bit boring the roles that we have. That really motivates me to do something different.

How do you feel about the finished film now?
Much better than when I first finished it, now that I am at a distance from it. When you first finish you just see everything you missed. I see something in it that's not just a short and it's very hard to capture it in that time frame. The father and some of the other characters are quite one-dimensional, it's basically the girl throughout, and that was not the intention. But for different reasons I ended up going that way while we were shooting. It's not the film that I had in mind, but then again I've never had that complete feeling after finishing a film. It's such an organic process, it depends who you work with, what you discover, why you're doing this story yourself as well.

So originally it was more about a group of characters?
Well the script was exactly how the film is which is why I'm trying to think, 'Did I see it as something that wasn't really there?' because we shot everything as the script is. But I was quite happy with the girl, her performance.

You never have it perfect, especially when you're just starting out, but then you see what you've achieved so you think, 'Alright, the next one will be better.'

What do you like about it now?

I wanted this to be centred on the characters, and that the camera and the look doesn't take over the story, which I've done with one of my films before. And I think I've achieved that.

In Cherish, *the actors were actually given time to act rather than chasing the narrative. It concentrates on the people.*

It took quite some time to make the actors understand they could do that, because they were used to a rapid pace. But that's definitely what I wanted. It's really a rewarding process actually.

How is Cherish *being marketed?*

I'm sending it to festivals myself, and it's a lot of work. It's difficult and time-consuming. Where should I send it? What's a good festival? Where does it fit? I have to force myself because my mind is already on what I want to do next. But in film if you don't know anybody, it doesn't do you much good to write or sit at home and do your work. You have to get the work out there.

Have you tried broadcast outlets?

I met someone from Channel 4 Film Lab at the Black History month at the Ritz. But he kept saying you have to be in the network, and there are only so many things that can get made, it's very limited – it was really disheartening. And I was asking how you get in the network, but didn't get an answer. I'm not blaming him personally, but I don't like the whole institutional funding thing because it makes people so passive. They always wait for things to happen, when they apply and don't get it, they just think, 'I'll reapply next year.' In New York, it's very different. You don't have public funding, so people are much more creative. It's good that those funding sources are there I suppose, but there are obviously reasons why certain people profit from it and others don't. So I won't rely on it, I'm not the one who gets all the funding books out. I have them but it's really the last option for me, although maybe that's naive.

What's happened for you since the film was released?

I'm writing this feature and it's difficult. It's been in my head for five years now but it's more like a state of mind than a real story, so I'm working back-wards. I have to find the story that will support the state of mind of this character I want to bring in.

I'm trying to get some work in terms of commercials and promos because I need some money. I'm hoping to do a snowboarding commercial for German cinema. I get to do my own concept, but the budget is still being negotiated.

And I hope to make something with some musicians I know. So these things are in the pipeline, although you never know until the final go-ahead.

This work is first of all a way of meeting a lot of people, and secondly a way to get professional experience as a director, even if it's not in drama. People just take you more seriously. You can get an agent and you learn a lot of tactical things that somehow you can apply, and you pay your bills. It won't pay for you to make your films but it will give you leeway to say, 'I'm not going to worry if I don't work for a month. I can do my writing and then maybe I'll do something else.'

Do you enjoy the writing part of the process?

Writing is the hardest thing of all. Because to write something original and gripping is difficult. I don't know whether it may come more naturally to other people. It's nice when you've got your story to the point when you've got your characters and what basically happens, then you can have fun and enjoy the next part, but the part from empty blank page to something, that's the part that's hard.

Keith Wright

Keith Wright has been making films since he was fourteen. He studied editing at the National Film and Television School and since 1996 has been alternating between editing other people's work and directing his own. The films we discuss are *Where's Bingo Betty?* (1998) and *Stan's Slice of Life* (1999).

What made you decide to make a short film?

I'd spent three years at film school working on other people's films, and when I left I had the sudden urge to make my own short film. I'd made short films before so I think it was only natural to want to direct something again.

What got you interested in film?

Ever since the day my parents rented their first video machine I was hooked on watching films and got really interested in how they were made. My parents used to have late-night screenings with their friends and I always used to creep down the stairs to try and get a peek at what they were watching. When they went to work in the day I used to dig out the films from a secret cupboard and watch them. Some of the first films I saw were *Frankenstein* (1931), *Dracula* (1931) and *The Evil Dead* (1982).

Just the idea of bringing people together into one place and having their undivided attention for nearly two hours was enough to convince me that this was what I wanted to do. I was immediately hooked into the idea of making my own films that people could watch at home.

Were your parents in the business?

No, my dad was from a steel background, manufacturing, and my mum worked in the local bank. It was quite difficult to get into the film industry because I wasn't in a film environment. When I was at school, I saw the careers advisor and said that I wanted to be a film director, and he said, 'Well, what about the steel industry?' I decided to save my pocket money up for a video camera, and once I'd got that I armed myself with various books on film-making and was able to teach myself how to make films. I'd get together at weekends with friends and we would just go off and make short films. Then I won a prize from the Institute of Amateur Cinematographers when I was fifteen, and that encouraged me to do even more.

You were working with video?

Yes, I did shoot a little bit on film, but I found the process really difficult because I like to see instant results. Plus it was really expensive to shoot film, whereas once you had a video camera it would only cost you a few pounds for a three-hour tape. The problem with shooting on video is that you can shoot tonnes and tonnes of footage and end up with an editing nightmare. So that was an early lesson to learn.

Describe Where's Bingo Betty? *and* Stan's Slice of Life *for us.*

Where's Bingo Betty? is a comedy about a down-to-earth northern man who claims his wife's been abducted by aliens. I decided to shoot it in the style of a spoof documentary. I liked the idea of trying to take an extraordinary and unusual story and play it in a realistic manner. It was shot for about £50 in one day with a domestic camcorder.

Stan's Slice of Life was a more ambitious project and is a much more gentle comedy drama, which tells the story of an elderly man who reminisces about his life on the anniversary of his wife's death. It was an attempt to make something a bit more serious and romantic.

How would you categorise yourself as a film-maker?

That's difficult to say at this early stage. All the films I've made up to now have had a comedy element. People say comedy is really difficult to do, but I find it comes quite naturally, every day I step out the door I see something that makes me smile. Comedy is all around us. I guess I have a way of framing those moments onto screen that seems to work with an audience. I always try and look for the telling details in a character or a place: I think that's part of me and my upbringing.

What do you aim to do in your work?

There are so many levels to film-making that it's very difficult to pin down one particular thing. But ultimately I want people to take something from my films. And if that's just the fact they had a good laugh then that's great. But it is important that the film has some kind of heart, something that hits a universal chord. Having said that I've never been too worried about the audience when I make something, because I feel that if you're guided by the judgment of the audience then it's not really your film. You have to go with your own emotions because today's audiences will spot a fake a mile off.

Describe the process of making Where's Bingo Betty?

When I came out of film school I decided that I needed to do a film to prove myself, I was a bit frustrated. I had no money, so I thought I'd do something using found footage. I discovered loads of discarded rushes in a skip at the back of the film school that were just going to be thrown away. I decided to try and pull all this material together and make something out of it. The school was going digital and was getting rid of old equipment, so I managed to get a pic sync and splicer. I sat at home for about two weeks spooling through all this dusty material, trying to come up with an idea.

There was one particular reel where this old guy was walking round his garden. It was a documentary project, I think. It really struck me. The film had a really strange look to it – the colours looked alien. That's when the idea for *Where's Bingo Betty?* struck. I started to work the material but soon found that I couldn't actually create what I wanted from the existing material. That's when I realised the only thing I could do was shoot it myself. I came up with the idea of using my girlfriend's stepdad, because he's quite a character, he came across as a real natural. That's how the idea came about, and it was quite an interesting process, not something that I've ever repeated. It's probably worth doing again, actually.

Where did you go from there?

I went straight into writing a script, I didn't do a treatment. It seemed very clear in my head, because I've got quite a visual way of working, I can see the things on the screen before I can write them. It was easier to just write the script and fine tune it along the way. It's a loose way to work and I find it more creative. I think I wrote the script in two days, and I sent that to Dennis (who played the lead role) a few days before we started shooting. What came out of the filming process was a slightly different film from what was scripted because Dennis would add his own little bits as we were shooting.

On the other hand, looking at *Stan's Slice of Life*, which was a funded project – instead of a budget of £50 for *Bingo Betty*, I had £10,000 – it was a very different process. I was constantly having to submit scripts to people who could give some kind of approval or some kind of feedback. That was definitely a new way of working for me, but it got to the stage where I had gone over fifteen drafts and completely lost the original plot. We were due to shoot in a week, and I still didn't really have a final draft.

How did you get the funding for Stan's Slice of Life?

I put *Where's Bingo Betty?* in for a competition called the David Altshul Award,

Where's Bingo Betty? (1998)

run by Southern Arts, and I was lucky enough to win. That led to the Carlton scheme organised with Southern Arts. Basically, you have to go in and present your idea and if they like it they'll give you £10,000. I submitted a complete script and got a friend to create some visuals. Because the script dealt with flashbacks, I wanted to give the film a distinctive style for each flashback, so it was important that I had those visuals to show people. What's always difficult about writing a script for me is trying to get other people to see what's in my head. I had storyboards for most of the sequences, and I had some mood boards. I created some video footage using clips from other films to show how I wanted to treat the flashbacks. It helped communicate the whole mood of the piece.

How did your production crews compare on the two films?

Quite drastically. On *Bingo Betty* it was just me and a camcorder. On *Stan* I had all the major crew members in place.

Did you select the crew?

Yes, they were mostly people I met at film school, people I knew I could trust, and they would recommend assistants and other people we might need. It all fell into place pretty smoothly and we all got along very well, which is important.

It was tough in a way, because I was always used to having control over every aspect of production and here I was dishing out all the key roles to other people. It's not that I didn't trust anyone, it was just a different approach to making a film for me. One thing that did shock me was the number of applications I got for actors. I put an advert in *PCR* and for the next four days the post van arrived with sacks full of mail and CVs. That was the moment that made me sit up and think, 'God, there are so many people out there wanting to do this!' People were almost pleading just to get an opportunity. It's a tough industry, even just getting a break is a struggle.

Did you have a producer for Stan?

Yes, although I did consider doing it myself at first. As I started to get the production up and running I decided I might jeopardise the film if I tried to do too much at once, so I got a producer on board. He wanted to do it and it was his first drama so it was a great learning process.

And Carlton and Southern Arts let you do that?

Yes, they were pretty good on that front actually. The only area where they really got involved was with the story. As long as I kept them updated on the production they were happy.

What did you hope to achieve with these two projects?

With *Bingo Betty* it was simply something that I wanted to do. But at the end of the day it does prove that you don't need a lot of money to make films.

That's an important point to make, because anybody who really wants to do it, can do it. You can get a camcorder for £200 or even borrow one. I just wanted to do something and prove that it could be done without spending a lot of money.

On *Bingo Betty* I was working pretty much on my own. On *Stan* I was working with a crew of ten to fifteen people, and we were shooting on film. For me, it was a chance to work more professionally and to collaborate with other key crew in a creative way. The real challenge was to try and keep the idea consistent throughout the whole process. Everything – make-up, costumes, locations, sound design, etc. – needs to look integrated.

Did you feel it was like a test to see if you were a 'proper' director?

Yes. But it was more personal, more about proving to myself that I could do what I had told people I could do, which put the pressure on at first. Then, once I started to get involved with the process, all that fades away and you're just getting on with the job. Also, you're spending other people's money, and you want to do it before they change their minds.

Did you consider the production in career terms – whether it would be a stepping stone to something?

Yes. I wanted to prove that I can do something using a professional crew – I think that's what people are going to be looking for. But also the main factor was telling the story and entertaining the audience.

Bingo Betty *was shot on video, wasn't it?*

Yes, it was shot on a domestic video camera. I wanted it to look like archive footage so I used a digital effect filter to add scratches and grain. It looks pretty good actually and certainly adds to the film's charm. I remember the original feeling that I wanted to achieve was what I'd seen in those rushes that I'd got out of the film school skip.

What was Stan *shot on?*

I originally wanted to shoot *Stan* on Digital Betacam to keep down costs. But at the end of the day I'm a big believer that the story should dictate the shooting medium and this project was definitely a film project. Because I had the money available I decided to shoot on Super 16mm. It was definitely the right decision.

I learnt my craft working with video but you still can't beat the look of film. One of my other recent shorts, *Long in the Tooth* (2000), was shot on film as well – on a wind-up Bolex.

What was the pre-production process like on Stan's Slice of Life*?*

It was very different from *Bingo Betty* because I was working with a producer and all the key creative personnel were on board for me to discuss things with and talk about ideas. And that was good, because there were things that came

out of those meetings with people that I probably wouldn't have thought of.
But it could also work against you, because it was very easy to lose the focus
of what you were doing. You could have a conversation with someone and
think, 'Oh, that's a great idea, I'll put that in,' and then suddenly everything
else around it doesn't quite work. So what happened with the script is that it
started off as a simple idea and it got really complex. As the shooting dates
got closer, the backbone of the film was changing from a lighthearted drama
to something that was darker and much more serious. What came out in the
end was a mix of both, and in fact the final scene was the only one that
remained from the first draft and you can tell. The tone of it is very different
and it doesn't really add to the story. But that's just what film-making is like,
when you're so close to it and you're whole life is swallowed up by this
process you just become blind to the whole thing.

Did you retain editorial control?

Yes, pretty much. There were times when Southern Arts would phone up and
say, 'We've read the new script and we think it could do with this.' There was
one particular instance where there was almost an insistence on a death scene
in the film, which I had originally scripted but I'd started to strip away because
I thought the sense of loss was already very apparent. We ended up shooting
the death scene and it was a very strong scene, it worked really well. It was
almost a shame to cut it in the end, but it did go because it was totally out of
context, it didn't have the right tone for the film. It was quite a good experience to have to do that; we spent a full day shooting this stuff, and I just
ended up stripping it out. The other reason was that the film was running over
slightly so we had to cut something anyway.

So that was a limitation – the duration?

Yes, it had to be exactly ten minutes.

Were there any other limitations?

We had to follow ITC regulations, because it was going to be broadcast. I was
given this massive handbook which outlined all these rules and regulations, I
took one look at it and threw it to one side. I'd got enough to think about.
The whole point of the scheme was that it should represent what it was like to
work in the television industry. There were all the technical aspects of it as well
– you can't shoot widescreen. In a way, something like that for me is quite an
artistic constraint, but what can you do? I had always seen the film as being
shot in a widescreen ratio. I liked the idea of creating something that was more
cinematic, but then like they said, this was television. So I had to bow to the
rules.

The last process was to take the finished film and have it technically
assessed. I went to Central in Nottingham with my tape. There's a guy who sits

in this fantastically air-conditioned room with all these buttons and monitors to make sure your final tape is up to scratch. You have to sit there while he watches it and scribbles down notes. It was pretty nerve racking, this guy is like God really, if it doesn't come up to scratch he'll just send you away to fix the problem which could cost you another two grand. Thank God he passed it. I remember being quite emotional because that was the final stage and there was nothing else to do but start thinking about my next project.

Do you think limitations can be useful?

Yes, there's always some kind of constraint. In *Bingo Betty* the constraint was that I didn't have any money, and I had to realise something that on paper probably looked quite expensive – it probably looked like £100,000 on paper. But that's good because it breeds creativity. Part of you has to think, and say 'Okay, I don't have the money to do this but I can do this in such a way.' Like when I was trying to work out how to make a UFO for *Bingo Betty*, I ended up going into Reading and buying two Yorkshire pudding tins for 50p. That's part of the creative process, I referenced them in the film and it became one of the film's funniest moments.

I also think I've been successful when I've worked quickly, when I've worked really fast and haven't had time to reflect on things, just follow my instincts. And I think that's probably my most valuable asset, to say 'I've got ten minutes to do this, how am I going to do it, how am I going to achieve it best.' That is really when film-making comes alive.

With Stan's Slice of Life *how long was it from your proposal being accepted to completion?*

In all it probably took about six months from script to screen. It was a fairly ambitious project really, mainly because the flashbacks required a variety of locations. We had a day's shoot on Worthing pier, a day's shoot in a derelict house in Marlow, which we had to decorate and dress. It had a nice garden, which we had to completely strip out and lay down a lawn and redecorate the shed. We had a day's shoot in a studio – all the scenes where we flashback to him meeting his wife for the first time were all shot in a studio. Then we had a day's shoot in a church, we had to stage a wartime wedding. And we had a day in a church hall – we had to recreate a cabbage contest, which was brilliant fun. There were about five or six different locations all spread about and a lot of people to organise.

The other thing was that I had to put my editing career on hold, in other words I wasn't able to earn any money for several months and on top of that I was actually putting my own money into the film for post-production.

How do you feel about the finished films now?

I was very happy with *Bingo Betty*, just because it made me laugh. It's done so well, it just keeps going really, and it's not a film that I ever pushed. I didn't do any publicity on it or anything, it just seemed to take on a life of its own. To me, that's testament to the fact that it's a good film because people enjoy it. It's not me saying 'Look at this, it's brilliant,' it's people saying 'Wow, look at this, it's brilliant.'

Stan was broadcast as part of a one-hour show. I've got mixed feelings about it, because I don't think the scriptwriting process was ever properly finished. From a technical point of view I'm really pleased with it. It looks much more expensive than it was. It can stand up to anything produced on a higher budget, and it was the first time I'd worked with professional actors and actresses, which is a necessary experience. It's important to try to get in front of the camera and work with actors – that's definitely something I need to do more of.

On the whole I think it was successful in that I completed the film. It went slightly over budget, which was a pain because I had to pay for it. But other than that everyone involved had good things to say about it so I can't complain really – it was a fantastic experience.

What surprises me about Bingo Betty *is that it's quite a complex piece of film-making which is often read as naive because of its references to B movies and the low-budget look of it.*

I think that's what's great about it though, because people are dragged into it. People really believe it, that this is a character who really has lost his wife. The fact that she's been abducted by what appears to be a giant Yorkshire pudding tin is neither here nor there. The core of the story is this man wants his wife back. Most of the people's reactions that I've had have suggested that on the one hand it's really funny but on the other it's quite moving as well. That undoubtedly comes from the performance, but also the idea, the structure of it.

You've done pretty well with the distribution of these two films.

Yes, *Bingo Betty* has basically sold itself. Recently it was on 'Shooting Gallery', Channel 4, they've bought the rights to it now. It's been shown at the NFT in front of *Billy Elliot*, it's been shown at Brief Encounters, the Edinburgh International Film Festival and other festivals all around the world and in the UK, and on a number of late-night television shows.

It's still early days for *Stan*. It went straight to television, it's done a few festivals and there's an Internet site that's interested in putting it on.

Are you happy with the audience that your films have reached?

It's always difficult to keep track of where your films are shown but on the whole I'm not that bothered who gets to see it as long as they enjoy it. I would hate to think I had wasted anyone's time. It's really good when I get to see my work with an audience just so I can judge the reaction. The experience I had with *Long in the Tooth* was great. It was accepted for the Wrangler Short Film Award and they screened it at the Odeon West End and it was packed. Just to be sat in there and watch the film on a massive screen was great – it was a real buzz. People were cheering when it won and that was a fantastic feeling.

Do you think about things like distribution when you're developing a project?

I haven't in the past but the more I learn about the industry the more I realise how important things like this can be. Distribution is a notoriously difficult area for most film-makers, it can be easy to fall into the trap of getting a quick return, especially if those debts are building up, and ending up with a bad distribution.

What do you think is the essence of a short film idea?

Something that's simple but extraordinary. Just as *Bingo Betty* is about a man that's lost his wife to aliens, *Stan* is about a man who reminisces about his incredible life, *Long in the Tooth* is about a guy who thinks he's a scarecrow. The core of these films is very simple but the execution and personal style are what brings it to life.

Notes

1. Lucia Zucchetti is quoted in Joost Hunningher, 'Putting Student Collaboration before Authorship', *Journal of Media Practice*, vol. 1, no. 3, p. 176.

4

Contemporary Film-makers and Shorts Production

What do we learn from these interviews? All accept that it is difficult to get funding, distribution is poor, and the financial rewards are negligible. All agree as well, though, that the short film is an opportunity. They provide a creative space, not necessarily a cut-price apprenticeship for mainstream cinema. This chapter reflects on the process of film-making from the points made in the interviews with film-makers, draws out the main points to be learnt from their practice and discusses some of the issues raised around production, funding and distribution.

The creative process

The ways in which film-makers find the germ of a filmic idea and nurture it are various. For most film-makers here, part of the idea or the form it takes comes out of personal experience, emotional states and memories, interacting with external events, situations and opportunities. Sometimes an external event, like the destruction of John Smith's neighbourhood by the building of a motorway, provide the initial impetus. The idea for Keith Wright's *Where's Bingo Betty?* came from found film footage, which created the style and central character of the finished piece. Occasionally, a funding scheme may provide the limitations or line of thought with which the film-maker experiments. John Smith's collaboration with the composer Jocelyn Pook came about in response to a BBC2 scheme. The result of the collaboration, *Blight* received worldwide acclaim and greatly increased his public profile, although he remains suspicious of the audience manipulation of which music is capable. The initial spark for Emma Calder's *The Queen's Monastery* was a commissioning requirement to work with a piece of out-of-copyright classical music. This gradually fused with feelings around relationships from her own experience and experimentation with style and visualisation.

Adaptation of an existing text allows a more cerebral approach. Minghella's creativity in *Play* is based on a close analysis of the meaning of Beckett's text and a deeply thoughtful and inventive approach to how this can be translated from theatre to film. Film-makers recognise that adaptations provide the opportunity to achieve a clearer perspective than their own, often partly autobiographical, material.

The creative process before the written word is the most amorphous and delicate.

The catalyst for an idea may be an object, photograph, existing film or music, anecdotes, an emotion, memory or event. It may arrive in the conscious mind fully fledged, or the film-maker may be more aware of the process taking shape. But film-makers are aware of the need to protect a new-born idea from over-analysis at an early stage.

In bringing a project from initial idea to completed film the balance between planning and spontaneity is different for each film-maker. Some, like Tessa Sheridan, prefer a long pre-production process where the idea evolves gradually, with a complete script in place before production starts. Others, like Nick Park and Emma Calder, develop the idea both before and during production – and the longer production cycle of drawn and model animation allows this thinking time. John Smith, who often works alone and on low budgets over an extended production time, develops ideas by alternately writing and filming. He may not know at first how he will use footage, but his process clarifies the theme of the piece.

However complete the script is before shooting, directors need to be flexible during production. Keith Wright talks about working with his lead actor to develop the dialogue during recording. Lynne Ramsay discusses how much she learnt from shooting the party scene of *Gasman* in an improvisational, documentary way – experience she then drew on for her first feature, *Ratcatcher*. And John Hardwick found it beneficial when disaster struck and he had to throw the shot list away, and felt he had found his real voice with *The Sweetness Lies Within*.

Directors learn that over-structuring the production process can deaden their responsiveness to actors, ideas or opportunities which arise during the shoot. An essential part of a director's development is to learn their most successful methodology, tracing their own path between planning and chaos, and to know when to stand firm and when to take on others' suggestions.

Short films, unlike features, do not carry the burden of massive budgets, years of work and responsibility to a large number of people for its success. As Anthony Minghella remarks about feature production, 'You go into a tunnel and you don't think you're ever going to emerge from it.' Shorts allow a lighter, faster, more exploratory approach. Even for directors like Minghella who have an excellent track record on features, shorts provide a necessary creative space.

The role of writing in the process is variable, and seems particularly marginal to the evolution of animation ideas. Both Nick Park and Emma Calder describe the development of characters and ideas through drawings and research, which gradually turned into the storyboard. Experimentation took place throughout both development and filming.

Film-making as a creative process is emphasised in all these interviews: the writer/director has to write it or work through pre-production in their own way in order to find out what it's about – they cannot know in advance. It is a learning process, full of experiment and innovation, and therefore the outcome can never be completely known. In spite of this, to trust in instinct and first ideas is essential. Although this is sometimes risky, and does induce fear and nervousness, it is often the basis of creativity.

Any attempt at analysing work processes in terms of gender will be reductive of the wide range of methodologies evident, but there seems to be a suggestion that there is often a link between theme, process and gender. Women seem more likely to take personal experiences and emotions as their source material (or perhaps are more ready to acknowledge these sources). The evolution of the idea for Emma Calder and Tessa Sheridan is exploratory and open, particularly in its early stages. They are self-aware in the way in which they bring to consciousness hidden feelings and thoughts to work with. In contrast, both Keith Wright and John Hardwick discuss accidentally discovering the benefits of a more playful or exploratory process than they would normally use, their pleasure in its outcome, and their intention to use such methods again. John Smith habitually uses a slow, thoughtful process, and the catalyst may be external events or internal emotions or memories. Winta Yohannes' experiences as a black woman living in a different culture, and issues of personal identity versus tradition, are central to her work.

There is also a suggestion that women may often be less comfortable with the conventional narrative structure, with its active protagonist, three-act structure and sense of closure. Lynne Ramsay enjoys exploring structures beyond the linear narrative, as we can see in *Kill the Day*. Emma Calder describes the balance achieved by turning to a male colleague for advice when faced with a narrative problem that needs clarification, although she is also aware that she will not put all his suggestions into practice. Tessa Sheridan thinks it important to leave the audience space to create their own meaning. But John Smith makes similar comments on his dislike of closed, unambiguous narratives, and is wary of music because of the way in which it directs the audience in how to look at a film (and much avant-garde filmmaking is about raising questions around meaning rather than providing solutions). Although we may see a cluster of tendencies connected with gender around creative processes and narrative strategies, there is a spectrum of practices rather than a clearly drawn dichotomy.

Commissioning and funding

Film-making, even for short films, is often an expensive process that needs the financial backing of others in order to be made and to be seen. The novelist can provide a finished version of their creation when seeking backing; the film-maker is dependent on others grasping the nature of their vision based often on just an idea. How to communicate a personal vision is a skill which most film-makers have to learn to gain funding, and there is much (unpaid) work to be done to prepare the material necessary for a proposal which will excite the jaded palettes of commissioners. There is a notable difference in the complexity of this process for Nick Park (getting the commission for *Creature Comforts* in the late 1980s) and Emma Calder (going through a similar process in the late 1990s) which illustrates the increasing bureaucracy of commissioning. There is more advice available now, but many film-makers require individual mentoring at some stage in their career to learn how to apply for funding successfully. Many funding applications presume an existing partnership between director, writer and production company which may dissuade people without these connections from applying. A more sympathetic approach would provide mentoring support and assistance in developing creative partnerships.

The tenuous nature of the creative process and the vulnerability of ideas needs to be remembered when we consider the nature of the commissioning and funding process. A fundamental question is, does the process impede rather than encourage creativity? Some of the films featured may not have been made without the commissioning requirements of a certain approach, but it may also distort as well as encourage. Particularly frustrating are short-lived schemes specifying theme or genre, which may show little respect for film-makers' personal concerns and do not allow time for ideas to mature. During production, the toughest film-makers learn how and when to negotiate without jeopardising their vision, but it is a painful lesson to learn. Directors who place undue importance on the opinion of commissioners or an imagined audience may dilute the film and lose its integrity, and it is sometimes argued that an over-awareness of the agendas of funding bodies may have a homogenising effect on shorts production.

If the film-making process is full of experiment and innovation, the outcome cannot be known. How then to put in place the detailed documentation – treatment, scripts, budgets – required by many funding agencies? Maggie Ellis of the LFVDA and Animate!, who was involved in commissioning both Emma Calder and Tessa Sheridan, is concerned about the obsession with scripts for shorts. As she comments, 'There are lots of ways of making films; only some of them are script-led. It can be over-bureaucratic to demand a full script as part of the commissioning process. We need to be flexible and only ask for a script where appropriate.'[1] Asking a film-maker to produce a written script before funding may be like asking a fine art practitioner to produce a written commentary before starting the work of art. It does not recognise the creativity of the process or the different characteristics of the visual and verbal media. For some film-makers it will be possible. For those using cinematic language in an exploratory way, it may well be impossible. And, with some notable exceptions, the more unusual or innovative an idea for a film is, the more difficult it is to persuade people to invest in it, and the more detail required to support the initial proposal.

Commissioners who are prepared to recognise potential qualities in film-makers, to invest in them, have confidence in their own judgment, and to take a risk by empathising with the film-maker's vision and remaining supportive until the project is complete, enable short films to be made which make full use of the form's potential. Experienced people who are not interested in making their own mark on a slate of films, but want to develop and mentor the individual talents of directors and writers, are working to raise the standards of film-making as a whole. Funders and commissioners need to be as open and flexible as possible, and drawn from a range of backgrounds, ages and interests in order to maintain the diverse nature of short film-making in Britain.

Diversity of the people selecting projects is particularly important at a time when the process is becoming more centralised and more funding partnerships are being set up. The fewer the agencies involved, the less room there is for a range of approaches, and the greater the risk that film-makers unable to conform to certain criteria will be prevented from working.

The relationship between amount of investment and involvement in the production process also seems to be imbalanced. As budgets are reduced, we see no change in the amount of detail required from the film-maker about outcomes. Theme- and genre-specific schemes are prevalent, constraining creativity in the short film and tending to inhibit its experimental potential. Experiments sometimes fail, but the film-maker will learn a great deal from the process and should not be prevented from working again if one film is seen as unsuccessful. The importance of these aspects will not be recognised if commissioners are judged purely on the amount of screen time they produce rather than the quality of the film-makers they have helped to develop.

Short film-making is often seen purely as a training ground for feature film-makers, which undermines the importance of short film as an art form in its own right. It also encourages short film funding to concentrate on younger film-makers. Not all short film-makers want to make features – although many do want the opportunity. People who have made feature films often want to continue to make shorts. Whether Britain will ever be able to have an economically sustainable feature-film industry is questionable. For all these reasons, short film-making must be invested in as an end in itself, and not as a cut-price apprenticeship to mainstream cinema.

Many film-makers fund their personal projects – particularly at the early developmental stage – by making commercials or music videos. As Tessa Sheridan remarks, it is useful experience in terms of both technical processes and building a team of people to work with. Jonathan Glazer comments on the high budgets available, which mean that the latest special effects and the ideal location can be achieved. It may also lead to a cross-fertilisation of ideas, so that working on music videos has encouraged John Hardwick in a more improvisational approach, or it may encourage directors to be more adventurous in terms of pace and use of editing techniques.

Jonathan Glazer's development has been in music videos and commercials, and his feature film, *Sexy Beast*, is remarkable for its seamless meshing of live-action and digital effects, and for the speed and economy of its narrative. In the same way that we can see in Lynne Ramsay's work the aesthetic of art student, photographer and documentary camera operator coming together (in the opening scenes of *Ratcatcher*, for instance), the pace and technical scope of Glazer's work stems from this background. Experience in commercials and music videos often has a positive effect on the style and aesthetics of British film directors.

Exhibition and distribution

It is difficult to obtain theatric exhibition for shorts. Few cinemas will take the risk to show anything but feature films and commercials. Schemes that distribute films with a feature such as Pathé and Short Circuit, and some individual cinemas that show short films regularly, are exceptions. This is a constrained space for shorts to work within, however, in terms of both duration and content. Anything over ten minutes is usually avoided as it disrupts the programme schedule. And as the shorts have to prepare the audience for the feature film, difficult or harrowing pieces are avoided. The style and subject matter of Emma Calder's *The Queen's Monastery* was seen as a suitable precursor to the feature film by cinema programmers, which led to increased distribution opportunities. Where shorts are shown before a feature, the feature film will be seen as the main event and the reason the audience is there; the short just a moment's entertainment beforehand. It is noticeable too that Short Circuit, who initially asked for films of up to ten minutes duration, are now more interested in three- or four-minute pieces as they are easier to persuade cinemas to take. As John Smith remarks, it would be good to see cinemas having regular or even occasional shorts-only programmes so that shorts can be shown on the big screen free of these limitations. Touring collections of shorts have proved popular with both audiences and cinemas. Audiences see a carefully selected range of films, many of which are difficult to see anywhere else. Organisation and publicity is centralised, which offsets some of the extra labour inherent in programming shorts rather than features for individual cinemas. It also raises profile, as it gives the opportunity for reviews to appear in the press. Given that commercial cinemas will not be interested in philanthropic gestures, short film seasons and programmes are more likely to be seen in the subsidised sector. Further support to such cinemas seems essential to ensure that the good work that already takes place can be expanded.

Film festivals enable some critical recognition, help to raise profile, and create a global market in short film. They do not, however, provide a regular opportunity for exhibition. Part of learning to make films comes from sitting with an audience watching the film. As Keith Wright says, it gives a buzz which makes the whole strenuous process worthwhile. It is also the way in which the film-maker can learn where they have communicated and where they have not, and this direct experience of an audience is irreplaceable. Many film-makers are dependent on local film clubs – often using portable film or video projection – for an opportunity to exhibit and to learn from audience reaction. The clubs also provide a supportive community for film-makers. John Hardwick, a member of the Exploding Cinema in London, has come to film-making through this route and the experience has helped him maintain his individualistic approach to the medium.

As Damien O'Donnell comments, digital cinema may open up opportunities for shorts as cinematic releases could be both cheaper and more flexible. At present, however, American feature films swamp British cinemas, and this domination of film culture is reinforced by much American Web-based material. In the circumstances, it is difficult to imagine how short film will find a niche when so many British feature films receive restricted release, or none at all. For an alternative digital exhibition network to exist and find an audience outside the mainstream, both funding and publicity (including a lively website presence) are needed.

Non-theatric opportunities for short film are proliferating as the take-up of the Internet and digital television expands, and digital technology allows the moving image to be shown in more and different environments. Many of the films discussed here have been purchased by Internet sites, and airline companies are discovering short film. Digital technology has also led to an improvement in the use of video in galleries, whether as part of an installation or on its own. This is an exciting space for film-makers who work outside mainstream narrative structure.

Television offers much wider audiences for short film than cinema, and many of the film-makers featured here have benefited from the funding and distribution initiatives television companies provide. Although seen as very expensive in terms of airtime, both BBC2 and Channel 4 accept that it is part of their remit to invest in film-making talent through shorts. Traditionally, they have been important commissioners: increasingly they are working in partnership to provide support – for instance, with the Film Council or with digital channels. Scottish Screen has an excellent history of developing talent, with initiatives for directors at different levels of experience. Channel 4's promotion of animation has been impressive, with regular scheduling (although late-night) of comedy, and a bracing mix of experimental and narrative work with information about film-makers and the animation processes.

Anthologies of short films scheduled late at night, although useful for existing fans, do little to widen the audience, however. Shorts would benefit from more flexible scheduling, perhaps using the most accessible shorts as a trailer for anthologies – after all, one of the good qualities of shorts is that they can be repeated without taking up too much time. Including popular forms such as music videos in anthologies may also raise the interest of a wider audience. Often the ways in which scheduling marginalises short film suggests that television companies think of shorts purely as a training ground for film-makers, and that they have little concern about building an audience. There is a need for a positive strategy from both programme-makers and schedulers if people are to discover the pleasures of short film and accept shorts as part of the viewing mix as they used to do at the cinema.

Shorts will become increasingly important with the proliferation of digital channels, although budgets will continue to be reduced. The explosion in the number of television channels has not been met with the same growth in either audiences or advertising revenue. In the short term co-productions between traditional and new channels have provided new opportunities for shorts, however, and the potential for future development.

With websites, CD Rom and DVD, moving image work can be produced and disseminated more cheaply than before. As the opportunities provided by interactivity are explored we are seeing a more exciting use of the medium, as Damien O'Donnell's work with Mike Figgis demonstrates. There has also been a growth in the use of CD and DVD Roms for interactive work.[2]

Digital film-making

All the film-makers interviewed here are interested in investigating the possibilities that digital technology provides, but feel that it depends on the nature of the project whether it is suitable or not. Some feel liberated by the possibility of obtaining good technical standards using their own resources, so freeing them from the commissioning process. Shooting may be quicker and less obtrusive, making a documentary style easier to achieve.

Damien O'Donnell's work for the *Hotel* website is an example of the advantages of using digital cameras. The outcome is Internet-based, and the qualities of hand-held, small-crew working gives an immediacy which fits well with the vérité style of the content and the small screen output. He found that digital technology loosened up the shooting process, enabling the director to concentrate on actors rather than worrying about lighting, and to set up and move quickly. He also comments on his enjoyment of the use of film and studio-based production for the Samuel Beckett short, however. Some film-makers are concerned that budgets will be reduced to levels that make the use of film impossible, while others are enjoying its potential to fuse special effects with reality, even to the extent of blurring the line between animation and live action.

Digital editing techniques can allow greater rapidity of process, enabling, for example, the rapid preparation of material for the *Hotel* website. As the process is not linear, it also allows easier experimentation with different structures and nonlinear narratives. Special effects are more accessible to the low-budget film-maker, and make work from home a realistic alternative to the hire of expensive post-production facilities. There is a side effect in that audiences may no longer know when an image is filmed in the real world or when it is computer generated. Nick Park's comment about computer-generated animation – that it lacks the human contact inherent in the model animation process – sounds a warning. Unless used carefully, computer-generated effects can lose the warmth of the human touch, and the result may be distancing for the audience.

Conclusion

The short is an opportunity for play and innovation, of condensed, elliptical, poetic film forms. It may be the site of concentrated communication between film-maker and audience, where a strong voice or individual vision is possible. That film-makers, commissioners, funders and distributors recognise the special qualities of short film is essential for its continued pivotal role in British film-making. It is also important that audiences' awareness of short film is raised through improved opportunities to view shorts both in cinema and on television. It is to be hoped that the Internet and digital projection may result in a wider base for a British film culture which includes shorts, rather than increased opportunities to view mainstream American features.

The combination of digital cinema projection, organisations like Britshorts (involved in the production, distribution and exhibition of short film) and clubs such as Exploding Cinema give the basis for a lively film-making community. Add to this the use of the Internet to reach an audience (which will grow as use of broadband increases) and an increasing number of television channels, and we see the conditions for a renaissance of interest in shorts. At present, this may be limited to an 'in crowd' of film-makers and fans, but the occasional scheme breaks out into wider public awareness when supported by print and television coverage. In future, we may see the evolution of a more widespread, dynamic film culture in Britain which brings together makers and audiences, although through digital technology and the computer rather than the flickering light of the film projector.

Notes

1   Conversation with Maggie Ellis of Animate! and the London Film and Video Development Agency, 7 December 2001.

2.   See Martin Rieser and Andrea Zapp (eds), *New Screen Media* (London: BFI, 2001) – book and accompanying DVD Rom.

5

How Shorts (Can) Get Made and Shown

Much of what is said in this book is inspirational. Great films made, often against the odds. Creative people able to pursue their film-making dreams and visions. Films shown to appreciative audiences. Short films made, not as calling cards but as ends in themselves. If what is said here encourages budding and existing film-makers to pursue their own short film plans this book will have served its purpose.

There is a need for home truths, however. It is difficult to make a good short film. If you make one it won't make you rich. In most cases, in fact, you will pay for it. There is no market for most short films. It is relatively easy to show your film to friends (you might even hire a cinema), possible to place it on the Internet, hard to get it on television, difficult to get it into festivals, and virtually impossible to obtain a cinema release. Despite the fact that the first films were shorts, and that until recently a short was a routine part of the cinemagoing experience, few shorts make it on to the big screen. The most popular shorts in recent years – the Wallace and Gromit films in the UK, *George Lucas in Love* (1999) in North America – have found audiences mostly through television, video and the Internet rather than the cinema.

We want to see more and better short films made and shown widely. Our aim in this final section is to provide some help in getting films made and seen. This is not a list of funding bodies, advice centres and television channels that have shown short films. This information exists in abundance, for example in the BFI's *A Filmmakers' Guide to Distribution and Exhibition*, and further information is included in Chapter 6. What we say here covers more the realities of getting support, putting a film in a festival or distributing it digitally. It is based on our management of Brief Encounters, experience of production – in universities and managing the Brief Encounters production project – teaching about the short film, and general interest in cinema. It reflects the discussions we have had with many film-makers and potential festival organisers seeking advice, and interviews with those involved in short film production, distribution and exhibition.

A word of warning. Writing about any aspect of the short film presently is akin to trying to predict the impact of sound films in the mid-1920s. Discussion is especially difficult around the Internet. The position changes rapidly, new sites are established regularly and change is a frequent occurrence. In summer 2001, Atom Films, the leading Internet webcaster, cut back its operations though it remains a leading Internet short film site. Similar problems exist with funding. Changes in television company ownership and programming priorities, and in organisations providing subsidy for cultural film production, make definitive statements difficult. With these caveats in mind we will try to help.

Despite all the difficulties, shorts are more important then ever. They are popular with aspirant film-makers, and with experienced feature film directors. Though no estimate is ever made – it would be impossible in terms of productions in higher education alone – it is clear that more shorts are made now than ever before. Most are poor and deserve obscurity. But the best continue to be made, and will continue to be seen.

After a century of short film production, many of the questions remain the same. The key issue is gaining advantage over others. How do I get my film made? How do I get it into a festival? Is there a television opportunity? Can it be shown on the Internet? Our experience tells us that there are no easy answers. It should be said right away, though, that unless you are a Keith Wright and can create magic out of nothing, and you want to make something special and get it shown, you will have to be a fundraiser, a marketer, a blagger, prepared to both break the rules and follow them where necessary. Above all, you need to be good at making friends, influencing people and building and maintaining partnerships.

Getting the film made

Some film-makers are happy to get on with it. Others make films because they are doing a college degree. Some – a lucky few – have a commission. Only a few film-makers will get support for their films, however. For the rest, where cost is an issue, funding has to be found. There is money out there. Media development and screen agencies, regional arts boards, local authorities, the Lottery, even private sponsorship have all helped create short films in the past. After seventy short films, though, Lottery-funded production stalled with the reorganisation of public funding agencies. Changes in regional funding and the television industry mean that it may be some time before new budgets are established so that shorts can be supported again. The Film Council is supporting shorts with new schemes announced on their website in 2001.

Film-makers need to be better prepared in making applications. It is difficult to sell an idea, and we do believe that some funding agencies need to work more closely with film-makers in developing, making and distributing projects. More risk-taking should be encouraged, funding provided for time and space to develop ideas, and mentoring. Film-makers have responsibilities too. Lessons include: always read the rules and understand the scheme; ensure that you are eligible; don't overly bother staff – but try to build a relationship with them; make sure that the budgets submitted add up. Above all – make refusal impossible, but never start a funding application with the claim that 'this is the greatest film you will ever see'. Similar lessons apply in approaching private companies. Kodak, who are keen on short films, and who provide, on occasion, discounted film stock, say film-makers seeking assistance need to talk with them first. Most of this is stating the obvious. Our experience suggests that the obvious is often missed or ignored.

Can short films be sponsored? There is an honourable history of the sponsorship of short films, including the support of the Post Office historically and companies like BMW, Levi's and others more recently. Every art form can obtain sponsorship, even the most difficult targeted at minority interests. Short films have yet to take advantage of this, though. Festivals, on the other hand, including short film festivals, have managed to generate significant private support: in the case of Brief Encounters, 70 per cent of income is from private sources. As the British Film Institute's *Low Budget Funding Guide* states: 'Filmmakers have not tended to be the first in the queue when talking to businesses about sponsorship, although there is no reason why film or video production should not be successful in this area.'[1] Some support from the private sector might be possible. There will only be limited cash, however, with most support being help in kind.

To succeed, film-makers need to become more aware of the needs of sponsors, and of funders. Chris Chandler, author of the guide, says that while 'short film-makers are getting better at blagging stuff and not paying for everything', they are 'very, very poor at getting sponsorship'.[2] One company that sponsored Brief Encounters said those seeking funds make fundamental errors. These include a failure to understand what the company is about and what the company wants; wrong timing (everyone needs a lead-in period); impossible requests. Simply by looking at a company, seeing what they would like out of the relationship, and building a partnership with them make success possible.

There have been many good examples of partnerships between companies, charitable trusts and short film-makers in recent years. Sadly, most have been short-lived. Initiatives involving BT Payphones, Channel 5, the *Daily Telegraph*, the *Independent on Sunday*, the Jerwood Foundation, Kodak and Warner's Cinemas have all seen major interest. The Jerwood Prize attracted 3,000 entries. Neither lasted more than one year, even though the two films that won were good films and deserved a wider release. The Jerwood Charitable Foundation, the First Film Foundation and BBC Drama Shorts now support the Jerwood First Film Shorts Prize.

Perhaps the most significant initiative was made by Levi's. Seeing a link between short films and those who buy its products, as well as wanting to get away from straight advertising, the company started to support festivals and show short films on monitors at their flagship London store. With Alliance Atlantis Releasing, Levi's then supported the production of four short films. Going against the trend of short films being seen as a cultural product for a few, Levi's insisted that the films be com-

mercially viable and shown in cinemas. Eventually, the films were released with features, they were shown on Virgin airlines and one helped open Film Four.

Though difficult to secure, funding does exist. At the same time the means to
make, distribute and exhibit short films are open now to virtually everyone for minimal cost. And the future promises digital editing, production, projection and direct
distribution. There is a downside. Short films may not get any better – any number
of terrible films that previously would have been sent deservedly to the loft will now
be available. And that brings us to a final point: make sure that the film is good,
especially the script. Attend all the workshops you can, take advantage of training
courses, watch short films, and feature films, and use script-reading services. These
are all simple guidelines, but they are often not followed.

Getting the film shown

Few want only to make a film. Most want their work to be seen by as wide an audience as possible. There are many options open to the short film-maker: send a video
round television, airlines, festivals, the cinema and the Internet. Only a very few
films will receive a cinema release. Some British chains, such as Zoo, and some
regional film theatres have an honourable history of showing shorts. But even here
opportunities are limited due to print availability – some prints cost more than the
actual production – and the difficulty of linking the short to a feature.

Recent experience suggests mixed news. The collapse of Jane Balfour Films
removed from the scene one of the few distributors willing to consider short films.
Better news is the launch of Short Circuit, a Lottery-funded partnership between
London Film and Video Development Agency, Yorkshire Media Production Agency
and Showroom Cinema in Sheffield, which aims to get short films into cinemas. It
is done for passion: no-one gets paid, but at least some films get seen. It is market-
ing-centred in that it links carefully the right short films to features. Most exhibitors,
they believe, want to show shorts. What they don't want is hassle or cost. The first
to be seen was *Love is All*, a three-minute animated film. *Suicidal Dog* (2000) went
out with *Chuck&Buck*. No films are more than ten minutes long.

Short Circuit is a good model. But the problems in establishing the project – in
addition to the National Lottery, funds come from the Arts Council of England,
European Regional Development Fund, Yorkshire Arts, North West Arts and the
Film Council – show how difficult it is to make short film distribution a sustainable
venture.

For most short film-makers, festivals still provide the main chance to show a film
at the cinema, even if it is only one or two screenings. There are some great short
film festivals: Clermont Ferrand, Oberhausen, Tampere, Brief Encounters in Bristol and Rushes Soho Shorts in London, and excellent short film programmes at
festivals in London and Edinburgh. Getting a film shown at a festival is hard though

– the ratio of films submitted to those shown is around ten to one in the Bristol experience, and likely to be much higher in the big international festivals. It should go without saying that the film should be good (though most aren't) and that festival rules should be followed.

We have been associated most with Brief Encounters – the Bristol Short Film Festival. Looking at the festival's history, its aims and some of the realities of getting accepted may help film-makers in their attempts to get films screened. Brief Encounters was established after the refusal of the International Animation Festival to return to the city. A Bristol short film festival was proposed initially by staff in Aardman and BBC Bristol. Originally anticipated as a one-off event to celebrate the centenary of cinema, good audiences in 1995 led to Brief Encounters being launched as an annual festival the following year.

Brief Encounters has been a great success. It has combined vision with pragmatism, careful financial management with proactive marketing, high-profile ventures with community and avant-garde presentations. It has no doubt been helped by Bristol being the home of many successful short film companies, including BBC Bristol, HTV, Aardman and the animation company bolexbrothers and by a business sector in the city that wanted to make things happen and were prepared to support new initiatives.

Around 180 films are shown annually. Most of these are new films. There are also retrospectives. Each festival focuses on a particular country or region – Ireland, France, the Nordic countries have all been featured, as well as film-makers including John Smith in 2000. Avant-garde film-makers have regular slots as do the best British and international films, and there are programmes dedicated to new student films and films from Bristol and the South West. In addition, as part of long-term audience development, an education programme with free film screenings, a pack and sometimes a video is run annually. Workshops on screenwriting, production and conferences on the National Lottery and short films and on developing sponsorship for short films have also been organised.

There are more lofty aims. These range from selling Bristol to the outside world as a centre for media production and a festival city to promoting future short film production. Though difficult to measure, these have been achieved. The profile of the city is stronger, with film-makers and the media. Audiences have also been good, reaching an average 70 per cent of capacity (the usual for independent films is 40 per cent). Animated Encounters, a partner festival launched in 1999, has been an even greater success.

It is not easy to run a film festival. It is not easy running any activity reliant on funding and sponsorship. Most major festivals are well established and benefit from the long-standing support of funders and sponsors. Even these find it difficult, however. Audience choice for leisure is much wider, and eagerly fought over. It is worth it, though: audiences experience new and classic films in the place where they should be shown. Many films stand out even years after being seen. The work of bolexbrothers and Aardman in Bristol, *Thirty-five Aside*, *Where's Bingo Betty?*, *Tout le Monde Descend* (*Last Stop*, 1997), (about a young African condemned by three bus inspectors to be deported for not having a ticket) and *Ballad of the Skeletons* (1997), Gus Van Sant's film of Allen Ginsberg reading his classic poem to a montage of news items and music by Philip Glass and Paul McCartney.

Festivals are exciting, and Brief Encounters is regarded highly. But most of the work is routine. The search for staff, volunteers and overall management takes up much of the time. As does the constant search for money. Only when this is done can programming begin. Programming can be exciting, but it is also dull. Watching 800 films annually is impossible, especially in the few months between submission date and decisions. It is often clear from the first few minutes if a film is going to make it.

Film-makers, and those wanting to run festivals, need to learn from this. Do build relationships with festival staff; do provide stills; do fill in the official entry forms. Most of all make good films. The best films in Brief Encounters capture the imagination right from the start. And don't ignore the short in short film. The best films are often those that are really short.

Television

So festivals provide one opportunity. Television is another, but here things look bleak. Short films used to find a welcome on terrestrial television, but such high-profile initiatives such as the BBC's *10 x 10*, which featured commissioned productions, and Channel 4's programme of shorts, *The Shooting Gallery*, either no longer exist or are shown at the television margins. Digital broadcasting is better. Film Four, MTV, BskyB and BBC Choice show shorts, and *Artsworld* is working in partnership with Rushes Soho Shorts.

As Keith Wright points out in his interview, there are good opportunities with regional independent television, with broadcasters linking with arts boards in the production of short films. HTV's *Western Lights* initiative is a good example of this.

HTV is also involved in partnership with Brief Encounters. They support the festival because there is a 'programme connect'. Each year, four programmes are broadcast about the festival – one a documentary, the others made up of films being shown in Brief Encounters. Not only does this publicise the festival, it also gives profile to the film-makers involved.

The short film and the digital revolution

So what is left: the Internet and the digital revolution. The digital revolution could create – some would argue is creating – a revolution in short film production, marketing, distribution and exhibition. A new democracy for independent film-makers has even been predicted. Some believe, indeed, that the Internet provides a whole new viewing experience, 'short attention span theater' according to a Warner Bros. executive.[3]

There is still no money, however. Though Internet companies have created a market, the first market for shorts since the early days of cinema, giving film-makers a choice of who to sell to, it is clear that the economics of the short film will not change. Competition for content turns traditional supply and demand theory on its head. Though a fee may be paid for some films, most film-makers will provide, often willingly, their work free of charge for exposure.

Given their length and potential audience, shorts, of all films, are most suited most to digital exhibition. In an interview for *Salon* magazine following Sundance 2000, Patrick Lynn from MediaTrip.com said that short films now have an excellent life. It's 'their day in the sun'. However, he feels that short film-makers have yet to see the opportunities of the Internet. Short film-makers make 'films for a reason, and one of the main reasons is to get some exposure. Now, another reason is to get some money up front. With the Internet, that can totally happen.' However, he is sceptical that there will ever be shorts in cinemas, as there used to be. They will certainly never replace advertising, which is lucrative. In the future 'if it's an "event" short film, you can help sell a feature by bringing in people that may want to see the short film'.[4]

How real is this revolution? After the initial hype – and there is a lot of hype out there – it is wise to take a more sober view. At the 2000 Sundance Film Festival there was much talk of the Internet boom. It was said that shorts had come of age. Dot.coms were everywhere and huge parties were hosted for new young film-makers. Unsurprisingly, there was a boom in submissions: 2,000 shorts were submitted – hundreds more than in 1999 – though only sixty-five were selected.[5]

A year later the position was not so good. The gold rush had subsided. In the intervening year, prominent sites had disappeared and Pop.com, Stephen Spielberg's Internet film site, had failed to materialise. There remained a touching hope, and not a little truth, to the failures though. A representative of Shortbuzz.com, which collapsed in 2000, claimed that 'Filmmakers are the big winners in the online experiment. Filmmakers have never had such opportunities. They can get more exposure from one day on the Web than in an entire year on the festival circuit.'[6] Sundance also kept faith with the potential of new technology with the launch of the Sundance Online Film Festival for six weeks in January 2001 with twelve shorts. This was not the first online festival. In March 2000, Yahoo! held their own online festival and followed this eight months later with the publication of a short film directory, a single point of reference for finding data on short films. Sundance believes that on-line film can help independent cinema. 'Regardless of how you and I feel about movies on the internet,' said Ian Calderon, the festival's digital initiatives director, 'the truth is that the internet is the off-off-Broadway of filmmaking today.'[7] His colleague, Shari Frilot, added:

> I think these digital filmmakers can take us back to exploring the potential of what independent cinema can do. With the commercialization of independent filmmaking, it has become more and more important for films to have stars and bigger budgets. But online, you don't need to worry about any of that. It's you, your computer, and your ideas.[8]

It is not just the re-emergence of independent film that the Internet promises. It is the opportunity to interact with the film, look at different viewpoints, even to experiment with different endings.

Getting the film on the Web is one matter. It is questionable, though, if people can watch it given that current technology makes viewing difficult. Even though most shorts shown on the Internet are less than ten minutes long, unless they are Flash animation, they take an age to download through the 56k modems most in use. The quality of some sites is good, though this does not make up for the poor quality of film presentation, at least as most people experience it at present. This will remain until broadband is more widely available.

There are success stories, though. The most important Internet short has been Joe Nussbaum and Joseph Levy's *George Lucas in Love*, a nine-minute short spoofing the feature hit *Shakespeare in Love* and the producer himself. Within nine months of being released on MediaTrip.com it had reached 1 million viewers and was also number one in the Amazon.com video charts. By January 2001 it had sold nearly 50,000 copies. Though *George Lucas in Love* is the exception, not the rule, and despite all the challenges of operating in the new world, some Web companies have succeeded in bringing short films to new audiences.

Who are the main players? Any record of short film on the Internet will be out of date quickly. A quick search hits fifty sites. There are sites commissioned by companies – BMW and Absolut Vodka; sites made up of college shorts; indie sites; sites devoted to films made according to Dogma 95 principles; sites devoted to a single film-maker or a single country; sites solely showing animation (especially Flash); sites showing material made solely for the Internet. There are sites linked to film festivals, sites devoted to underground and black film sites.

Three leading companies are Atom, ifilm and The Bit Screen. Atom aims to be 'a leading entertainment provider for businesses and consumers' (*www.atomfilms.com* and *www.shockwave.com*) and offers games, films and animation products. In addition to the Internet, Atom uses television, airlines and mobile devices to distribute product. In April 2001, Atom was claiming 10 million unique viewers, with 6 million showings of short films monthly. Sixteen- to thirty-year-olds make up most of their audience.

In addition to investors, Atom's financial support comes from syndication rights, with sales of films to airlines and television, sponsorship and some advertising (Atom believes that shorts could even play in petrol stations and lifts). Sponsors include Swatch, Ford and Volkswagen. They have commissioned Bernardo Bertolucci and David Lynch to make ten-minute films in a new series. Atom also supports new film-makers. In September 2000, with Birken Interactive Studio, the on-line entertainment company established by Leonardo DiCaprio, Atom launched the Savage Sideshow, an on-line short film festival. In December 2000, it announced the first community-selected 360-degree short film which allows viewers to watch the film from different directions. Building on Amy Talkington's *The New Arrival* (2000), the first 360-degree film, Atom's 'Insiders' chose Joe Riley's *Coming of Age* (2000) as the award winner.

ifilm (*www.ifilm.com*) was launched in October 1998. It claims to be 'the leading authority for the emerging world of internet film, and the most popular online resource for film fans, film-makers and entertainment-industry professionals'.[9] Its mission is 'to enable the discovery of new talent'.[10] It has links to over 15,000 Internet films, aiming to put on the site any film received within twenty-four hours. ifilm has twelve special-interest channels, including drama, erotica, experimental, action, gay and lesbian, spoof, and sites on special communities such as women's film and teens. It has a range of partnerships with Yahoo! and the Independent Film Channel. ifilm established a partnership with AMC Theaters in 2000 to ensure that films they stream can be shown first at a cinema so that they qualify for Academy Awards. AMC want to 'tap into the creative explosion occurring online among filmmakers'.[11]

The Bit Screen (*www.thebitscreen.com*) is seen as the arthouse equivalent to the more commercial Atom and ifilm (though these distinctions are meaningless when you see what is on offer). What it does differently is to exhibit films made especially for the Web. Nora Barry, the creator, sees similarities between the early days of the Web and the early days of cinema. She says:

> We've come to view those early films as art, while the overall perception of Internet films is that they are 'flash animations' created by 21-year old kids. And yet, in a way, that [perception] is unfair because it implies that Internet films will not evolve past where they are now to become art in their own right … I don't imagine those early filmmakers knew they were creating something that would later be viewed in museums. Those films are very crude, both technologically and narratively. And yet … we see the foundations of all the beauty and special effects that we do not take for granted in cinema. So the crudeness doesn't matter – it's part of what makes those films so fascinating. . . . I can see some of those foundations being laid in these early Internet films.[12]

Internet writer Michael Wolff gives a less sanguine view. 'On the one hand,' he says,

> you have the explosion of content from, quite literally, millions of new content creators.
> And on the other hand, you have the constant fracturing of the audience base. And on a
> weird third hand, you have the traditional content producers desperately trying to find a
> place, and constantly reassuring themselves that there will be a place, for the old, brand-
> name, big-money content. The end result, I think, is that we are heading towards a hitless
> world in which the content that survives is the content that is produced most cheaply.[13]

One interesting entrant into Web shorts is BMW, which has hired major film-makers
to make a series 'The Hire' about cars. Directors include Ang Lee, John Franken-
heimer and Guy Ritchie. The main outlet for the films, which are really commercials,
has been *www.bmwfilms.com*. However, some have been shown at Cannes. There
has even been a trailer.

BMW, Atom and others represent one end of the Internet shorts spectrum. It is
useful to look at how Brief Encounters has tried to use the Internet and digital technology. Though there has been talk of having a Web-based film festival and live
streaming of events and films, it is in the production of very short films and in marketing that the festival has embraced digital technology. Depict! – the short, short
film competition – was set up for the second festival. Originally inviting photosto-
ryboards of up to thirty-six photographs, the competition in recent years has called
for the submission of short films, most of which are shot digitally, of up to ninety
seconds. Inevitably, though, it is in marketing where Brief Encounters has used the
Web most effectively with its own website (*www.brief-encounters.co.uk* and its partner site, *www.animated-encounters.co.uk*). Brief Encounters has built partnerships
with Internet companies, most notably Atom (at least until the company retrenched
in 2001 and the relationship ended).

So the news is mixed, as always with short films. Sites are available, some pay-
ment is made in some cases, and shorts have a higher profile than ever before.
Broadband technology will create a better viewing experience. Whether you will
want to watch them, or be allowed to, is another matter. A film would have to be
very short to be seen in a lift and at a gas station. Will employers tolerate their staff
logging off from work, logging on to the Net, to watch *George Lucas in Love*, some
animation, or the latest *Angry Kid*? And what about the audience? The viewing
experience will be limited, confined to a tiny screen, where the carefully crafted film
will be reduced to its minimum to fit the technology. Even as a 'lean-forward
medium' it resembles television ultimately and is perhaps worse: there is no substitute for seeing a film – any film – on the big screen with an audience. There is also
the problem of few having access to the broadband networks needed for speedy

download, though this will arrive eventually, and is already present in some commercial companies and universities, substantial markets in themselves.

Yet the Internet is of value. It promotes short films more than the cinema does, and provides often the only opportunity to see shorts in a sustained way outside of festivals and television. But it will not create the stream of income needed to make short films, nor pay for them in full after production in all but very special cases. In terms of short films, the Internet will play a role in marketing and distribution, perhaps a pre-eminent role eventually, but it will always be the junior partner of cinema, as the creativity starts with the film not the Web. Finding support for films to be made and getting them shown in cinemas remain the key issues. What should not be ignored is the potential of Web-only films and art. Using the capacity of the Internet to create new work is one of the opportunities open to film-makers and artists. The Film Council's New Cinema Fund to support innovative shorts using digital technology will provide increased resources.

What should be done?

To take advantage of this intensely competitive position, film-makers, distributors, exhibitors and funders need to work together. It is essential that there is better training for short film-makers that goes beyond the one-day festival course. Training should be in screenwriting, but it should also be in management and marketing. Short Circuit needs to be expanded and there should be better support for short film festivals.

There is a wider need. Funding bodies need to launch a major marketing and education programme about short films to convince people that they are worth watching and persuade distributors and exhibitors that they are worth showing. More research is needed also. There is only limited information available on the history of shorts, and no regular database of films made or in production. This offers fertile ground for universities seeking projects for students. Why not go further and establish a centre for the short film, which could be an archive, research group, training centre and act as an advocate?

Conclusion

For film-makers, the key lesson from all the interviews, and from the wider research, is to keep at it. Those who are committed can create films, but partnerships need to be built and relationships nurtured. Short films remain essential. Cinema would not only be a poorer experience without shorts, it simply wouldn't exist. Short films are essential for the future development of the moving image and of film-makers. They are as necessary and as valuable now as they were at the very beginning of cinema.

Notes

1. See Chris Chandler, *Low Budget Funding Guide, 98/99* (London: BFI, 1998).
2. Interview with Chris Chandler, 1998.
3. J. Banister, quoted in J. Geirland, 'Short Attention Span Theater', *Salon.com*, 21 July 1999.
4. Quoted in M. Ebner, 'Who Wants Short Shorts?', *Salon.com*, 31 January 2000.
5. R. Lyman, 'Ferocious Buzz at Sundance, for Better or for Worse', *New York Times*, 20 January 2000.
6. Quoted in M. Hart, 'A Comeback for Short Films is Linked to the Web', *New York Times*, 14 January 2001.
7. Quoted in J. Silverman, 'Sundance is Online's Big Chance', *Wired News*, 18 January 2001.
8. Ibid.
9. From ifilm website.
10. Jon Fitzgeraldi, ifilm's vice president of programming, quoted in J. Spingarn-Koff, 'Net Films Score Oscar Loophole', *Wired News*, 23 June 2000.
11. Ibid.
12. Quoted in S. Rea, 'Internet Festival Heralds Democracy in Filmmaking', *The Philadelphia Enquirer*, 19 March 2000.
13. Quoted in Q. Curtis, 'Coming to your screen.com', *Daily Telegraph*, 26 February 2000.

6

Short Film-making Resource Guide

This guide provides details of websites, funding sources, short film festivals (and festivals that have significant short film programmes), short film distribution agencies and journals. Though extensive, we would not claim this guide to be definitive. New websites set up regularly (often disappearing just as quickly), and others change over time. Moreover, links change: by the time of publication, 'linkrot' may have set in. In addition, ongoing developments in public funding in the UK will mean that many organisations change their names, and in some cases their contact details by the end of 2002.

ON-LINE FILMS
The following websites were on-line in October 2001.

Afilmcinado.net
http://www.afilmcinado.net
A site for watching and submitting independent films using RealPlayer and QuickTime.

always independent
http://www.alwaysindependentfilms.com
Aims to develop new revenue and distribution opportunities, and provide an exhibition platform for independent entertainment creators with a library of over 2,000 feature-length films, short films, animation and TV-like series available to view in streaming formats.

Apple iMovie Gallery
http://www.apple.com/imovie/gallery

Showcase of professional and amateur works created using iMovie.

AtomFilms
http://atomfilms.shockwave.com/af/home
Web film site that is part of AtomShockwave, an independent company that has an extensive catalogue of game, film and animation content distributed across the Internet, broadband services and mobile devices, as well as traditional outlets.

BijouFlix
http://www.bijoucafe.com
Works as a virtual cinema co-op, allowing customers to find cinema works available at three fee levels (free, micropay and all access) while also allowing the makers to directly profit each time their films are viewed.

The Bit Screen

http://www.thebitscreen.com
A showcase for original Internet short films and Web series, adding new programmes each week.

BMW Films

http://www.bmwfilms.com/site_layout/index.asp
Featuring short films by award-winning directors.

BritShorts

http://www.britshorts.com
Offers British and European short films, industry news, production news and a facility to both read and write reviews.

Camp Chaos

http://www.campchaos.com
Offering regularly updated Flash-animated shows and games, Camp Chaos was officially launched in July 1998 and became an incorporated animation and film production studio in January 1999.

Cinema Now

http://www.cinemanow.com
Broadband movies on demand, including shorts.

Culturejam

http://www.culturejam.com
An on-line, on-going festival and showcase for independent streaming media that includes features, shorts and episodic A/V adventure that aim to subvert mainstream media culture.

DFILM

http://www.dfilm.com
DFILM's site lets visitors download movies from its travelling and on-line festival, read interviews with directors talking about how their films were made, buy and sell equipment or trade tips with other DFILM members, and get information on how to create digital film themselves.

Director Unknown

http://www.directorunknown.com
A collaborative venture in which a group of film-makers got together one day a month to shoot an episode for a thriller series, the name of the writer/director of each episode being drawn from a hat.

Evan Mather

http://www.evanmather.com
The official distribution channel for digital films made by film-maker Evan Mather.

filmfilm.com

http://www.filmfilm.com
Produces, promotes and screens independent film via the Internet. It provides tools, webspace, viewing and reviews.

Film Four

http://www.filmfour.com/screeningRoom/sr.jsp
Short films, trailers, clips, submissions and competitions.

Flash Film Festival

http://www.flashfilmfestival.com
Site for a conference dedicated to
supporting the community of designers
and developers using Macromedia
Flash and other products that write
using the Macromedia SWF format.

Get Out There

http://www.getoutthere.com/index2.cfm
BT site that includes opportunity to view
and vote on film shorts and animations.

hahabonk

http://www.hahabonk.com
A UK-based producer of cross-platform
entertainment programming, for
customers including BBC, Channel 4,
the Paramount Comedy Channel,
Freeserve and PlayUK.

Heavy.com

http://www.heavy.com
Site offering films, music, games and
shows, and a monthly bonus box in the
mail to premium members.

HotWired: Animation Express

http://hotwired.lycos.com/animation
Gathers together a collection of
animations on the Web, offering films
by up-and-coming animators as well as
seasoned professionals, longer stories
as well as 'quick hits', and work by
Pixar Animation Studios and Spike and
Mike's Festival of Animation.

Hypnotic

http://www.hypnotic.com/index.asp
An entertainment and marketing

services company distributing one of
the world's largest libraries of short
films and animations. It works with
emerging film-makers to acquire,
develop, produce and distribute
independent films, television properties
and commercials.

Icebox

http://www.icebox.com
Original animated shorts and webisodes
by established talent, such as the
creators of popular television shows like
The Simpsons and *Frasier*, as well as the
best work from emerging writers.

Icuna

http://www.icuna.com
Offers subscribers access to one-
minute films every working day, and
has a website that includes an archive
of films and a chat room.

ifilm

http://www.ifilm.com
Offers independent films with an on-
line video on demand library.

in-movies

http://www.in-movies.co.uk
Highlights British short films, as well as
offering news, script submission,
competitions, and a film forum.

Intensity TV

http://www.kqed.org/tv/productions/
intensitytv
KQED short film anthology series
presents a selection of films from
around the globe.

JibJab

http://www.jibjab.com/jibjab.html
An interactive and broadcast animation
studio offering cartoons, screensavers,
e-cards and downloads.

mainestream.nu

http://www.mainestream.nu
Streaming short films and music by
Maine-based artists.

Mediatrip

http://www.mediatrip.com
Produces original entertainment to
create franchise characters and
properties.

The New Venue

http://www.newvenue.com/index2.html
Features short independent films for
the Internet and the Palm OS which
aim to break aesthetic and technical
barriers.

Newmediaman

http://www.newmediaman.com
Digital short films by Vasily Shumov
and other members of a media arts
group.

Pitch TV

http://www.pitchtv.com/issue004/
index.html
A New York City-based studio using
the Internet to experiment with
presenting new work on the Web. It
also offers a festival of short films, an
on-line magazine, Flash samples and a
spotlight on independent film-makers.

plugincinema

http://www.plugincinema.com
UK-based Internet exhibition plus
information and discussion group.

The Quickie

http://www.thequickie.com
Billed as one of the Internet's premiere
cartoon animation sites.

Reel Screen

http://www.reelscreen.com
A creative community and business to
business operation, providing a free
platform for new film-making and
composing talent by broadcasting
media on-line.

ShortTV

http://www.shorttv.com
An independent short film channel and
Internet company.

Shortvillage

http://www.shortvillage.com
Features short films, film-maker
interviews, production tips, a database
of players, an opportunity to test ideas
and projects, and discussion.

sputnik7

http://www.sputnik7.com/
index-menu.jsp
A broadcast network offering a mix of
independent music, film and anime
programming via interactive video
stations, audio stations, videos on
demand and digital downloads.

StudentReel.com

http://www.studentreel.com
A place for student film-makers to showcase their work, including categories such as 3D computer, live action, stop motion and experimental.

The Surrey Stick Figure of Death

http://www.c-cat.demon.co.uk/theatre
A one-man-band operation from David Thorpe who animates a weekly cartoon of stick-figure massacres.

The Sync Online Film Festival

http://www.thesync.com
Offers shorts and serials, using RealPlayer, aimed at the needs and expectations of the Net-generation audience.

Undergroundfilm.com

http://www.undergroundfilm.com
Site creating an on-line film community by showing the work of independent film-makers.

Urban Chillers

http://www.urbanchillers.com Shows short urban myth horror movies and welcomes contributions from film-makers.

Urban Desires

http://www.urbandesires.com/
index_flash.html
Showing made-for-Web experimental film using QuickTime.

Urban Entertainment

http://www.urbanentertainment.com
A production, exhibition and distribution company focused on African American and urban-themed entertainment content across multiple platforms and distribution channels.

Waking Streams

http://www.wakingdream.net/streams
A repository for streaming media content, and a showcase of films and videos created by TMTV Productions.

ON-LINE FILM DIRECTORIES

4mp.com

http://www.4mp.com
The official guide for Rich Media sites featuring entertainment, business, knowledge, chat and shopping.

Episodic: Online Soap Opera Review

http://www.episodicreview.com
Articles, coming attractions, episode recaps and reader critiques of Web soap operas and dramas.

Internet Soap Operas

http://goan.com/soap.html
Guide to weekly Web shows.

National Archive of Film Shorts (NAFS)

http:www.nafs.co.uk
A free depository of shorts of 30 minutes duration or less made by UK-based independent film-makers. Offers a catalogue, database and annual awards.

Soap Operas on the Web

http://home.earthlink.net/~merlin200
Short reviews and links to Web-based soap operas and comedies.

Yahoo Shorts

http://movies.yahoo.com/shorts
A guide to short films on the Web, with browsing by genre, featured shorts and sites, chart listing and player downloads.

FUNDING SOURCES FOR SHORT FILMS IN THE UK AND THE IRISH REPUBLIC
Animate!

http://www.animateonline.org
Provides funding and advice for UK animators.

The Arts Council of Northern Ireland

http://www.artscouncil-ni.org
Lottery funding is available to formally constituted organisations as well as film production companies whose principals live, work and are resident in Northern Ireland for tax purposes. All genres and subject matter are considered, including single feature films, drama series, short films, experimental films, documentaries and animation. Digital media productions will also be considered, where there is a high proportion of moving image content. Short films intended exclusively for broadcast or release on video are excluded.
The Arts Council of Northern Ireland
MacNeice House
77 Malone Road
Belfast
BT9 6AQ
Tel: 0 28 90 385200
Fax: 0 28 90 661715

The Arts Council of Wales

http://www.ccc-acw.org.uk
Lottery funding for film production in Wales is intended to increase the overall level of film production and contribute to the growth of a national film industry which reflects Welsh society and culture. Script development awards are also available.

There is a Lottery division at each of the council's area offices.
9 Museum Place
Cardiff
CF10 3NX
Tel: 02920 376500
Fax: 02920 221447
e-mail: information@ccc-acw.org.uk

6 Gardd Llydaw
Jackson Lane
Carmarthen
SA31 1QD
Tel: 01267 234248
Fax: 01267 233084

36 Prince's Drive
Colwyn Bay
LL29 8LA
Tel: 01492 533440
Fax: 01492 533677

Cineworks

http://www.cineworks.co.uk/
Glasgow Media Access Centre,
3rd Floor, 34 Albion Street
Glasgow
G11 1LH
Tel: 0141 553 2620
Fax: 0141 553 2660
e-mail: CineworksFilms@aol.com

A short film production initiative which commissions original and innovative films from emergent Scottish talent.

Commedia Millennium Awards

http://awards.commedia.org.uk/index2.htm
Community Media Association Head Office tel: 0114 279 5219
Community Media Association, London tel: 020 7700 0100 x234
Offers grants for individuals and small groups of individuals who want to make a media production that will be of benefit to the community. This is an initiative of the Community Media Association with funding from the Millennium Commission.

English Regional Arts Boards

http://www.arts.org.uk
The ten English regional arts boards are partners with the Arts Council of England, the Film Council and local authorities in developing, sustaining and promoting the arts in England. The money is used to fund arts organisations and individual artists working in a wide variety of art forms including film. Each regional arts board will have its own funding procedures and criteria, and should be contacted individually for information on funds that might be available. From April 2002 all regional arts boards joined the Arts Council of England in one unified structure. At the time of writing, no changes had been made to contact details of individual arts boards. This is expected to take place by the end of 2002. In the meantime, the regions and their contact details are as follows:

East England Arts
http://www.eab.org.uk
Cherry Hinton Hall, Cherry Hinton Road, Cambridge, CB1 8DW
Tel: 01223 215 355
Fax: 01223 248 075
Minicom: 01223 412031
e-mail: info@eearts.co.uk

East Midlands Arts
http://www.arts.org.uk/directory/regions/east_mid/index.html
Mountfields House, Epinal Way, Loughborough, Leics, LE11 0QE
Tel: 01509 218 292
Fax: 01509 262 214
e-mail: info@em-arts.co.uk

London Arts
http://www.arts.org.uk/directory/regions/london/index.html
2 Pear Tree Court, London, EC1R 0DS
Tel: 020 7608 6100
Fax: 020 7608 4100
Textphone: 020 7608 4101
e-mail: info@lonab.co.uk

Northern Arts
http://www.arts.org.uk/directory/regions/northern/index.html
Central Square, Forth Street, Newcastle upon Tyne, NE1 3PJ
Tel: 0191 255 8500
Fax: 0191 230 1020
e-mail: info@northernarts.org.uk

North West Arts Board
http://www.arts.org.uk/directory/regions
/north_west/index.html
Manchester House, 22 Bridge Street,
Manchester, M3 3AB
Tel: 0161 834 6644
Fax: 0161 834 6969
Minicom: 0161 834 9131
e-mail: info@nwarts.co.uk

Southern Arts
http://www.arts.org.uk/directory/regions
/southern/index.html
13 St Clement Street, Winchester,
Hants, SO23 9DQ
Tel: 01962 855 099
Fax: 0870 242 1257
e-mail: info@southernarts.co.uk

South East Arts
http://www.arts.org.uk/directory/regions
/south_east/index.html
Union House, Eridge Road, Tunbridge
Wells, Kent, TN4 8HF
Tel: 01892 507 200
Fax: 0870 242 1259
e-mail: info@seab.co.uk

South West Arts
http://www.swa.co.uk
Bradninch Place, Gandy Street, Exeter,
EX4 3LS
Tel: 01392 218 188
Fax: 01392 229 229
Minicom: 01392 433503
e-mail: info@swa.co.uk

West Midlands Arts
http://www.arts.org.uk/directory/regions
/west_mid/index.html
82 Granville Street, Birmingham, B1 2LH
Tel: 0121 631 3121
Fax: 0121 643 7239
Minicom: 0121 643 2815
e-mail: info@west-midlands-arts.co.uk

Yorkshire Arts
http://www.arts.org.uk/directory/regions
/york/index.html
21 Bond Street, Dewsbury, West
Yorkshire WF13 1AX
Tel: 01924 455 555
Fax: 01924 466 522
Minicom: 01924 438585
e-mail: info@yarts.co.uk

The Film Council
http://www.filmcouncil.org.uk
Film Council
10 Little Portland Street
London
W1W 7JG
Tel: 020 7861 7861
Fax: 020 7861 7862
e-mail for general enquiries: info@
filmcouncil.org.uk
The Film Council has been established
by the Department for Culture, Media
and Sport (DCMS) as the strategic
body for the UK film industry, and is a
Lottery distributor for various new
production and productions funds. Of
particular interest to film-makers are
the following:

The Development Fund
Contact:
development@filmcouncil.org.uk
This fund aims to broaden the quality,

range and ambition of British film projects and talent being developed. More specifically, the aim is to raise the quality of screenplays produced in or from the UK through strategically targeted development initiatives engaging with the industry at first on a project by project basis.

The New Cinema Fund

Contact: newcinemafund@filmcouncil.org.uk

This fund aims to encourage unique ideas, innovative approaches and new voices. Its initial funding programmes include:

New Cinema Fund/Film Four Lab Joint Shorts Scheme

Contact: shorts@filmcouncil.org.uk

The New Cinema Fund and Film Four Lab are each investing £250,000 a year divided between four major schemes. Neither the Film Council nor Film Four Lab will be accepting any applications directly but will instead be working with production companies to manage and deliver the schemes. Details are available on the Film Council website.

New Cinema Fund – Digital Shorts Funded Regionally

The New Cinema Fund has selected organisations in each region and nation of the UK to work with as partners to enable film-makers to make innovative shorts using digital technology. Information on digital shorts and who to apply to in each region is at

http://www.filmcouncil.org.uk/funding.lasso?p=newdsrf.

First Light

A pilot project running from April 2001 to the summer of 2002 (now in its second year) aimed at giving seven- to eighteen- year-olds the chance to make a digital short film. Further information is available at http://www.filmcouncil.org.uk/filmmakers/firstmovies.html.

The First Film Fund

http://www.firstfilm.co.uk
First Film Foundation
9 Bourlet Close
London
W1P 1PJ
Tel: 020 7580 2111

The First Film Foundation is a charity that exists to help new British writers, producers and directors. Schemes include the Jerwood First Film Shorts Prize and the Studio Film Completion Fund.

first take films

http://www.firsttakefilms.com/frames.htm
first take films Limited
Anglia House
Anglia Television
Norwich
Norfolk
NR1 3JG
Tel: 0 1603 756 879
Fax: 0 1603 767 191
e-mail: firsttake@angliatv.co.uk

A cultural agency whose principal function is 'to facilitate, encourage and promote the creative arts of film, video and moving image production in the East of England'. The agency commissions approximately ten films each year for Anglia Television made as independent productions, and runs a scriptwriting development programme for new screenwriters and a number of training and development schemes for writers, directors and producers. Also responsible for the East of England Media Production Fund (a joint venture of the Eastern Arts Board and Anglia Television).

The Irish Film Board
http://www.filmboard.ie
Rockfort House
St Augustine Street
Galway
Ireland
Tel: +353 91 561398
Fax: +353 91 561405
e-mail: info@filmboard.ie
Provides loans and equity investment to independent Irish film-makers to assist in the development and production of Irish films. The Short Cuts scheme aims to add to the range and scope of Irish short film-making and to encourage new talent in all areas of film production.

The London Film and Video Development Agency
http://www.lfvda.demon.co.uk/
114 Whitfield Street
London
W1P 5RW
Tel: 020 7383 7755
Fax: 020 7383 7745
Provides funding, information, advice and professional support to makers of independent film, video and television in London.

MEDIA
http://www.mediadesk.co.uk/media.taf
This five-year programme of the European Union aims to strengthen the competitiveness of the European film, TV and new media industries and to increase international circulation of European audiovisual product. All MEDIA guidelines and application forms are published as single documents known as Calls for Proposals. There are four UK offices:

MEDIA Desk England
http://www.mediadesk.co.uk/england
c/o Film Council
10 Little Portland Street
London
W1W 7JG
Tel: 020 7861 7507
Fax: 020 7861 7867
e-mail: england@mediadesk.co.uk

MEDIA Antenna Wales
http://www.mediadesk.co.uk/wales
c/o SGRIN The Bank
10 Mount Stuart Square
Cardiff Bay
Cardiff
CF10 5EE
Tel: 02920 333 304
Fax: 02920 333 320
e-mail: antenna@sgrinwales.
demon.co.uk

MEDIA Antenna Scotland
http://www.mediadesk.co.uk/scotland

249 West George Street
Glasgow
G2 4QE
Tel: 0141 302 1776/7
Fax: 0141 302 1715
e-mail:
media.scotland@scottishscreen.com

MEDIA Services Northern Ireland
http://www.mediadesk.co.uk/
northernireland
c/o Northern Ireland Film Commission
21 Ormeau Avenue
Belfast
BT2 8HD
Tel: 02890 232 444
Fax: 02890 239 918
e-mail: media@nifc.co.uk

Scottish Screen
http://www.scottishscreen.com/index.taf
Scottish Screen
249 West George Street
Glasgow
G2 4RB
Tel: 0141 302 1700
Fax: 0141 302 1711
e-mail: info@scottishscreen.com
Scottish Screen has taken over the
distribution of National Lottery
funding for film production in
Scotland from the Scottish Arts
Council. Their short film schemes
include Tartan Shorts, $8^{1}/_{2}$ and New
Found Land.

Regional Screen Agencies:

EM-Media
http://www.em-media.org.uk

35–7 St Mary's Gate
Nottingham
NG1 1PU
Tel: 0115 950 9599
Fax: 0115 958 3250
e-mail: info@em-media.org.uk

**London Film and Video
Development Agency**
http://lfvda.demon.co.uk
114 Whitfield Street
London
W1P 5RW
Tel: 020 7383 7755
Fax: 020 7383 7745

Northern Film and Media Office
http://www.arts.org.uk/directory/regions
/northern
Central Square
Forth Street
Newcastle-upon-Tyne
NE1 3PJ
Tel: 0191 269 9200
Fax: 0191 269 9213

North West Vision
http://www.arts.org.uk/directory/regions
/north_west
109 Mount Pleasant
Liverpool
L3 5TF
Tel: 0151 708 8099
Fax: 0151 708 9859
e-mail: andrewp@ftcnorthwest.co.uk

Screen East
http://www.screeneast.co.uk
Anglia House
Norwich

NR1 3JG
Tel: 0845 6015670
Fax: 01603 767 191
Screen South
http://www.screensouth.org.uk
Folkestone Enterprise Centre
Shearway Road
Folkestone
Kent
CT19 4RH
Tel: 01303 298 222
e-mail: info@screensouth.org.uk

Screen West Midlands
http://www.screenwm.co.uk
Third Floor, Broad Street House
212 Broad Street
Birmingham
B15 1AY
Tel: 0121 643 9309
Fax: 0121 643 9064

South West Screen
http://www.swscreen.co.uk
St Bartholomews
Bristol
BS1 5BT
Tel: 0117 952 9977
Fax: 0117 952 9988
e-mail: info@swscreen.co.uk

Yorkshire Screen Commission
The Workstation
15 Paternoster Row
Sheffield
S1 2BX
Tel: 0114 279 6511
Fax: 0114 279 6511

CINEMA EXHIBITION

Many of the above websites carry short
film schemes which include theatric
release and/or distribution on
videotape and DVD.

Short Circuit

UK scheme which selects films of ten
minutes or under to be distributed with
features. See the website for details.
http://www.shortcircuitfilms.com

Some independent cinemas are
interested in showing shorts, for
example:

City Screen

86 Dean Street, London, W1D 3SR.
Tel: 020 7734 4342

The Showroom, Sheffield

Paternoster Row, Sheffield, S1 2BX.
Tel: 0114 275 7727

Zoo Cinemas (formerly Oasis)

20 Rushcroft Road, London, SW2 1LA.
Tel: 020 7733 8989

SELECTION OF FESTIVALS
SHOWING SHORT FILMS
Alcala de Henares Film Festival

http://www.euro-red.com/alcine
Short film festival in Spain.

American Short Shorts Film Festival

http://www.americanshortshorts.com
A touring festival for short American
films in Japan.

Animated Encounters

http://www.animated-encounters.org.uk
Festival of animation, predominantly shorts.

Bfm International Film Festival

http://www.bfmfilmfestival.com
UK and international black films, including shorts and animation.

Black Point Film Festival

http://www.blackpointfilmfestival.com/home.htm
A celebration of independent film, video, music and art that is scheduled to debut in Lake Geneva, Wisconsin, in 2002 and includes a short film section.

Brief Encounters

http://www.brief-encounters.org.uk
Competitive festival showcasing the best in British and international short film-making and featuring an array of UK and world premieres.

Cinematexas International Short Film Festival

http://www.cinematexas.org
Festival in Austin, Texas, with an international and student competition.

Cinequest

http://www.cinequest.org/
San Jose film festival including a short film section.

Clermont-Ferrand International Short Film Festival

http://www.clermont-filmfest.com

Competitive festival that includes a short film market.

Cork International Film Festival

http://www.corkfilmfest.org/flash/index1.html
Features a short film competition and documentaries.

Crested Butte Reel Fest Short Film Festival

http://www.crestedbuttereelfest.com
Festival in central Colorado focusing on the categories of animation, comedy, drama/narrative, experimental and documentary.

Exploding Cinema

http://www.explodingcinema.org
A London-based open-access initiative showing fifteen to twenty short films, videos and related performances.

Film Nite

http://www.killingtimepictures.com/filmnite
Monthly showcase of short films shown in Wilmington, North Carolina.

Flickerfest

http://www.flickerfest.com.au/html_site/index.htm
Short film festival touring Australia.

Girona Film Festival

http://www.gna.es/festivalgirona
European film and video shorts with Jewish themes in Girona, Spain.

Hi Lo Film Festival
http://www.killingmylobster.com/
product/hilo/2001.html
Annual event in San Francisco
showcasing short films 'with high
concepts and low budgets'.

Huesca Film Festival
http://www.huesca-filmfestival.com
Film festival in Huesca, Spain.

Interfilm Berlin
http://www.interfilmberlin.de
Annual short film festival in Berlin.

International Hamburg Short Film Festival
http://www.shortfilm.com/start.html
Site offers information about the
agency and its short film festival.

Iowa Independent Film and Video Festival
http://www.uni.edu/~martin/iifv.html
Featuring short films and videos from
Midwestern producers/directors.

Jaffas Down the Aisle
http://www.jaffasdowntheaisle.com.au
Promotes independent film, theatre and
multimedia, particularly Australian, and
holds a yearly festival of short films.

Kino Film
http://www.kinofilm.org.uk
Manchester's international short film
and video festival.

Krakow Short Film Festival
http://www.shortfilm.apollo.pl

One of Europe's oldest short film
festivals, founded in 1961.

Los Angeles International Short Film Festival
http://www.lashortsfest.com
An annual festival and a monthly short
film showcase held the last Sunday of
every month.

Manhattan Short Film Festival
http://www.msfilmfest.com
Screenings in Union Square Park, New
York City.

MisFit Short Film Festival
http://www.ualberta.ca/~filmzone/
Misfit/misfit.htm
Annual short film and video
competition hosted by the University
of Alberta Film Zone each May.

New York Exposition of Short Film and Video Festival (NY EXPO)
http://www.nyexpo.org
The longest-running annual festival of
independent short film and video in
the USA.

Oberhausen International Short Film Festival
http://www.kurzfilmtage.de

One Minute Film Festival
http://www.uol.com.br/minuto
Brazilian festival.

Phat Shorts
http://www.phatshortsfestival.com
Short film festival held in New York City.

PitchTV

http://www.pitchtv.com
A live event in New York City to coincide with the monthly on-line festival.

Raindance

http://www.raindance.co.uk
Britain's only film festival dedicated entirely to independent films, including shorts.

Riverina Flickers

http://www.flickers.webfront.net.au/index 2.html
Short film festival and competition in Australia.

Roma Independent Film Festival

http://www.riff.it
Monthly screenings and annual awards in Italy.

Rushes Soho Shorts Festival

http://www.sohoshorts.com
Competitive festival screening shorts in a variety of Soho venues.

São Paulo International Short Film Festival

http://www.terra.com.br/curtas/2001/e_kc_capa.htm
The leading event for the short format in Latin America, the São Paulo International Short Film Festival is also an international meeting place for the exchange of cultural, political and financial experiences.

Short Attention Span Film and Video Festival

http://www.dreamspan.com/shortspan/index.cfm
Touring film and video festival.

Shorts International Film Festival

http://www.shorts.org
Festival dedicated to the art and craft of the short film held in New York City.

Slamdance

http://www.slamdance.com
Independent festival held in Utah that coincides with Sundance.

Slamdunk

http://www.slamdunk.cc/festivals
Another Utah festival held concurrently with Sundance.

Summer Shorts

http://www.summershorts.com/index.shtml
Short film festival usually held in the Hamptons, USA.

Sundance

http://www.sundance.org
Indie features and shorts festival, Salt Lake City, USA.

Tampere International Short Film Festival

http://www.tamperefilmfestival.fi
International and Finnish competition sections.

Uppsala International Short Film Festival
http://www.shortfilmfestival.com/

Vila Do Conde International Short Film Festival
http://www.curtametragens.com
International and Portugese short films.

Yorkton Short Film and Video Festival
http://www.yorktonshortfilm.org
The longest-running festival of its kind in Canada.

Zinebi
http://www.zinebi.com
International festival of documentaries and short films in Bilbao, Spain.

OTHER INTERNET SOURCES OF INFORMATION
Animate!
Provides details of events, festivals, news, information and opinion, links, and a selection of animation.

British Film Commission
http://www.britfilmcom.co.uk
Aims to promote the UK as an international production centre, and provides links to the UK Film Commission Network and other industry-related sites. Gives support and advice to film-makers.

British Film Institute
http://www.bfi.org.uk
Site includes information on film-making and the film industry, film education and an on-line library catalogue.

Euclid international
http://www.euclid.co.uk
Providing European and international information, news and analysis for the arts and cultural sector.

Exposure
http://www.exposure.co.uk
An Internet resource site for film-makers.

Netribution
http://www.netribution.co.uk
Information on funding, statistics, contacts, events and film links.

New Producers Alliance (NPA)
http://www.newproducer.co.uk
National membership and training organisation for new producers.

Producers Alliance for Cinema and Television (PACT)
http://www.pact.co.uk
Membership organisation for producers that runs courses and events.

Shooting People
http://www.shootingpeople.org
Crews for low-budget productions and film-making advice.

Short Circuit
http://www.shortcircuitfilms.com
Provides resources, information and contacts for British makers of short films.

The Short Film Bureau
http://www.shortfilmbureau.com
A non-profit organisation set up to

raise awareness of the short film among a wider audience and provide support and advice to short film-makers.

Six Degrees
http://www.6degrees.co.uk
Independent film information including courses, web-links and forum.

PRINT PUBLICATIONS
Magazines:
bfm (black filmmaker)
Magazine for black film-makers. Also organises the bfm International Film Festival.
e-mail: bfm@teleregion.co.uk.
Tel: 020 8527 9582
Suite 9, 5 Blackhorse Lane, London, E17 6DS

Filmwaves
Quarterly magazine for independent film-makers.
e-mail: filmwaves@filmwaves.co.uk.
Website: www.filmwaves.co.uk.
Tel: 020 8906 4794
Obraz Productions Ltd, PO Box 420, Edgware, HA8 OXA

Vertigo
For film-makers and audiences.
e-mail: vertigo.lusia@lineone.net.
Website: www.mondialonline/vertigo
Vertigo Publications Ltd, Lusia Films, 20 Goodge Place, London, W1P 1FN

Booklets:
A Filmmakers' Guide to Distribution and Exhibition
Available on the BFI's website and from the BFI Exhibition Development Unit, Regional Arts Boards, regional screen agencies and national film bodies.

First Facts
Information on funding, professional training and developing a career in the film industry.
First Film Foundation, 9 Bourlet Close, London, W1W 7BP
e-mail: info@firstfilm.demon.co.uk.
Website: www.firstfilm.co.uk.
Tel: 020 7580 2111

The Low Budget Funding Guide
Available from the Film Council on www.filmcouncil.org.uk

Bibliography

Barr, Charles, (ed.), *All Our Yesterdays* (London: BFI, 1986)

Bendazzi, Giannalberto, *Cartoons: One Hundred Years of Cinema Animation* (London: John Libbey, 1994)

Box, Sydney, *Film Publicity: A Handbook on the Production and Distribution of Propaganda Films* (London: Lovat Dickson, 1937)

Chandler, Chris, *Low Budget Funding Guide, 98/99* (London: BFI, 1998)

Cook, David A., *A History of Narrative Film* (New York: W.W. Norton & Company, 1990)

Cook, Jim and Jim Hillier, 'The Growth of Film & Television Studies 1960–1975' (London: Film and Television Studies in Secondary Education Conference Paper, 1976)

Cooper, Pat and Ken Dancyger, *Writing the Short Film* (Boston: Focal Press 2000)

Cornwell, Andrea, *First Facts* (London: First Film Foundation, 2000)

Eisenstein, S. M., *The Short Fiction Scenario* (London: Methuen, 1988)

Ettedgui, Peter and Paul Kemp Robertson, *The Commercials Book* (Crans: Rotovision SA, 1997)

Fiddy, Dick, *Pop Video Exhibition Catalogue* (London: MOMI, 1992)

Fletcher, Winston, *A Glittering Haze: Strategic Advertising in the 1990s* (London: NTC Publications, 1992)

Frith, Simon and Howard Horne, *Art into Pop* (London: Methuen, 1987)

Gable, Jo, *The Tuppeny Punch and Judy Show* (London: Michael Joseph, 1980)

Giles, Jane, *A Film-makers' Guide to Distribution and Exhibition* (London: BFI, 2001)

Goodwin, Andrew, 'Music Video in the (Post)Modern World', *Screen*, vol. 28, no. 3 (1987)

Henry, Brian (ed.), *British Television Advertising, The First 30 Years* (London: Century Benham, 1986)

Lord, Peter and Brian Sibley, *Cracking Animation* (London: Thames & Hudson, 1998)

Manvell, Roger, *Art & Animation* (London: Halas & Batchelor, 1980)

Mulvey, Laura, *A Short History of the BFI Education Department* (unpublished paper, 1994)

Pilling, Jayne (ed.), *A Reader in Animation Studies* (London: John Libbey, 1997)

Rees, A. L., *A History of Experimental Film and Video* (London: BFI, 1999)

Rieser, Martin and Andrea Zapp (eds), *New Screen Media* (London: BFI, 2001)

Robinson, Mark, *100 Greatest TV Ads* (London: HarperCollins, 2000)

Street, Sarah, *British National Cinema* (London: Routledge, 1997)

Toulet, Emmanuelle, *Cinema is 100 Years Old* (London: Thames & Hudson, 1995)

Filmographies of Contributing Film-makers

EMMA CALDER

Ikla Moor Baht Hat (1981) – shown at
the ICA and other galleries
Madame Potatoe (1983) 6 minutes –
Director. Shown at the Tate Gallery
1984 (Music for Modern Americans)
(1983) 11 minutes – Director.
Produced by Eduardo Paolozzi/Royal
College of Art
Springfield (1986) 6 minutes – Director.
Silver Plaque, Chicago
The Drummer (1989) 7 minutes – Co-
director with Ged Hancy (Magic
Mirror Award)
The Queen's Monastery (1998)
6 minutes – Director (Silver Hugo,
Chicago; Silver Prize, Dresden; Best
Professional Film, Bradford
International Film Festival; Special
Jury Prize, Zagreb)

JONATHAN GLAZER

Commercials:

Caffreys, *Occasion, New York*
Carling, *H20*
Guinness, *Swimblack* (D&AD – Silver
– Outstanding Direction 2000;
Creative Circle Gold, Silver Alec
Ovens Memorial Honour – Best
Direction 2000; Gold, British
Television Advertising Awards 2000)
Guinness, *Surfer* (1999) – Director
(Gold Lion, Cannes Advertising
Festival; Grand Prix, Kinsale Festival;
British Television Award ITV Award –
Outstanding Commercial; 7 Creative
Circle Golds, including Best
Direction; Channel 4 – voted Best
Advertisement Ever by viewers;
Selected for Design Council's
Millennium Products Exhibition;
D&AD – 4 Silvers, 2 Golds – Most
Outstanding Direction, Most
Outstanding TV Commercial over 60
seconds)
Guinness, *Dream Club* (2002) –
Director
Levi's, *Kung Fu, Space Odyssey* (2002) –
Director
Nike, *Parklife* (1997) – Director (Gold,
British Television Awards, 1998;
Creative Circle – Best Direction;
D&AD – 3 Silvers – Direction, Best
TV Commercial, Best Cinema
Commercial)
Stella Artois, *Last Orders* (Creative
Silver – Best TV Commercial 2000:
Silver, British Television Awards
2000)
VW Polo, *Protection*
Wrangler, *Whatever You Ride* (2001)

Music videos:

Blur, *The Universal* (1995) – Director
Massive Attack, *Karma Coma* (1995) –
Director

Jamiroquai, *Virtual Insanity* (1996) –
Director (Best Pop Video 1997; 4
MTV Awards – Best Video, Best
Cinematography, Best Special
Effects, Best Breakthrough Video
1997; MVPA [Music Video
Producers' Association] Best
Overall Video 1997; Billboard
Music Video Awards – Director of
the Year 1997)
Radiohead, *Street Spirit* (1996) – Director
(MusicWeek C&D [Creative &
Design] Awards – Best
Rock/Alternative Video 1996, Best
Video 1996)
Radiohead, *Karma Police* (1997) –
Director
Unkle, *Rabbit in Your Headlights* –
Director (D&AD – Silver –
Outstanding Direction; MVPA –
Best International Video 1999)

JOHN HARDWICK
Glottis (1997) 12 minutes – Director
F Canal (1998) 1 minute – Director
Wet Work (1998) 13 minutes –Director
*No animals were harmed in the making
of this film* (1999) 3 minutes –
Director
The Place of Last Things (1999) 50
minutes. Documentary
Broth (1999) 18 minutes. Short for
performance artists The Spunk Flakes
To Have and to Hold (2000) 13 minutes
– Writer/Director (Best Director,
Short Film, Buenos Aires Film
Festival 2001; Third Prize, Emden
Film Festival 2001; Audience Prize,
Cambridge Film Festival 2001)
Wormcasts (2000) 11 minutes – Director

Mule (2001) 14 minutes – Director
John has made about 15 music videos
for a number of bands, including
Hefner, Travis, James, The
Bluetones, Blur, The
Propellerheads, Cecil and Orbital,
as well as two commercials.

ANTHONY MINGHELLA
Living with Dinosaurs (1989) 52
minutes – Writer
Truly, Madly, Deeply (1991) 106.5
minutes – Writer/Director (BAFTA
Film Award)
The English Patient (1996) 162 minutes
– Writer/Director (9 Academy
Awards, including Best Picture and
Best Director; 2 Golden Globe
awards; 6 BAFTA Awards; The
Writers Guild of America Award –
Best Screenplay; Directors Guild of
America – Best Director; and others)
The Talented Mr Ripley (1999) 139
minutes – Writer/Director
(American National Board of
Review – Best Director; ShoWest –
Director of the Year 2000)
Comic Relief – The Wall (1999) 4
minutes – Director
Jubilee 2000, (2000) 3.25 minutes –
Director
Play (2000) 16 minutes – Director

DAMIEN O'DONNELL
Booth (1992) – Writer/Director (Best
Irish Short Film, Galway Film
Festival 1992; Best Short Film, Irish
Student Film Festival 1992)
Thirty-five Aside (1995) 27 minutes –
Writer/Director (Best New Director,

The Talent, BBC2; 3 prizes at the
Clermont-Ferrand Film Festival)

Danger Doyle's Doo (1996) 29 minutes
– Director

Chrono-Perambulator (1998) 11 minutes
– Director

East is East (1999) 96 minutes –
Director (BAFTA – Best British
Film 2000; Prix Media 2000)

What Where? (2000) 13 minutes –
Director

Hotel Website (2001) – a website for
the Mike Figgis film.

Damien has also made a number of
commercials.

NICK PARK

Lip Synch – Creature Comforts (1989) 5
minutes – Director/Animator
(Academy Award – Best Short
Animated Film 1990)

A Grand Day Out (1989) 23 minutes –
Director/Animator (BAFTA – Best
Short Animated Film 1990)

The Wrong Trousers (1993) 29 minutes –
Director/Animator (with Steve Box)

A Close Shave (1995) 31 minutes –
Director/Animator (with Steve Box,
Lloyd Price, Peter Peake and Gary
Curetan)

Chicken Run (2000) 84 minutes – Co-
Director (with Peter Lord); Co-
Producer (with Peter Lord and
Dave Sproxton)

Music videos:

Peter Gabriel, *Sledgehammer* (1986) 4
minutes – Animator (with Peter
Lord, Richard Goleszowski and
Brothers Quay)

Commercials:

Oberlin (1986) – Animator

Angel Delight, *Magician* (1987) –
Animator

Manchester Evening News, *Get in the
Know* (1987) – Animator (with
Peter Lord, Richard Goleszowski
and Barry Purves)

Duvivier, *Mosquito* (1987) – Animator

Duracell, *Spider* (1987) – Animator

KP Appleyard, *Temp-tation* (1989) –
Animator

Isseo, *Bahlsen* (1989) – Animator

Electricity Board, Heat Electric *Pablo*,
Frank, *Vicky* (1990) –
Director/Animator

Access, *Hotel* (1990) – Animator (with
Rose Hackney Productions)

London Zoo, *Introduction* (1990) –
Director/Animator

Electricity Board, Heat Electric *Frank 2*
(1991) – Director/Animator

Electricity Board, Cook Electric
Penguins 1 and 2 (1991) –
Director/Animator

Electricity Board, Heat Electric *Pablo 3*
(1993) – Director/Animator

LYNNE RAMSAY

Small Deaths (1995) 10 minutes –
Writer/Director (Jury Prize, Cannes
Film Festival; First Prize, Pantin
Film Festival, Paris)

Kill the Day (1996) 18 minutes –
Writer/Director (Jury Prize,
Clermont-Ferrand Film Festival;
First Prize, Brest Film Festival)

Gasman (1997) 15 mins – Writer/
Director (Jury Prize, Cannes Film
Festival; Best Short Film, Scottish

BAFTA; Best Short Film, BAFTA
Kodak Prize; Best Short Film,
BAFTA Nomination)

Ratcatcher (1999) 93 minutes –
Writer/Director (Shortlist Sundance
Film Festival, International Script
Prize; Official Selection, Cannes
Film Festival; Special Mention, 'Un
Certain Regard' Prize; Opening
Film, Edinburgh Film Festival;
Guardian Best Director Prize,
Edinburgh Film Festival; Herald
Angel Award for Excellence,
Edinburgh Film Festival; Best New
Director (Douglas Hicox Award),
BIFA; Best Director, Chicago Film
Festival; Best Film, Sunderland
Trophy, London Film Festival; Best
British Director, London Film
Critics Circle; Nominated, BAFTA
2000 Alexander Korda Award for
Best Film; Winner, BAFTA 2000
Award for Best Newcomer; Winner,
BBC 2 Visual Arts Award for Best
Film; Grand Prix Award at the IFF
Bratislava 2000)

Morvern Callar (to be released in 2002)
93 minutes – Writer/Director

TESSA SHERIDAN

Feed Me (1990) 20 minutes –
Writer/Director

Smokescreen (1991) 30 minutes –
Director

Alien Corn (1992) 23 minutes –
Writer/Director (First prize and
Special Award, Krakow Film Festival
1993; Special Commendation,
Chicago Film Festival 1993; First

Prize, Best Short Feature, Hungary
Film Festival 1994)

The Chocolate Acrobat (1995) 40
minutes – Writer/Director

Is it the Design on the Wrapper? (1997)
7 minutes – Writer/Director (Palme
d'Or, Cannes Film Festival 1997;
BBC Award – Best Drama, London
Short Film Festival 1997; Best Short
Film, LA International Short Film
Festival 1997)

The Lizard Lover (1998) 30 minutes –
Screenwriter

South in my Soul (1999) 5 minutes –
Writer/Director

Since 1997, Tessa has made a number
of TV commercials, including Caisse
D'Epargne Bank, Pontins, Stork
and Boots.

JOHN SMITH

Triangles (1972) 3 minutes – Director

Someone Moving (1972) 5 minutes –
Director

The Hut (1973) 5 minutes – Director

Words (1973) 7 minutes – in
collaboration with Lis Rhodes

William and the Cows (1974) 6 minutes
– Director

Faces 1 (1974) 11 minutes – Director

Faces 2 (1974) 3 minutes – Director

Associations (1975) 7 minutes –
Director

Leading Light (1975) 11 minutes –
Director

Nine Short Stories (1975) 3 minutes –
Director

Subjective Tick-Tocks (1975) 11 minutes
– Director

The Girl Chewing Gum (1976) 12 minutes – Director

Summer Diary (1977) 30 minutes – Director

Gardner (1977) 6 minutes – Director

Hackney Marshes (1977) 2 versions – 15 minutes and 30 minutes – Director

7P (1978) 7 minutes – Director

Blue Bathroom (1979) 14 minutes – Director

Celestial Navigation (1980) 10 minutes – Director

Spring Tree (1980) 3 minutes – Director

Shine So Hard (1981) 32 minutes – Editor/Director

Light Sleep (1981) 6 minutes – Director

Shepherd's Delight (1984) 35 minutes – Writer/Director/Photography/Editing

Om (1986) 4 minutes – Director

The Black Tower (1987) 24 minutes – Director/Cast member

Dungeness (1987) 12 minutes – Director

Slow Glass (1991) 40 minutes – Writer/Director/Photography/Editor

Gargantuan (1992) 1 minute – Writer/Director/Editor

Home Suite (1994) 96 minutes – Director

Blight (1996) 14 minutes – Director/Photography/Editor (Best European Short Film, Cork International Film Festival 1997; Golden Dove – Best Short Documentary, Leipzig International Festival 1997; Gold Plaque – Best Experimental Film, Chicago International Film Festival 1997; Best Experimental Film, Uppsala International Short Film Festival 1997; 2 prizes and an Honourable Mention, Oberhausen Short Film Festival 1997; Special Critics Award, International Biennale of Film and Architecture 1997; Short Film Prize, Hamburg International Film Festival 1998; Audience Prize, Bangkok Experimental Film Festival 1999; Special Mention, Architektur & Film Festival, Regensburg 2000)

The Kiss (1999) 5 minutes – in collaboration with Ian Bourn (Third Prize, Palermo International Video Art, Film and Media Festival 2000)

The Waste Land (1999) 5 minutes – Director

Regression (1999) 17 minutes – Director (International Short Film Festival Prize, Oberhausen Short Film Festival 2000; International Jury Special Mention, Cork International Film Festival 2000)

Lost Sound (2001) 28 minutes – in collaboration with Graeme Miller

KEITH WRIGHT

The Mind's Eye (1996) Director (with Rob Richardson)

Legend of Roy (1997) Director (with Rob Richardson) (First Place, Festival of Fantastic Films)

Where's Bingo Betty? (1998) 9 minutes – Director (David Altshul Award; BAVA Best Comedy)

Stan's Slice of Life (1999) 10 minutes – Director

Long in the Tooth (2000) – Director (Wrangler Short Film Award)

WINTA YOHANNES

Do Your Thing (1995) 12 minutes –
    Writer/Director
Blues is My Middle Name (1998) 12
    minutes – Writer/Director
Cherish (2000) 17 minutes –
    Writer/Director
How (2001) 3-minute MTV music
    video for Harry Turn

Index

Italicised page numbers denote illustrations

Aardman Animation 12, 23, 24, *26*, 134
  Wallace and Gromit 28, 129
  see also Lip Synch series
Absolut Vodka 136
Academy Films 86, 87
advertising and commercials 8, 13, 14, *16*, 52, 102
  see also Surfer
advertising magazines 15
Alien Corn (Sheridan, 1992) 21, 41, *42*, 46, 48, 49
Alliance Atlantis Releasing 131
American Beauty (Mendes, 2000) 60
Anderson, Lindsay 7
Anger, Kenneth ix
Angry Kid 138
Animate! 123
Animated Encounters 133
animation xv, 8, 11–13
Arts Council of England 6, 77, 80, 81, 84, 85, 98, 132
Artists' Film and Video Committee, Arts Council of England 77
Artsworld 134
Association of Cinematograph, Television and Allied Technicians 9
Atom Films 59, 129, 136, 137, 138
avant-garde film xv, 2, 10, 18–19, 122

Baker, Bob 32
Ballad of the Skeletons (Van Sant, 1997) 134
Barry, Nora 137
Beatles, The 17
Beckett, Edward 69
Beckett, Samuel 1
Beckett Shorts 22, 23, 66–77, 127
  distribution 70, 76
  funding 66–7
  see also Play and *What Where?*
Betjeman, John 15
Beware of Trains 37
Biggar, Helen 9
Birken Interactive Studio 137
Biographic 12
Bit Screen, The 136, 137
Black Tower (Smith, 1987) 3, 22, 80
Blackton, James Stuart 11
Blast Theory 93
Blight (Smith, 1996) 22, 77–85, *78*
  as protest film 82
  budget 80
  funding 80
  music in 82, 84
  production 79, 81, 82
  sound 81
  writing 77–8
  see also John Smith
Blindfold 41, 52
Bluebottles (Montagu, 1928) 7
BMW 131, 136, 138
Bohemian Rhapsody 17

Bolexbrothers 134
Bonehead 41
Bourn, Ian 86
Box, Steve 32
Brakhage, Stan ix
Bread (1939) 7
Brief Encounters Short Film Festival 2, 118, 133–4, 129, 131, 132, 133–4, 138
  and Internet 138
Bristol University 9
BAFTA 59
British Broadcasting Corporation 36, 40, 57, 85, 126
BBC Choice 134
BBC Drama Shorts 131
BBC Short Film Festival 51
British Film Institute 6, 10, 53, 98, 100
  BFI New Directors Award 93
  Film Poem tours xiv
British Kinematograph Sound and Television Society 9
British Screen 6
Bryher xiii
BSkyB 134
BT Payphones 131
Britshorts 128
Brothers Quay xiv
Bug Boy Gull Girl 43, 47
Buñuel, Luis viii
Burrows, Saffron 65
Bush, Paul xiv

Calder, Emma 13, 21, 22, 32–41, 120, 121, 122, 123, 125
  creative process and 34–6, 37–8
  filmography 159
  IMAX film development 41
  research for films 39
  see also The Queen's Monastery
Calderon, Ian 135
Calderwood, Andrea 59, 60
California Cooper J., 104
Campbell, Walter 86
Campion, Jane x
Canadian Film Board 12
Carlton 114
Carnival in the Clothes Cupboard 12
cartoon 35
Carty, Tom 86
C.O.D. – A Mellow Drama (Richards, 1929) 7
Chandler, Chris 131
Chain xiv
Channel 4 8, 16, 22, 25–6, 30, 30, 32, 35, 37, 51, 52, 59, 63, 66, 70, 109, 126
Channel 5 131
Chaplin, Charles 1
Cherish (Yohannes, 2000) 22, 102–10, *105*
  acting in 109
  budget 107
  casting 107
  original idea 103–4
  problems in production 107
  production 106
  summary of film 103, 106
  writing of film 104–6, 107
  see also Winta Yohannes
Chien Andalou, Un (Buñuel, 1929) viii, 18, 19
Children's Film Foundation ix

Clermont-Ferrand festival xiv
Close Up xiii
Cohen, Jem xiv
Cohl, Emile 11
Colgan, Michael 22, 66, 69, 71
Coming of Age (Riley, 2000) 137
commissioning and short films 122–5
Cook, Jim 10
Cooper, Arthur Melbourne 11
Colour Box, A (Lye, 1936) 12
Corsican Brothers, The (Smith, 1897) 6
creative process and short films 120–2
Creature Comforts (Park, 1989) 23–32
  Channel 4 and 25–6, 30, 123
  distribution 31
  idea for film 24
  making of 24
  production 30
  storyboarding and 28
  see also Nick Park
Cripps, Julian 32, 36, 37

Daily Telegraph 51, 131
Dali, Salvador viii
David Altshul Award 112
Davies, Paul 99
Davies, Terrence xii
Depict! 138
Deren, Maya ix, 18
DiCaprio, Leonardo 137
Dickenson, Desmond 7
digital film-making 83–4, 127–8
Disney ix, 11, 12
distribution of short films 40, 51–2, 59, 70, 76, 85–6, 109, 118–19, 125–7, 132–4, 152
Dog Star Man (Brakhage, 1964) ix

Dogma 61, 64
Douglas, Bill xii
Dreams of Toyland (Cooper, 1908) 11
Duchess of Malfi, The 61
Duna Bull (Henson, 1971) ix

Eady Levy 6, 10
East is East (O'Donnell, 1999) 60, 61, 66, 69, 71
Edinburgh Film Festival 101, 118, 132
Ellis, Maggie 36, 123
English Patient, The (Minghella, 1996) 21, 76
European Regional Development Fund 132
Everyday (Richter, 1929) 7
Exploding Cinema 93, 128
Exorcist, The (Friedkin, 1973) 79

Fairy Godmother, The (Smith, 1898) 6
Far Side, The 31
FAT – Fashion, Architecture, Taste 93
Faust and Mephistopheles (Smith, 1898) 6
Feiffer, Jules 43
festivals, short film xiv, xv, 40, 51, 59, 109, 118, 125–6, 131, 132–4, 135, 152–6
Figgis, Mike 60, 61, 62, 63, 127
film clubs 126
Film Council, The 7, 126, 130, 139
Film Four 59, 100, 132, 134
Film Four Lab 98
First Film Foundation, The 131
Flaming Creatures (Smith, 1963) ix

Franju ix
Free Cinema Movement xi
Frilot, Shari 136
funding short films xiii, 6,
    37–8, 46, 47, 49, 54–5,
    56, 60, 66–7, 68, 80,
    84–5, 93, 98, 107, 109,
    112, 122–5, 146–52
  fear that funding leads to
    self-censorship 49
  in-kind support 47, 48, 49
Funny Games (Haneke,
    1997) 100

Gargantuan (Smith, 1992)
    85
Gasman (Ramsay, 1997)
    21, 52–60, 121
  background to film 53–4
  budget 56
  development 54–5, 56
  distribution 59
  funding 54–5
  narrative and gender in
    59–60
  production 57–8
  story 54
  see also Lynne Ramsay
General Post Office Film
    Unit, 7, 12
George Lucas in Love
    (Nussbaum, 1999)
    129, 136, 138
Gertie the Dinosaur (McCay,
    1914) 11
Gilliam, Terry 15, 56
Ginna, Arnoldo 11
Ginsberg, Allen 134
Girl Chewing Gum, The
    (Smith, 1976) 18, 22
Glasgow School of Art 9
Glass, Philip 134
Glazer, Jonathan 2, 22, 86,
    124, 125
  creative aims 91
  filmography 159–60
  'political' issues in film-
    making 91–2
  views on collaboration
    86, 92

Glazer, Jonathan *cont.*
  views on music videos
    92–3
  see also Surfer
Glottis (Hardwick, 1997) 93
Godfrey, Bob 12
Grand Day Out, A (Park,
    1989) 23, 31
Great (Godfrey, 1975) 12
Green, Jonathan 62
Greenaway, Peter xii, 10
Grierson, John 7
Griffiths, Keith xv
Guardian, The 51
Guinness 86–90
Gutch, Robin 98

Halas and Batchelor 12
Haneke, Michael 100
Haney, Ged 13, 32, 33, 34,
    38, 41
Hanley, Jimmy 15
Hard Day's Night, A (Lester,
    1964) 17
Hardwick, John 22,
    93–102, 121, 122, 124,
    125
  budgets 100
  collaborators 94–5
  early work 93
  filmography 160
  pre-production work 95
  views on films 95–6
  views on length of short
    films 101
  writing 94
  *see also The Sweetness Lies
    Within* and *To Have
    and to Hold*
HTV 134
Harrison, Jon xv
Harrison, Rachel 95
Haunted Hotel, The
    (Blackton, 1907) 11
Hayek, Salma 63
Hell UnLtd (McLaren,
    1936) 7, 9, 19
Help 17
Henry's Cat 12
Hepworth, Cecil 12

Hepworth Manufacturing
    Company 5, 6
Herzog, Werner 102
Hickey, Lee 62, 64
Hillier, Jim 10
Hornby, Nick 70
Hotel (Figgis, 2002) 22
    60–6, 65, 69, 127
  budget 63
  development 62–3
  production 62–3, 64
  summary of film 60–1
  see also Damien O'Donnell
Hughes, Enda, 62, 63, 69

Ifans, Rhys 64, 65
ifilm 136, 137
Imax 41
Independent Film Channel
    137
Independent on Sunday 131
Institute of Amateur
    Cinematographers 111
Internet and short film 1,
    16, 51, 59, 62, 125,
    127, 128, 129, 132
  and animation 13
  and music video 17,
    134–9
  problems with speed 136
  quality of viewing
    experience 141–6
  see also Hotel
Irish Film Board 66
*Is it the Design on the
    Wrapper?* (Sheridan,
    1997) 2, 21, 41–52, 45
  casting 44–5, 47
  creative process 43–4
  development and 46–7
  distribution 51
  with *Shine* 51
  with *Big Night* 51
  funding and 43, 49
  London Film and Video
    Development Agency
    and 43
  problems with 48–9
  production 47–8, 49, 50
  see also Tessa Sheridan

Janáček 34
Jane Balfour Films 51, 132
Jarman, Derek 10
Jazz Singer, The (Crosland, 1929) 17
Jennings, Humphrey ix
Jerwood Charitable Foundation, The 131
Jerwood First Film Shorts Prize 131
Jetée, La (Marker, 1962) viii
Jolson, Al 17
Joseph, Verona 107
Julien, Isaac 8, 10

Karma Sutra Rides Again (Godfrey, 1971) 12
Keaton, Buster 1
Kiddigraphs (1922) 12
Kilano, Buffalo 88
Kill the Day (Ramsay, 1996) 21, 53, 56, 59, 122
Kino 7
Kiss, The (Bourn, 1999) 86
Kitson, Claire 32, 35
Kodak 131
Korine, Harmony 102

Langdon, Harry 1
Larkins 12
Laurel and Hardy 1
Lee, Spike 108
Lerner, Keith 12
Lester, Richard 7
Levi's 131–2, 131
Levy, Joseph 136
Lewis, Gary 67, 69
Lip Synch 23, 24
Little Nemo (McCay, 1910) 11
Little Red Riding Hood (Dyer, 1922) 12
Lizard Lover, The (Sheridan, 1998) 52
London Film and Video Development Agency 43, 49, 132
London Film School 8
London Film–makers' Co–operative 7

London International Film School 102, 103
London Production Fund 36, 37
Long in the Tooth (Wright, 2000) 23, 115, 119
Lord, Peter 12, 24, 26
Lothar, Suzanne 100
Love on the Wing (McLaren, 1938) 12
Lovebytes Media Art Festival xv
Lucanus Cervus (Starewich, 1910) 11
Lumière Brothers ix, 5
Lye, Len 12
Lynch, David x
Lynn, Patrick 135

McCartney, Paul 134
McCay, Winsor 11
McDermott, Sean 95
McGinley, Sean 67
McKissick, Barbara 57
McLaren, Norman 9, 12
Maloney, Alan 66, 69
Marker, Chris viii
Matches, An Appeal (Cooper, 1899) 11
MediaTrip.com 135
Méliès, George ix, 5
Mentoring support, need for 123
Meshes of the Afternoon (Deren, 1943) ix, 18
Minghella, Anthony 2, 21, 23, 71–7, 120
aims in filming *Play* 75–6
approach to *Play* 71–6
filmography 160
involvement in Beckett 71
views on distribution 76
views on shorts 76
see also Play and Beckett Shorts
Montagu, Ivor 7
Morph 23
Morvern Callar (Ramsay, 2002) 21, 52

Mule (Hardwick, 2001) 101
Mullen, Peter 67
Mulloy, Phil xiv
MTV ix, 17, 134
music video 16–18, 22, 124, 92
and animation 18
My Ain Folk (Douglas, 1973) xii
My Childhood (Douglas, 1972) xii
My Way Home (Douglas, 1978) xii

National Film and Television School 8, 9, 23, 52, 106, 110
National Film Finance Corporation 6
National Lottery 6, 36, 40, 85, 130, 132, 133
New Arrival, The (Talkington, 2000) 137
New York Post 15
Nicholas, Bianca 44, 45, 47, 48
Night and Fog (Resnais, 1955) ix
Night Mail (Jennings, 1936) ix
Noah's Ark (Cooper, 1906) 11
North West Arts 132
Nussbaum, Joe 136
Nwimo, Stella 50, 51

Oasis Cinema Group 40
Oberhausen Festival xiv, 132
O'Donnell, Damien 2, 22, 60–71, 127
filmography 160–1
involvement in *Hotel* 60–1
views on Beckett 66
views on digital film-making 61, 63, 65, 66
views on Dogma 64
views on shorts 70–1

O'Donnell, Damien *cont.*
  see also Hotel and *What Where?*
Ogborn, Kate 98, 101
Oh Dreamland! (Anderson, 1954) 7
On Probation 27

Paris Texas (Wenders, 1984) ix
Park, Nick 21, 23–32, 121, 123
  animals in 24–5, 29
  filmography 161
  influence of *The Far Side* 31
  inspiration for film 24, 29–30
  model animation and 23–4
  use of depth of field 27–8
  wish to work again with shorts 32
  see also Creature Comforts
Parker, Alan 10, 15
Passion Pictures 41
Pathé 125
Paul, Robert 5
Peace and Plenty (Montagu, 1939) 7
Pearly Oyster Productions 13, 32, 37
Penny Lane (1967) 17
Petit, Chris xvi
Play (Minghella, 2000) 71–7, 120
  production 130–2
  see also Anthony Minghella
Polanski, Roman x
Polygamous Polonius (Godfrey, 1959) 12
Pop.com 135
Pook, Jocelyn 77, 80, 81, 82, 120
Post Office 131
Potter, Sally 8, 10
Presley, Elvis 17
Puttnam, David 10, 15

Queen 17
Queen's Monastery, The (Calder, 1998) 21, 32–41, 120, 125
  aims of film 39
  distribution 40
  with *Love is the Devil* 40
  with *My Name is Joe* 40
  Janáček and 34
  lottery application 36
  music in 34
  production 38
  research 36, 38
  story 32–3
  use of watercolours 33–4
  views on funding conditions 37
  writing 35, 36
  see also Emma Calder
Quinn, Joanna 8

Rabbit in Your Headlights (Glazer, 1999) 22
Ramsay, Lynne x, xii, 8, 18, 21, 52–60, 121, 122, 125
  aims in making *Gasman* 57, 58–9
  background to *Gasman* 52–3, 55
  control of film-making 58
  filmography 161–2
  influence of Maya Deren 18
  use of photographs 55
  view of *Gasman* 58
  view of short films 54
  see also Gasman
Ratcatcher (Ramsay, 1999) 52, 55, 59, 121, 125
Regent Street Polytechnic (then Polytechnic of Central London, then University of Westminster) 9
Reisz, Karel 7
Rescued by Rover (Hepworth, 1905) 6
Resnais, Alain ix
Richard, Cliff 17

Richter, Hans 7
Riley, Joe 137
Riverchild Films 52
Roobarb 12
Rose, Colin 36, 37, 38
Royal College of Art 9
Royal Television Society 9
RTE 66
Running Jumping Standing Still Film (Lester, 1959) 7
Rushes Soho Shorts 132

S4C 34
Salmon, Danny 95
Scorpio Rising (Anger, 1963) ix
Sankofa Films 47
Sang des Bêtes, Le (Franju, 1948) ix
Saturday Night and Sunday Morning (Reisz, 1960) 7
Schlesinger, Derrin 94, 98
Schwimmer, David 63
Scottish Screen 126
Scott, Ridley 10, 15
Screen 10
Sexy Beast (Glazer, 2001) 86, 92, 125
Sheridan, Tessa 2, 21, 22, 41–52, 121, 122, 123, 124
  background influences 41–3
  filmography 162
  views on finished film 50–1
  work since *Wrapper* 52
  see also The Sweetness Lies Within
Shannon, Roger 98
Shooting Gallery, The 134
Short Circuit 125, 132, 139
Short films and avant-garde 18–19
  and class 6
  commercial sponsorship 16
  and education 8–11

Short films and avant-garde
   cont.
  gender 59–60, 108, 122
  and history 5–20
  intrinsic value or stepping
   stone? 23, 49, 59,
   76–7, 85, 103, 115,
   124
  and length 101–2
  and politics 7
  and propaganda 1
Shortbuzz.com 135
Showroom Cinema 132
Sight and Sound xvi, 10
Silverlaski, Pat 107
Slade, The 9
Slater, Ben xv
Slow Glass (Smith, 1991) 85
Smith, Debbie 29, 31
Smith, G. A. 6
Smith, Jack ix
Smith, John xv, 3, 18, 22,
   77–86, 120, 122, 125,
   133
  aims in work 84
  budget for *Blight* 84, 85
  development as film-
   maker 83
  digital film-making 83–4
  distribution and 85–6
  filmography 162–3
  future plans 86
  idea for *Blight* 77
  Pook, Jocelyn
   collaboration 80
  views on *Blight* 79–80, 81
  views on short film 82–3
  see also Blight
Sortie d'usine (Lumière,
   1895) 5
Sound on Film scheme 80
Southern Arts 114
Speaking with the Angel 70
Spike and Mike 40
Springfield (Calder, 1986)
   40
Sproxton, Dave 12, 24, 26
Stan's Slice of Life (Wright,
   1999) 23, 111–19
  distribution 118–19

Stan's Slice of Life cont.
  funding 112–13
  production 112, 114, 117
  summary of film 111
  see also Keith Wright
Starewich, Ladislas 11
Strawberry Fields Forever
   (1967) 17
Strong, Mark 64, 65
Sundance Film Festival
   135
Sundew 52
Surfer (Glazer, 1999) 2, 22,
   86–93, *89*
  background to film 86, 87
  budget 87
  production 87–91
  special effects 89–90
  storyboarding and 86, 87
  see also Jonathan Glazer
Sweetness Lies Within, The
   (Hardwick, 1998) 22
  aims of film 121
  development 93–4
  distribution 95
  pre-production 95
  see also Tessa Sheridan
Swimblack 86

Tait, Margaret xiii
Talkington, Amy 137
Tampere Festival xiv, 132
Tartan Shorts 54, 56, 57
television and short films
   126, 134
  see also Channel 4 and
   BBC
Thirty-five Aside
   (O'Donnell, 1995) 2,
   134
Three Little Pigs, The (1922)
   12
Time Code (Figgis, 2000)
   60
Time Out 51
To Have and to Hold
   (Hardwick, 2000) 22,
   96–102, *97, 99*
  budget 98
  funding 98

To Have and to Hold cont.
  idea 96–7
  production 98–101
  see also John Hardwick
Todd, Peter xiv
Tout le Monde Descend
   (1997) 134
Train Trouble 12
Trainspotting (Boyle, 1996)
   52, 59
Truly, Madly, Deeply
   (Minghella, 1991) 76
Tusalava (Lye, 1929) 12

Van Sant, Gus 134
Vertical Features Remake
   (Greenaway, 1978) xii
Virgin Airlines 132
Vision On 24
Volcano Theatre Company
   99–100
Von Trier, Lars 102

Walk Through H, A
   (Greenaway, 1978) xii
Walter Thompson, J. 12
Water Wrackets (Greenaway,
   1978) xii
We are the Lambeth Boys
   (Reisz, 1958) 7
Webster, John 61
Western Lights 134
What Where? (O'Donnell,
   2000) 66–71
  budget 68
  distribution 70
  production 66–7, 68–70
  see also Damien O'Donnell
Where's Bingo Betty?
   (Wright, 1998) 22, 23,
   111–19, *113*, 134
  distribution 118–19
  production 112, 114
  summary of film 111
Williams, Abby 62
Williams, Heathcote 65
Wilson, Rodney 80, 81
Woodcock, Fiona 32, 38,
   41
Woolf, Michael 138

Workers' Film and Photo
    League 7
Wrangler Short Film Award
    119
Wright, Keith 22, 110–19,
    120, 121, 122, 125, 134
aims in film-making
    114–15
audiences and 111–12
filmography 163
on film-making 111
inspired by classic
    Hollywood horror films
    110
views on distribution 119
views on short film 119

Wright, Keith *cont.*
    working with video 111
    see also Stan's Slice of Life
        and *Where's Bingo Betty?*

Yahoo! 135, 137
Yohannes, Winta 21, 22;
    102–110, 122
aims with *Cherish* 108
background 103
cultural identity and film-
    making 108
filmography 164
gender and 108
views of finished film
    108–9

Yohannes, Winta *cont.*
    views on short film 110
    work since *Cherish*
        109–10
    writing feature 104

Yellow Submarine (1967)
    12
Yorkshire Arts 132
Yorkshire Media Production
    Agency 132

Zoo 132
Zucchetti, Lucia 23, 57